A Manager's Guide to Hiring the Best Person for Every Job

A Manager's Guide to Hiring the Best Person for Every Job

DeANNE ROSENBERG

JOHN WILEY & SONS, INC.
New York • Chichester • Weinheim • Brisbane • Singapore • Toronto

Library of Congress Cataloging-in-Publication Data:

Rosenberg, DeAnne.
   A manager's guide to hiring the best person for every job /
DeAnne Rosenberg.
     p. cm.
   Includes index.
   ISBN 0-471-38074-1 (paper : alk. paper)
   1. Employment interviewing. 2. Employee selection. I. Title.
HF5549.5.I6 R674 2000
658.3'1124—dc21

                                    99-051372

Printed in the United States of America.

10 9 8 7 6 5 4 3 2 1

*To Myron Lewis, my significant other,
without whose encouragement, nagging, support,
nudging, assistance, badgering and love this book
would never have been written.*

Contents

Foreword

We are barraged in the marketplace with financial advice on how to limit losses and maximize profits. Much as we might like to put our heads in the sand or just muddle through, rather than learn new techniques and approaches, businesspeople are constrained to heed at least some of that advice. Our fiduciary responsibility to shareholders impels us to learn the skills and knowledge to act in a fiscally responsible manner. These skills are not innate; they are learned. Each new MBA, corporate officer, or venture capitalist understands the concept of the bottom line. But the smaller business, the partnership, or sole proprietorship is equally concerned about business expenses. In fact, the smaller the business, the greater effect financial losses will have on the business's viability.

From kindergarten on, we are given problems to solve. We set our goals, gather, examine, and evaluate all relevant information, and determine means of reaching a recommended course of action. In the business world, we are also faced with problems to solve—from organizing the sales campaign to determining the production schedule to implementing a distribution plan. To resolve each problem, we assess our goals and aspirations and evaluate possible means of approach. We thoroughly develop all the ways in which our goal can be effected, weighing the chances of success of each. Then we choose from among the best solutions. We consider this to be a rational and reasonable approach to business management.

Why then, do managers, particularly in businesses without a thorough personnel function, hire employees by the seat of their pants? Why is it that we do not take the same careful approach to hiring and orienting new employees that we take with our new marketing strategy, for example?

DeAnne Rosenberg, in this carefully organized guide, tells us that one of the primary reasons for this is that there have been few, if any, simple resources for middle managers to rely on when making their employment decisions. Further, and contrary to what we may have thought, this knowledge, like much of our business knowledge, is learned, not innate.

Here is your opportunity! As employers, will we be proactive in seeking out competent assistance, or will we merely be reactive to someone whose resume seems to fit the bill? Common sense would tell us that the former approach is a better managerial tool. And how will we conduct an interview? Frankly, will we even conduct it or will we allow the applicant to organize it for us? Starting with the Master Match Matrix™, a clever but easy-to-use schema for organizing, conducting, and evaluating an interview, managers will be able to carry forward a speedy, thorough, well-researched, and professional review, gearing discussion to the specific skills necessary to the job and matching the person with the company, as well.

Upper-level managers may make decisions about the ultimate direction in which a company may move forward, but it is middle management that is tasked to strategize how the business will actually get there. Hiring is not normally considered a primary task for the working manager; perhaps a course is offered in college or graduate school, but little emphasis is placed on it. This guide offers you, the working manager, a simple strategy that you can use over and over again, to assist in the hiring process. It is a tremendous advance in the field of personnel management.

But let's get to the bottom line. This guide urges managers to strongly consider the financial consequences of making a mistake in hiring. For the newly hired employee who is not really qualified for the position, the business bears the lost expense of salary while the employee founders, the expenses of advertising, searching, interviewing, and training a second candidate, and the lost profits from the lost business during the period of the poor employee's probationary period. Think, too, of the effect of a poor employee on the morale (and consequently, productivity) of other, more appropriate employees. Even for the employee who is qualified for the position, there is a risk of a quick turnover if the employer has not adequately assessed the career goals and aspirations of the employee.

Utilizing her skills and experience in interviewing, personnel management, and systems analysis, the author has put together an effective, understandable, and sensible guide for managers. If you learn only the most minimal of skills from this book, you will have saved your business a considerable sum of money. Read the book with vigor. It may even be your fiduciary responsibility!

Lewis H. Kerman

(Mr. Kerman is an attorney, real estate consultant, and full-time member of the faculty at Rutgers Graduate School of Management.)

Preface

Many years ago, as a job seeker, I discovered that, except for the professionals in the personnel or human resources department, most folks really didn't know much about how to interview effectively. People would ask questions that confirmed the data already supplied on the resume. Then they would ask questions that prompted pleasant conversation but that had nothing to do with the position for which I was applying. Generally, interviewers were not at all concerned about my career goals or job preferences, even though these are the keys to long-term retention. Instead, they only seemed interested in learning if I could handle a few finite tasks. Sometimes an interviewer focused only on a single aspect of my background, ignoring all other facets of my experience. Occasionally it felt as if the people charged with conducting the interviews really weren't sure what they were actually seeking in a candidate. Many interviewers asked for information that, if answered, would put my candidacy in a negative light. It seemed unlikely in this atmosphere that I would ferret out a job that matched my objectives. I therefore decided to attempt self-employment as a speaker and lecturer on—you guessed it—interviewing.

The course I developed and still present from time to time is called *Getting a Job*. It is designed for job seekers and coaches candidates in how to take control of the interview so that they thrust such topics as their primary strengths and career aspirations into the forefront of the interview in case the interviewer does not ask for it. The course also includes a section covering the questions candidates should ask to be certain that the position meets their goals and expectations. Attendees are prepared to answer intelligently such dumb questions as, "How are your people skills?"

There is even a portion in the course on how to respond to trick questions, which are queries with a hidden agenda. There is also a section on how to uncover exactly what the interviewer thinks they want in a candidate and how to portray themselves as that very individual. The inevitable result is a job offer.

A few years into this activity, a former student asked me to come into the corporate setting and teach his managers how to interview so that they would not be victimized by the tactics taught in *Getting a Job*. My research for developing such a course involved audio- and videotaping hundreds of actual interviews.

What became immediately obvious from listening to the tapes was how unprepared most managers were. A great deal of time was spent asking questions that served no purpose except perhaps to fill in the time. Interviewers would miss pivotal information because they were not really listening to their candidates. Instead of listening, most interviewers were working on question generation. They wanted to be ready to immediately throw another question at the candidate as soon as he or she stopped talking. It became clear to me that managers needed to prepare their questioning strategy *before* going into the interview. That way their attention would be focused on listening to the candidate's responses.

For preparation, managers in the taped interviews would use the candidate's resume along with a job description that was generally out-of-date as the foundation for their interviews. Some managers used a list of desired competencies that related to a previous jobholder's achievements. This current candidate's job success, however, would not depend on the old job description, his or her resume (professional obituary), or a previous candidate's competencies, but rather on how well he or she met the manager's expectations one year down the road. Moreover, because every candidate's resume was different, managers were using a shifting target as the basis of their interviewing activity rather than a solid, firmly based foundation of requirements and expectations. So, I realized that along with a prepared questioning strategy, managers needed some definitive guidelines for interview preparation that would be grounded in performance expectations and the competencies necessary to meet those expectations.

Since candidates might be strong in some areas and quite weak in others, there had to be some mechanism that would tell an interviewing manager what the trade-offs were. The Master Match Matrix™ (see Chapter 3) solved those problems.

From reviewing the research videotapes, I also began to understand the relationship between the candidates' spoken word and their body language. Therefore, one entire chapter of this book (Chapter 6) is about reading body language during the interview. In addition, it became evident from watching the videotapes how clearly a candidate's personality and motivational drive came through in the interview. If managers knew what to listen for, they could easily avoid hiring individuals who would create behavior problems in the workplace. This information, which is grounded in the work of David McClelland (from his motivational theory known as "The Need for Achievement," in *The Achieving Society* [New York: Irvington Press, 1975]), is discussed in Chapter 8.

This book contains an abundance of questioning tactics and ploys. There is also an extended appendix of questions (over 800 open-ended questions) organized by competency. To help you get a good start on your planning, there are chapters on setting the stage and how to structure the interview so that you cover everything within a 40-minute time frame. There is also a plethora of information regarding the legal restrictions and pitfalls that surround interviewing. In other words, this book will prepare you to interview competently and hire accurately the first time. Between these covers are all the tools and techniques I have been teaching managers for the last 28 years in my two-day interviewing workshop.

As an operating manager, your organization anticipates that you will at some point interview and select people to add to your staff. Moreover, your organization probably assumes that you already know how to do this proficiently. Do you?

Perhaps you recognize how difficult it has become in today's world to remove marginal or troublesome performers. It would make sense, therefore, that you guarantee yourself of competent interviewing skills so that you only select the best people for your staffing needs. No management function is more critical than the hiring of competent, productive employees who will be vigorous contributors in the years to come. No matter how good a manager you may be, you still cannot do all the work yourself. You have to depend on others—your staff. If they do a good job, you look competent; if they do a poor job, you seem inept. Your staff is the lifeblood of your career. They can either impede or advance your career.

What you need, and what this book provides, is an easy-to-use strategy along with a step-by-step guide for navigating through a rational process of meticulous preparation. It is a logical, intelligent, and repeatable system that recognizes two significant items:

1. You want to spend a minimum amount of time on the interview.
2. You want a strategy that generates superior results *every* time it is used.

This book will demonstrate that all you need is 30 minutes of thoughtful preparation, 10 good questions, and 40 minutes for the interview to do the job. The strategy is flexible and can be easily implemented to target your individual needs and specifications no matter what skill set or employment experience you are seeking in a candidate. It is a practical—not a theoretical—approach to interviewing. It will provide you with the essential tools and insight necessary to interview and hire candidates who will give you maximum productivity with minimum aggravation while at the same time giving your organization an optimum return on payroll dollars.

DeAnne Rosenberg
Widow's Cove, Wareham, Massachussetts
www.managementsense.com

Chapter

Introduction

■ BACKGROUND

Although they are used in nearly all selection processes, face-to-face interviews coupled with personal and/or business references are the *least accurate predictors* of future job performance.[1] As illustrated by the interview provided later in this chapter, you can easily see why. This dreadful statistic is further borne out by the experience of many human resource professionals and various investigations on the subject. Among the many reasons cited for this ominous situation are the following:

- Ineffective analysis of the candidate's background.
- Inappropriate selection strategies used in the decision process.
- Confusion and lack of clarity regarding expectations.
- Ignoring the fact that the successful candidate must have a very steep learning curve.
- Irrelevant job description and/or skill set.
- Failure to ensure that the values of the candidate and the organization mesh.
- Forgetting to ascertain whether the selected candidate has the capacity to learn.

Studies from the U.S. Department of Labor indicate that 50% of all new hires leave the job within the first six months.[2] Many quit because the position turns out to be something other than what was described (sold) to them in the interview. Some leave because they object to how they are being managed. Others are relieved of their duties because they prove themselves unfit for the jobs for which they were hired. Moreover, no amount of training seems to be able to correct a poor hire. At an average salary of $50,000 year, companies pay astronomical sums for their hiring errors (see Table 1.1).

According to studies from the Center for Creative Leadership in North Carolina, 50% of the senior executives hired today will fail in their new positions.[3] Generally speaking, however, these individuals will remain with the organization, forcing their staffs and colleagues to work around their inefficiencies. Even though a combination of methods may be used to make the selection (e.g., testing, personal interview, and psychological profile), the final determinant and principal criteria used to differentiate the successful candidate from all the others are usually the following:

- The person who will best fit into the culture.
- The candidate who will most likely be approved of by the key decision maker.

It is the mission of this book to rectify these dreadful statistics. The personal interview can and should be an accurate predictor of future job performance if preceded by a precise analysis of the position and impeccable, thoughtful preparation prior to the interviewing event. The process advanced in this book contains three basic steps:

1. Analyzing the core responsibilities of the position.
2. Determining what skills, knowledge, experience, attributes, and competencies are needed to meet those responsibilities.
3. Generating appropriate questions that, when answered, will provide solid evidence of the candidate's possession or lack of the required qualities.

All the analysis and preparation must be done prior to speaking with a single candidate. In this way, the basis for the interview becomes the requirements for the position rather than the candidate's resume and background.

Table 1.1   The Price Tag on Turnover

The U.S. Department of Labor statistics indicate that 50% of all new hires leave their jobs within the first six months. At an average salary of $50,000 year (for a supervisory candidate or a junior-level engineer), you may be throwing away a great deal of money on hiring errors that should not have happened.

The categories and percentages shown in this table are based on a study done by The Society for Human Resource Management; the actual financial data is based on a yearly salary of $50,000 a year for a candidate who does not require relocation.

Category	Percentage of Salary	Cost in Dollars
Cost of inadequacy of the new employee (12 months)	[46%]	$23,000
Cost of assistance by coworkers closely associated with the new employee (12 months)	[33%]	$16,500
Cost of declining productivity of departing employee (1.5 months)	[6%]	$3,000
Cost of shift of attention from the work to the departing employee by coworkers (11% over 1.5 months)	[2%]	$1,000
Cost of leaving the position vacant or functioning with stopgap measures (13 weeks)	[50%]	$25,000
Cost of processing both the departing employee and the new employee by human resources department	[3%]	$1,500
Cost of recruitment (newspaper ads, agency fees, etc.) and screening of applicants by human resources department	[10%]	$5,000
Cost of operating department time in processing and orienting the new employee (49 hours)	[8%]	$4,000
Cost of relocation		$0
Total cost		$79,000
Ratio of costs to average salary		1.58

Source: Douglas Phillips, "The Price Tag on Turnover," *Personnel Journal (Society for Human Resource Management)*, December, 1990, pp. 58–61.

This book describes a logical, intelligent, repeatable strategy that is easy to apply. It is a system that recognizes the following:

- As a hiring manager, you want to spend a minimum amount of time on the interview.
- Whatever system you use must generate superior results *every* time it is used.

This book will demonstrate that all you need is 10 good questions and 40 minutes to do the job.

■ YOUR USUAL STRATEGY FOR HIRING

When you are involved in selecting people for key positions on your own staff, your primary concern is to hire *failure-proof candidates*. Perhaps you feel that the success or deficiency of the selected candidate may have a considerable effect on your own career.

Because the process of selecting the right person for the job is based on a process of risk aversion, the most attractive candidates are probably those whom you have observed in other positions, perhaps as temporary workers, trainees, or summer interns. Should this method fail to uncover a suitable candidate, you may try asking close friends and colleagues whose opinion you trust to recommend possible candidates. Should these efforts fail to locate an appropriate candidate, you will attempt to look for candidates whose background and experience indicate that they have handled similar tasks and activities in prior jobs. Your assumption is that if the candidate did it before, surely he or she can do it again for me.

During the actual interviewing process, you will evaluate candidates on items that may not have very much to do with the requirements for the position, such as the following:

- School attended and grade point average attained.
- Whether the candidate articulates a knowledge of function specific task skills (i.e., uses the appropriate jargon).
- The candidate's level of interpersonal skills.
- Whether the candidate displays good communication skills.

In so doing, you are ignoring the characteristics that can point you to the successful candidate.

■ KEY ITEMS FOR LONG-TERM SUCCESS

The following three items are not generally considered in the interview process but actually prove to be the most important of all in terms of long-term success:

1. The candidate's ability to learn.
2. The candidate's values.
3. The candidate's cognitive ability.

The Importance of the Candidate's Ability to Learn

Organizational impatience is a by-product of the short-term mentality that plagues most of society today. Therefore, a candidate's ability to learn and learn quickly becomes critical to his or her success. It used to be that people had a honeymoon period of one year in which to assimilate themselves into the inner workings of the organization and make some decisions about how they wanted to shape their jobs. For today's lucky candidate, that period has been compressed into a few weeks at best. Not only do the new hires have precious little time to grasp the job, they are expected to produce results almost immediately.

The Importance of the Candidate's Values

There must be a commonality of conviction between the candidate's personal values and the values cherished by you and the organization. Such concerns are not usually addressed in the interviewing process, but only after hiring has taken place. Then it becomes a major issue. Values are a key component of strategic thinking and problem solving. They determine how the organization wants its people to make decisions. When it becomes apparent that the values of a person differ with those of the organization, the person is generally pressured to resign.

The Importance of the Candidate's Cognitive Ability

It is a rare event for an interviewer to consider the depth of a candidate's wisdom and acumen. Yet this is another area that becomes an important factor in long-term job success. Any experienced candidate has made his or her share of mistakes. When competent candidates make mistakes, however, they acknowledge, accept, and attempt to learn from them. Candidates who reject their mistakes by blaming others or stating that their organization was at fault do not have the capacity to learn. They have never accepted responsibility for their mistakes; in their mind, they don't make mistakes. Therefore they have nothing to learn from those negative situations (except that other people don't know what they're doing). If given a responsible job, they will most likely fail at it.

When an employee acts, two capacities are utilized: the technical ability to do the work (the necessary knowledge and skills) and the thinking (decision making) about how to do it. The latter involves an overview or structure of concepts that is used to evaluate situations and guide actions. Such a structure is the result of prior experiences—particularly failures. The experiences and learnings have been incorporated into a thought process that the person uses to evaluate future situations and guide future actions. A candidate who is highly skilled at decision making will demonstrate a well-developed and evolving overview about what he or she is doing and how various work challenges should be dealt with.

An astute interviewer should ask candidates about their blunders, examine what they learned from them, and how what was learned influenced later decisions. Desirable candidates look at a mistake as feedback rather than as a failure, regard every job assignment as developmental, and seek out challenging opportunities where the pressure to learn will force them to grow professionally and stretch their capabilities.

Why a Candidate's Level of Intelligence Is Critical

Often the perfect candidate (in terms of skills, experience, etc.) is hired and, as inconceivable as it may seen, within six months, it becomes apparent that the person hired doesn't have the right skills to handle the position. The reason is that, whereas the job description used to delineate the vacancy contained information regarding specific tasks, title, compensation, desired personal characteristics, and reporting relationship, there was precious little information regarding competencies, sagacity, expected results, and future needs. The selected candidate, therefore, was actually hired on the basis of a finely tuned job description that reflected yesterday's needs.

The skill set of the selected candidate, therefore, became immediately obsolete and meaningless in terms of future needs. Moreover, there was probably no attempt to ascertain whether the candidate could, if the situation required it, recast and retool him- or herself in order to adapt to a changing environment. With so many organizations transforming themselves these days, there is no question that the candidate of today must be able to do the same, or be out of a job tomorrow.

■ THE CHALLENGE

The big question then becomes what you should be looking for in candidates that assures you that they can handle the job at present but which also shows that they are equipped for tomorrow's responsibilities—responsibilities that are not yet known. Such a candidate exhibits the following qualities:

- Has broadly based rather than narrowly specialized knowledge.
- Knows many strategies and techniques within the discipline.
- Believes in the same values the organization admires.
- Is a fast and perpetual learner, resilient in the face of failure.
- Demonstrates flexibility.
- Looks at change as a challenge rather than as a disaster.
- If going into a leadership role, has superior management skills.

As the hiring manager (i.e., the person who needs a new employee), you start the process by providing the human resources department with a vague description of what you want in a candidate. It then becomes the task of the human resources department to provide you with a short list of suitably talented candidates from which to choose. Obviously, the human resources department cannot do a competent job without an adequate and clearly delineated description of the specific skills and experience you require. If all you tell the human resources department is that you "need another pair of hands in here before the end of the month," and from that they produced an appropriate short list of candidates, the interviewing process will invariably break down at this point.

As a typical manager in today's world, your life is a running battle with inherited troops and their marginal competencies and/or bad attitudes. You may well understand the importance of prudent hiring. You may acknowledge that the workforce is the lifeblood of your organization. You may realize that it is impossible to manage effectively without being able to hire effectively. However, you will also insist that you have no time to devote to preparing for an interview.

If you do not prepare, however, your interview might proceed something like the one that follows. The interview includes many of the most common mistakes likely to occur in a typical off-the-cuff interview. The tragedy is that an inappropriate person will be hired as a result of this interview.

■ A TYPICAL INTERVIEW

Interviewer: Hi! Glad you could come in to see us today. I'm George Winggit. I manage this section. [*Extends hand*]

Candidate: Hi. I'm Nancy Doall. Nice to meet you. [*Extends hand*]

Interviewer: So . . . make yourself comfortable. Did you have any trouble finding us?

Candidate: No, not at all. Your assistant's directions were very clear.

This is a nice way to start the interview—an attempt at rapport. The candidate, however, needs to know how the interviewer intends to conduct the interaction. Rapport is not about making friends with the candidate. Neither is it about playing psychologist to the candidate's anxiety. Establishing rapport is

(Continued)

(Continued)

accomplished by stating at the onset of the meeting how the interview will be structured. The interviewer might say, "At Junkit Manufacturing we try to match a person's strengths to our job needs. Now in order for me to assess whether we have the right job for you, I need to know something about you. I need to know about your previous job experiences, maybe something about your goals and career plans, and maybe a little about how you spend your nonwork time. Suppose you start by telling me about your responsibilities at Lowe Bidd Construction."

Interviewer: Good. Good. I'd just like to take a few minutes here to refresh myself on your background. [*Looks at the candidate's resume*] So, I see here that you live about 20 miles from our facility.

Thirty seconds into the interview, it becomes obvious that the interviewer has not prepared himself for the discussion. He is forced into using the candidate's resume as the springboard for the interaction rather than a meticulously developed job specification or list of requirements.

Candidate: Yes. I'm not far away at all.

Interviewer: Good. Good. And I see here that you graduated from Dummer Thandirt University.

If the interviewer begins the process by examining the candidate's resume and then asking questions that relate to the resume information, the interviewer has created a moving target as the basis for the interview. Every interview, then, is about the candidate's resume rather than the requirements of the position. The job requirements, however, are what should provide the foundation for the interview. Only then is it truly possible to evaluate one candidate versus another.

Candidate: Yes.

Interviewer: So did my niece. She has lots of good memories of the place.

Candidate: I really enjoyed my years there, too.

Interviewer: She spoke of a bar just off campus—the Dungeon, I think she called it.

Candidate: Oh yes. That was the campus hangout.

Interviewer: Do they still sell those huge roast beef sandwiches for three dollars?

> *The interviewer has become a victim of the "halo effect." This happens when the interviewer finds something in the candidate's background that matches something in his or her own (such as attending the same university or having grown up in the same town). That similarity gives the entire interview a golden glow so that, when negative information surfaces, the tendency of the interviewer is to play it down or ignore it.*

Candidate: Probably. Your niece must be a recent graduate because they were only a dollar fifty when I was there, and that was 10 years ago.

Interviewer: Ruth—that's my niece—applied for a waitress job there to help with college expenses, but the Dungeon refused to hire her.

Candidate: I understood that the Dungeon had an agreement with the university not to hire any of the students.

Interviewer: Oh really? Perhaps Ruth wasn't aware of that. She thought they didn't hire her because she looked so young.

Candidate: What was Ruth's major?

> *This conversation is wasting both the interviewer's time and the candidate's time. Moreover, it has nothing whatever to do with discovering whether this candidate is a good fit for the vacancy.*

Interviewer: She started out in science—chemistry or biology, I think. In her third year she switched majors and went into prelaw. Now she's at Columbia University Law School.

Candidate: Your family must be very proud of her. Law is a great profession for a woman. It's hard to believe that just 20 years ago, there were very few female lawyers and today . . .

Interviewer: Yes, that's true. I see here [*looks at the candidate's paperwork*] that your major was marketing.

> *The interviewer keeps repeating the information on the resume or application. This wastes everyone's time, but it is an excellent ploy for someone who is not prepared to conduct an interview. Unfortunately, such an approach may signal the candidate that the organization has no real interest in him or her.*

Candidate: That's right.

Interviewer: Did you enjoy that?

> *This is a useless question because it provides no substantive information. A better question might be, "What was the most significant concept you learned from your marketing studies?"*

Candidate: Yes. It was very interesting.

Interviewer: So how did you happen to apply for this job?

Candidate: I have always heard great things about the company, but it was really your newspaper ad that intrigued me.

> *The interviewer should ask, "What have you heard about us?" or "What was it about our ad that intrigued you?"*

Interviewer: This company has always enjoyed a great reputation because of what it offers its employees. We have a very generous benefit package that is presented in a menu format.

The interviewer is selling the organization too soon. Telling the candidate all the things that interviewer believes make the position challenging, rewarding, advantageous, and exciting will not make it attractive to the candidate no matter how enthusiastically the interviewer imparts the information. The only way to find out what excites a candidate about a job—any job—is to allow her to tell her own story.

This allows each employee to tailor their benefits according to their own individual needs. For example, I have a benefit package that includes a 401(k) savings plan, health care coverage, and life insurance. My assistant's package contains tuition reimbursement, AAA coverage, and membership in a health club. I don't know what your plans are for your own career but the best thing about working here is the formalized mentor program. Every new employee is given the opportunity to work closely with one of our senior executives. In other words, you will not be just another cog in the wheel here.

Here is an excellent opportunity to ask the candidate what her career plans are, what she is looking for in a job, and how she would know his firm could offer her that kind of challenge. The interviewer might say, "What are you looking for in a job?" (or looking to avoid) and "How would you know that we could provide you with that kind of opportunity?"

You will have the continued support of a senior person whose sole function will be to help you with such things as experience options, career choices, educational opportunities, and so forth.

Promotions and raises are made on the basis of both performance excellence and the willingness to take risks. That last item I think is the most unusual of all.

> *The most common error interviewers make is talking too much. The most important skill in interviewing is listening. The only time the interviewer can listen to a candidate is when the candidate is speaking. Talking too much (more than 20% of the time) is a sure way to fail in obtaining any meaningful information.*

Should you take a calculated risk in your job and things not work out—as long as you can justify your decision—you will not be penalized, reprimanded, or castigated. In fact, risk takers are valued here. We believe that risk taking is what keeps us ahead of our competition.

Candidate: That's absolutely amazing.

Interviewer: It certainly is. That's what makes us so special. It states in your resume [*looks at the candidate's resume*] that you have been employed by Lowe Bidd Construction as a . . . "Buying Specialist"?

Candidate: Yes. That's right.

Interviewer: What exactly is that? Your resume says you examined building contracts and arranged for the purchase of any unique specialty items that were specified in the documents.

> *The interviewer continues to waste time by repeating the information on the candidate's resume. A better approach might be to ask, "Walk me through what you did as a buying specialist."*

Candidate: Yes. That's right.

Interviewer: Were you involved in price negotiations and bargaining? Did you act as a purchasing agent for the company? Were you responsible for selecting vendors? What about commonly used items that were not specifically stipulated in the contracts?

> *Here the interviewer asks several related questions at the same time. Most candidates, when faced with multiple questions, will only respond to the last one in the series. The others go unanswered. Because the first question in the string is generally the most critical one, the interviewer fails to obtain significant information. A good question might be, "Tell me about your experience with price negotiations."*

Candidate: We had our usual suppliers for those items.

Interviewer: In your resume it states that you manage others. How many people do you actually supervise?

Candidate: I have one permanent employee, and from time to time when the work is especially burdensome, they give me another person on a part-time basis.

> *The interviewer fails to follow up on the candidate's interesting use of the word* burdensome. *An effective follow-up question might be, "Burdensome?"*

Interviewer: So you do know how to supervise others?

Candidate: Yes.

Interviewer: And supervision will not present any problems for you?

> *This is a useless series of questions because it does not provide any substantive information.*

Candidate: No problems.

Interviewer: In this job you will have a staff of four. Will that present any difficulties for you?

> *If the candidate wants the job, she must answer affirmatively, "No problems."*

Candidate: No. Not at all.

Interviewer: What did you like best about your job with Lowe Bidd?

Candidate: Well, I'm a very independent person, and at Lowe Bidd they left me pretty much on my own.

Interviewer: So you like to work without supervision and make your own decisions?

> *Here the interviewer makes an assumption. This is not what the candidate said. There are no facts on which to base this impulsive inference. It would be more effective to ask, "Please give me an example of how you operated independently at your previous job."*

Candidate: Yes, I do.

Interviewer: Do you consider yourself a self-starter or someone who needs a managerial nudge every now and then?

Candidate: I am definitely a self-starter.

> *This question does not give worthwhile information because it telegraphs the desired response. Moreover, the answer, although obvious, is not (or cannot be) checked for truthfulness.*

Interviewer: That's good, because we value self-starters and independent thinkers.

> *Here the interviewer might have said, "Give me an example of a situation at Lowe Bidd where you had to be a self-starter."*

    In this position, negotiating with our suppliers will be a critical part of your duties.

> *It is a major mistake for the interviewer to say anything that might be interpreted as a commitment for employment. He should have said, "a critical part of the duties in this position."*

As a manufacturing operation, what we pay for parts often determines our profit margin. This is quite different from what you did at Lowe Bidd. Do you think you could handle it?

Candidate: Yes, of course.

Interviewer: So negotiating won't present any problems?

This sequence of questions serves no purpose except to take up time while the interviewer is mentally engaged in devising his next question. Without adequate preparation—which includes a preselected battery of questions—the interview will probably contain many such irrelevant questions to hide the fact that the interviewer is preoccupied with question generation.

Candidate: Well, my boss thought I was pretty good at it.

Interviewer: How do you feel about your negotiating skills?

Candidate: I think I am a very good negotiator.

Interviewer: I figured as much. You look the part.

Candidate: Do I?

Interviewer: Oh, yes. You have that straight-in-the-eyeball look, along with a firm, confident voice. I take it that you did negotiate with suppliers on price.

Interviewers too often make impulsive conclusions and generalizations based on a candidate's physical characteristics. It shows how interviewers' biases may work against them by influencing them to hire a candidate based on appearance ("looks the part"), verbal facility ("thinks well on their feet"), apparent values ("sounded honest and forthright"), or superficial behavior ("looked me straight in the eye").

Candidate: Well . . . um . . . err . . . now and then.

Interviewer: What else did you negotiate on?

Candidate: Most often on terms, sometimes on delivery dates, and once in a while on shipping costs.

Interviewer: So negotiating will not present any problems for you?

Here is another assumption followed by an obvious hesitation by the candidate (known as "free information") that should be followed up. The interviewer might ask, "Tell me about your favorite price negotiation strategies" or "Describe a particularly challenging negotiating situation." He needs to obtain a clearer picture of what and how she actually negotiates. The question he used is useless.

Candidate: No.

Interviewer: What about human relations?

Candidate: I beg your pardon?

Throughout this interview, there are abundant examples of poor sequencing of questions. This one is particularly noticeable. When an interviewer's questions jump from area to area, the result is superficial data from many areas of the candidate's background but no in-depth knowledge of any one area.

Interviewer: What I mean is, how do you get along with all the people you work with—not just the suppliers and customers, but internally, especially with coworkers and upper management?

Candidate: I never had any problems. We all got along well.

Interviewer: Did you ever have a conflict situation with any of your coworkers?

Candidate: Well, umm, no, not really.

Here, the candidate gives an evasive response that should be pursued. This question should have been, "Tell me about a time when you had a conflict situation with a coworker. How did you handle it?" The difference is between reaching for the

(Continued)

(Continued)

candidate's actual experience and finding out if the candidate knows the textbook answer. The interviewer has not discovered anything about the candidate's ability to manage conflict.

Interviewer: Suppose you did have a conflict with someone; how would you handle it?

Candidate: I'd go talk with the person and see if we could work things out.

Interviewer: We go to great lengths to ensure that every department works together for the good of the company. We regard cooperation and teamwork of critical importance here.

Candidate: I think that's very important too. At Lowe Bidd, my boss used to say all the time that interdepartmental cooperation was job number one.

Interviewer: Are you a team player or do you consider yourself as more of a loner type?

This question gives no worthwhile information because it telegraphs the desired response. If the candidate wants the job offer, she must affirm that she is a team player. A question such as, "What responsibilities do you believe you have toward your peers in other areas of the company?" might bring forth interesting information. After the candidate answers, a good follow-up question might be, "How were those responsibilities carried out?"

Candidate: I think I am a very good team player.

Interviewer: That's good. Your success here will depend on that. Was there anything you particularly did not like about your job with Lowe Bidd Construction?

Here the interviewer has again said something in a way that might be construed as a commitment for employment. This is

(Continued)

> *(Continued)*
>
> *also another example of poor sequencing of questions. Without designing a structure beforehand that controls the flow of the exchange, the interviewer skips from one topic to another, gaining only shallow information about the candidate's experience and abilities.*

Candidate: Nothing really . . . except that . . . well . . . there are always times when tempers get short because there's more to do than one can possibly accomplish within the allotted time frame.

Interviewer: But that's a part of every job, isn't it?

Candidate: It doesn't need to be if everyone would just do their job and make a little effort at being organized.

Interviewer: I think you're absolutely right about that. For some people, however, being organized is almost impossible.

> *Here the interviewer gives the candidate evaluative feedback. It is not the function of the interviewer to hold up his or her end of the conversation by commenting on, agreeing with, or disputing what the candidate has said. The interview is not a social event; the interviewer's opinions are of no concern here.*

Candidate: I'm a very organized person. I plan my work carefully so that every detail is handled in an orderly manner and each project is completed on time. It really bothers me when other people's lack of planning puts me under pressure.

Interviewer: How did you handle that kind of pressure?

> *This is a good question.*

Candidate: I just did my job. If it was necessary, I just worked overtime. But everything was completed when it was supposed to be.

Interviewer: Did you talk to those people who created the problem?

> *This is a good follow-up question.*

Candidate: I didn't want to make matters worse. If I made them angry, they could make things very difficult and unpleasant for me.

> *This very interesting response should be thoroughly examined. It may have a bearing on how the candidate typically handles conflict. The interviewer fails to follow up by asking, "How do you determine which difficult situations require you to speak up?"*

Interviewer: What was the most difficult part of your job with Lowe Bidd Construction?

> *This is a good question.*

Candidate: Client specification changes.

Interviewer: I thought you didn't interact directly with customers.

> *This is a good follow-up to gain clarity on what was said.*

Candidate: No, never directly, but sometimes clients would make changes to their contract specifications after everything had been negotiated and purchased. Making those revisions created a ton of extra paperwork, to say nothing of the problems it created with the suppliers, especially if they had already started production of the items I had originally ordered. Believe me, it was a mess.

Interviewer: But you took care of it.

> *Why not ask the candidate, "How specifically did you handle such situations?"*

Candidate: Yes. I had to. That was my job.

Interviewer: We consider our suppliers every bit as important to the success of our business as our customers.

> *This is information the candidate does not need at this point.*

We try to build long-term relationships with both groups. We will happily make a supplier our exclusive source on a particular part if they give us both their best price and a product that meets our specifications. Our customers make us their sole source when we show that we offer a quality product—in other words, a product that meets their specifications.

> *The interviewer is talking too much.*

When problems occur with either group, it is critical that we resolve the issues without alienating either party and, of course, without putting the company in a financial hole.

Candidate: That's really interesting. At Lowe Bidd, we were encouraged always to shop around for the best price.

Interviewer: Did you ever visit any of Lowe Bidd's construction sites?

> *Here is another poor transition.*

Candidate: Yes. Once in a while.

Interviewer: Did you enjoy that?

> *This is a useless question because it doesn't generate any useful information. A better question here would be, "What did you learn as a result of your site visits?" or "What purpose did your site visits serve?"*

Candidate: Yes, I did. It was always very interesting to see how the items I had purchased for the building actually got incorporated into the final product.

Interviewer: Well, unfortunately, you won't be able to identify the individual parts you negotiate for in our finished products. Everything's internal. However, you will be expected to visit the production lines frequently to get a feel for how everything comes together. The line foreman can then show you what happens when we get parts that don't quite meet specifications.

> *The interviewer is talking too much. Here again is an imbedded assurance of employment.*

How would you feel about that?

Candidate: Sounds great! I'm sure I'd enjoy that very much.

> *This is another question that serves no purpose except to take up time. The question telegraphs the desired response; if the candidate wants the job offer, she must answer in the affirmative.*

Interviewer: I've seen the name of the company at many commercial building sites in the city. Was Lowe Bidd involved in other types of construction?

> *This is another bad segue. In addition, the new topic doesn't add any information to the evaluation process.*

Candidate: You mean like private homes?

Interviewer: Yes.

Candidate: No. Just commercial.

Interviewer: How long have you been with Lowe Bidd?

> *Here we have a series of direct questions that limit the amount of information received. They also discourage the candidate from speaking freely, prevent the interviewer from learning how the candidate thinks, and, when used back-to-back, make the exchange seem like an interrogation rather than an interview. Moreover, the answers to all of these questions can probably be found on the resume.*

Candidate: About 11 years. It was my first job out of college.

Interviewer: Have you been in purchasing all that time?

Candidate: No.

Interviewer: How long have you been in the purchasing role?

Candidate: Just the last three years.

Interviewer: What did you do before that?

Candidate: I sort of ran the office operations.

> *What does "sort of ran the office" mean? This interesting comment needs to be explored.*

Interviewer: It states on your resume [*looks at the candidate's resume*] that you are looking for a "better opportunity"?

Candidate: Yes. I want something more challenging, and your position sounds like something I would find both challenging and rewarding.

Interviewer: What made you decide that your present position no longer held any challenge for you? Did you suddenly feel that things were becoming routine? Did you ask your boss for more challenging assignments? Did your job change recently?

> *The interviewer has again asked several related questions at the same time. When faced with multiple questions, the candidate will invariably respond only to the last one in the series. Generally, the first question in the series (an open-ended question) is the most important one, and it goes unanswered.*

Candidate: Yes, it did.

Interviewer: How did it change?

Candidate: The federal restrictions and building codes regarding fire safety and such have created more standardization requirements on the kinds of items I was in charge of purchasing.

Interviewer: Did that mean you had fewer sources from whom you could purchase items? Or was it that there were fewer specialty items that could be specified in the building contracts? Or was it that you had to determine whether the specialty item designated actually met code?

> *These are multiple-choice questions for which the interviewer has furnished the candidate with a handy laundry list of possible responses. Because it is the interviewer's population of responses, one can't be sure what the candidate's real answer is.*

Candidate: Mostly the second—fewer items could be designated.

Interviewer: Why did you find the job less rewarding? Was it because you had a decreasing amount to do? Was it because you had fewer opportunities to make decisions? Or was it because you feared your job might be eliminated?

Candidate: There was less decision making.

Interviewer: Here's an interesting question for you. Suppose you went to the North Pole for six dark months of solitude. You would have all the provisions necessary to sustain life, but you could take only three personal computer disks with you. What three would you take and why?

Many interviewers have a "magic question" that they like to ask. Such questions, when answered, are supposed to provide penetrating information regarding the candidate's psyche, personality, and general attitude toward life. This is such a question. It is really an excuse for not doing the difficult investigative work an effective interview requires.

Candidate: The Holy Bible for inspiration, the *Encyclopedia Britannica* for mental stimulation, and something on exercise and fitness to help keep me physically fit.

Interviewer: We all have strengths and weaknesses. Tell me about your weaknesses.

This is a favorite question for most interviewers. It actually says, "Please give me a reason for not hiring you." A bright candidate would have to be an idiot to respond to that question honestly. What candidates usually do is pick a strength that they think the interviewer values and talk about that in seminegative terms. A better question might be, "What do you consider your greatest strengths to be?" followed by "Where do you feel less competent?"

Candidate: People tell me I'm relentless on details; that I overdo it sometimes.

Interviewer: Do you think you overdo it?

Candidate: No. Never. It's what they pay me to do. That's my job—making sure that all the items specified in the contract are purchased exactly as the contract stipulates. My coworkers are not held to the exacting standards that I am. They just don't understand.

> *This comment should be followed up. A good question might be, "Please give me a specific example that illustrates how your standards were exact while the standards of others were not."*

Interviewer: I'm delighted to hear that you are detail oriented. Attention to details will be critical in this job. As you may already know, in manufacturing, one part that is just a little too large or a wee bit too small may make the entire product fail. Sometimes, a supplier will try to push a part on us that doesn't quite meet spec.

> *The interviewer is talking too much.*

They may even offer the parts to us at a reduced price. The person in this job must be able to refuse those parts without alienating the supplier. There aren't many suppliers who make the parts we use, so we have to be careful how we say "no" when parts don't meet spec. Do you think you could handle that kind of thing?

> *This is another question that provides no worthwhile information. If the candidate wants the job offer, she must answer in the affirmative. The interviewer should ask, "When a supplier did not meet your expectations, how did you handle that situation?"*

Candidate: Absolutely!

Interviewer: Suppose you had a supplier that wanted you to accept a load of parts that did not quite meet spec. How would you handle that?

Candidate: I'd tell him we could not accept the shipment and risk jeopardizing our production. However, if it did happen again, I'd look for another supplier.

Interviewer: Would you threaten him with that?

Here the interviewer misses a great opportunity to role-play with the candidate, where the interviewer takes the role of the devious supplier.

Candidate: Probably not.

Interviewer: Did situations like this happen to you at Lowe Bidd?

Candidate: I really wasn't dealing with those kinds of specifications. My suppliers might want me to accept brass-plated fixtures when the contract specified solid-brass fixtures. One time a supplier offered me a give-away low price on ceramic tile when the contract specified a particular brand of linoleum.

Interviewer: Did you present the option to your boss or the client?

Candidate: No. I didn't have any dealings with the clients. I just made sure that what was specified in the contract got purchased.

Here is the second example where the candidate had an opportunity to use some initiative and step beyond the narrow boundaries of her job to negotiate or problem solve. Once again she chose not to do so.

Interviewer: Well, do you have any questions for me?

Candidate: Yes, I do. Does this job require knowledge of accounting procedures?

Interviewer: Well, you know, I'm not sure. I don't think so. You would be expected to understand exactly what we need and how much we should pay in order that the finished product can be competitively priced. That way we can make a reasonable profit on it.

> *The interviewer is not 100% clear on what a candidate for this position must have (competencies, knowledge, or skills) in order to be successful in the job.*

Candidate: Would I be told what that price was?

Interviewer: Not exactly. You would be working with our suppliers, our engineering team, and of course the production manager. It would be a team effort to secure the best part for the lowest price.

Candidate: A team effort? That sounds . . . um . . . quite . . . um . . . challenging.

> *This is free information and should be followed up with a question such as, "What do you think would be especially challenging about working that way?"*

Interviewer: You've worked on teams before where all members participated in the decision-making process, haven't you?

> *This is a poor question as illustrated by the response to it. A more effective question might be, "Describe a situation where you worked on a team where decision making was involved."*

Candidate: Oh, yes.

Interviewer: Do you prefer working alone or in a team?

Candidate: Well, it all depends on the task involved. Some tasks are most effectively handled by one person. Other tasks are better handled by a team.

> *The candidate did not answer the question. The interviewer did not follow up. An appropriate follow-up question might be, "Give me an example of a situation where you were working with a team on a problem that might have been better handled by a single individual."*

Interviewer: Do you have any other questions?

Candidate: Yes. When do you expect to be making a hiring decision?

Interviewer: Probably by the end of next week. However, if you do not hear from me or human resources by that time, please feel free to give me a call. I want to thank you very much for coming in to see us today. I am very impressed with your background and experience. I do think you would fit right in here, but I still have several other candidates to interview.

The interviewer should not say anything that could be interpreted as a commitment to hire.

Candidate: Thank you very much for the interview. I shall look forward to hearing from you.

■ NOTES

1. David DeVries, "Executive Selection: Advances but No Progress," *Issues and Observations Newsletter* (Center for Creative Leadership) 12, no. 4 (1992):2–5.
2. Reported by Edward Betof, *Just Promoted! How to Survive and Thrive in Your First Twelve Months as a Manager* (New York: McGraw-Hill, 1995).
3. Melvin Sorcher, *Predicting Executive Success: What It Takes to Make It in Senior Management* (New York: Wiley, 1985); David DeVries and Randall White, "Making the Wrong Choice: Failure in the Selection of Senior-Level Managers," *Issues and Observations Newsletter* (Center for Creative Leadership) 10, no. 1 (1990): 1–5; DeVries, "Executive Selection."

■ REFERENCES

Betof, Edward. *Just Promoted! How to Survive and Thrive in Your First Twelve Months as a Manager.* New York: McGraw-Hill, 1995.
Campbell, Richard, and Valerie Sessa. "Choosing Top Leaders: Learning to Do It Better." *Issues and Observations Newsletter* (Center for Creative Leadership) 15, no. 4 (1995):1–5.
Carbonara, Peter. "Hire for Attitude, Train for Skill." Fast Company, August–September 1996, pp. 73–81.
Charan, Ram, and Geoffrey Colvin. "Why CEO's Fail." *Fortune,* June 1999, pp. 69–78.
DeVries, David. *Executive Selection.* Greensboro, NC: Center for Creative Leadership, 1993.
———. "Executive Selection: Advances but No Progress." *Issues and Observations Newsletter* (Center for Creative Leadership) 12, no. 4 (1992):1–5.
Dou, Alan. "Planned People Obsolescence." *Training Magazine,* February 1995, pp. 54–58.
Phillips, Douglas. "The Price Tag on Turnover." *Personnel Journal* (Society for Human Resource Management), December 1990, pp. 58–61.
Sessa, Valerie, and Richard Campbell. *Selection at the Top.* Greensboro, NC: Center for Creative Leadership, 1997.
Sessa, Valerie, and Jodi Taylor. "Choosing Leaders: A Team Approach for Executive Selection." *Leadership in Action Newsletter* (Center for Creative Leadership) 19, no. 2 (1999):1–6

Sorcher, Melvin. *Predicting Executive Success: What It Takes to Make It in Senior Management.* New York: Wiley, 1985.

White, Randall, and David DeVries. "Making the Wrong Choice: Failure in the Selection of Senior-Level Managers." *Issues and Observations Newsletter* (Center for Creative Leadership) 10, no. 1 (1990):1–5.

Chapter 2

Setting the Stage

■ VICTIMIZATION OF THE (UNTRAINED) INTERVIEWER

Employment is a risky business because you are buying something before you know how well it will work. If you were purchasing an expensive piece of equipment, such as an automobile, you might first read articles telling you about repair costs, mileage, resale value (the equivalent of resume information), and so on. If you had a friend who owned a similar model, undoubtedly you would ask about their experience with the car (the equivalent of references).

Yet, when it comes to the employment process, if the people doing the interviewing are unskilled in the process, they will make the decision to hire based on 20 or 30 minutes of conversation in which they do most of the talking. Because they are so busy running their mouths, they will not really learn anything about the candidate. In addition, they will probably allow themselves to be victimized by the apparent relevance of experience, education, and verbal agility.

Apparent Relevance of Experience

According to various employment statistics, the average U.S. worker remains in the same job about 18 months to 2 years.

32

When a person is unsophisticated in the interviewing process and sees a resume describing a candidate who changes jobs every two years, he or she is reluctant to interview such an applicant. "Job-hopper" is the traditional assessment. The interviewer concludes that, as soon as this candidate is trained and reasonably capable at the job, he or she will walk out the door.

Of course, it is not a certainty that a job-hopping candidate will leave after two years. It isn't certain that such a candidate would remain longer than two years, either. The percentages, however, clearly show that the majority of resumes indicate job changes about every two years. It is truly a rare occurrence to see a resume that shows the candidate has spent five or more years at the same position.

The reason people change jobs often is relatively simple. If you wish to entice a person to leave a job—in which they are moderately happy—to join your organization, you must offer them at least 10 to 15% more cash in the hand. If an employee is doing a terrific job, the most the immediate manager can give them as a merit increase in today's world is 6 to 8%. So, in order to keep pace financially with the marketplace, people feel forced to change jobs periodically.

Conventional wisdom in the personnel arena recognized long ago that so-called job-hopping may not be a complete negative. Candidates who change jobs periodically can offer valuable knowledge and problem-solving skills to an organization—as long as their employment remains within an equivalent range of endeavor—because they have experience with a variety of diverse yet related issues. Length of time on a particular job may be meaningless; you must look further than dates to assess the validity of what appears on the surface to be an important consideration.

Suppose one day the ideal candidate (on paper) with the appropriate skills, experience, qualifications, and background sits down in front of you. The candidate has been in the same job for five years. You think to yourself, "At last, the perfect candidate! Here is someone who has proven their reliability by maintaining a stable, consistent background." Shouldn't you be asking yourself if this block of time represents one year of experience repeated four times or five full years of solid, in-depth growth, development, and seasoning?

Apparent Relevance of Education

The untrained interviewer will ask every recent graduate, "What was your grade point average?" The belief is that the brightest students will make the best employees. In addition, every organization has a hierarchy of preferences etched in stone regarding the assorted institutions of higher learning. Graduates from the various Ivy League schools are at the top, whereas graduates from the local state system are at the bottom. The rationale is simple. If someone with a 4.0 grade point average (GPA) from MIT is hired and fails miserably at the job, the person who selected that candidate can hide behind the excuse that he or she had in fact hired the crème de la crème. No one could have predicted that such a consummate candidate would fail.

Of course, those from the preferred institutions of higher learning and those at the top 10% of their graduating class come into the labor market with high salary expectations. Because all succeeding levels of compensation are based on the inaugural sum established at the start of employment, these people begin expensive and remain expensive.

These bright graduates are impressive in the interview; they speak with clarity and confidence. You are inspired, convinced that they should be a part of your organization. "What can we do to entice you to join us?" you might ask. These brilliant candidates want to know if the company will fund a master's degree in business administration for them at night school.

If these smart candidates follow the pattern of the majority of U.S. workers, you can anticipate that they will leave your organization within two years. Essentially, then, your company will be investing in the education of people who, once that investment was made, take their new knowledge and use it for the benefit of some other organization. These recent graduates want to extend their four years of successful experiences at an educational institution by continuing their educational process. Why not? It makes sense—for them.

By tracking the success rates of their recent hires, many companies have discovered that the achievements on the job of these exceptional candidates were no better or worse than those of other less exceptionally equipped candidates. Many researchers in the field have evidently come to the same conclusion. In fact, if you were to compile a list of research studies that reveal how GPA and success on the job have zero correlation, it could go on for pages.

Those candidates whose GPA history fell in the 50 to 80% range turn out to be a real bargain in terms of compensation issues. These candidates have salary expectations that are not as great as those who are more brilliantly educated. In addition, no candidate in this group will expect your organization to invest in continuing education as a condition of employment. When these candidates are asked if they have any interest in continuing their formal education by attending graduate school at night, they may avoid answering directly. Instead, they may assure you that they are ready to roll up their sleeves and get started on a career. They may have spent four years listening to "How come you're not as bright as Alice," "How come your grades are not as good as Alvin's," and so on, and they are sick of hearing it. They are ready to change their focus to something for which the possibilities of challenge and success might be more rewarding than their educational experiences.

Why aren't GPAs more accurate predictors of job success? Perhaps it has its roots in the way our educational system works. To facilitate the evaluation of test materials, the educational system has devised multiple-choice questions for which a selection of responses, including the correct one, is already supplied (A, B, C, D, none of the above). The problems encountered at work, however, rarely come with the possible solutions already provided. The candidate, once hired, is expected to generate solutions. Maybe it all comes down to a matter of being able to connect a number of disparate pieces of information to come up with a solution rather than the simple act of memorizing separate pieces of data.

The Apparent Relevance of Verbal Agility

An untrained interviewer may enjoy visiting with candidates. Presumably they are more comfortable with talkers. Sales candidates are always a big favorite. In fact, the most-difficult person for many interviewers to talk to is probably the quiet type.

Because, as an interviewer, I had a preference for verbal people, my hit rate (number of successful hires) was not very good. A person with a glib tongue and a polished supply of baloney would always succeed at getting my recommendation that they be hired, whereas the quiet, nervous, and less-verbal person would not. This happened even when the particular vacancy would have been best served by a complete introvert. So often I was told, "That candidate really did quite a snow job on you."

As an astute interviewer, you must understand completely that *the most important skill in interviewing is listening,* not cultivating a friendly conversation. The purpose of the interview, at least initially, is not to exchange facts. It is to glean sufficient information about the candidate to ascertain whether he or she meets the basic qualifications for the job.

It is also important that you listen without judging the candidate. After all, he or she may be nervous and ill at ease or may not be feeling well. Perhaps the candidate got a speeding ticket on the way to see you. Moreover, in most instances, you are not going to be working cheek by jowl with this person. Your personality preferences don't matter. What does matter, however, is whether the candidate meets the requirements of the job. The issue of personality fit is a consideration that should be explored at a later time in the hiring process. (See Chapter 8 for a more complete discussion of personality fit.)

■ BASIC CHARACTERISTICS TO LOOK FOR IN YOUR (IDEAL) CANDIDATE

You should have some specific characteristics in mind to seek in every candidate you would consider to be a potential addition to your team. This is especially true when examining professional- or managerial- (and supervisory-) level candidates. Such characteristics are critical in those who will be charged with leading the organization into the future. The first and most important of these is a continuing interest in learning and growing. Technology is forcing tremendous changes in the workplace. The rules are being rewritten. The so-called ideal candidate should make certain that they sustain a continuing state-of-the-art skill level. This includes being computer literate.

The second characteristic is flexibility in workplace situations coupled with a strong sense of personal ethics. The ideal candidate must be comfortable with change, chaos, and ambiguity. An inability to handle the stress that occurs when things are in flux can destroy a person's effectiveness. You should expect that the ideal candidate does not look to the world for his or her identity and purpose but instead looks within. An open mind is a great asset, but it should be grounded in a foundation of self-knowledge and personal integrity.

A third characteristic is the acknowledgment that relationship building and maintenance is crucial to job success. Even if the organization is *not* organized into teams, you should expect the ideal candidate to understand that no one accomplishes anything without help from others. This is more than the issue of being a team player. The ideal candidate knows the importance of being a proficient negotiator who can give and take when it comes to decision making, sharing scarce resources, and integrating his or her priorities with those of others. He or she recognizes that the way one's own priorities and concerns are addressed is based on the quality of the relationships developed with coworkers. He or she also understands that rapport is established through good communication skills and taking the time to listen to and act on the concerns of others.

The fourth characteristic is about motivation, taking the initiative and being a self-starter. It is about being able to sustain efforts without requiring a boss's prod every once in a while. It is knowing how to motivate oneself to do what needs to be done regardless of personal likes or dislikes. The ideal candidate perceives how to maintain a high degree of energy and enthusiasm to carry him- or herself through those periods of dedicated drudge until the assigned goals have been achieved.

A fifth characteristic concerns seeking feedback from the person to whom one reports. Your ideal candidate should realize that feedback is a gift and therefore exhibit a history of seeking it regularly. Such a candidate perceives that people cannot correct or change something without fully understanding what the problem is and the effect it is having on them, the organization, and their career. They would therefore understand that it is one's responsibility to refrain from becoming defensive but instead to seek clarification by asking questions.

Finally, your ideal candidate should possess a systems point of view. He or she perceives that a change in one area will inevitably affect something in another area and further understands that there is an underlying relationship between people and events that goes beyond cause and effect. This is especially true in the area of decision making. Decisions do not occur in a vacuum. When there are levels of interdependence in an organization, competent decision makers must always consider how their decisions will impact other people and functions in the organization.

■ THE FOUR TRADITIONAL CRITERIA USED FOR SELECTION

Historically, determining who is to be employed, at what level, and for how much compensation, was the function of the human resources department. Human resources also shouldered the responsibility of ensuring a level of organizational consistency with regard to job requirements, candidate skill sets, and compensation levels. In order to promote a level of consistency in the interviewing process itself, the human resource function used four criteria as the foundation of the evaluation strategy:

1. Personal preferences of the interviewer.
2. Personality traits of the candidate.
3. Educational background of the candidate.
4. Behavioral skills of the candidate.

Personal Preferences of the Interviewer

Untrained interviewers will hire people most like themselves. Perhaps we feel more comfortable with those who think like we do or who share a similar background or experience. Although it has been said that opposites attract, in the employment situation, it is really true that similarities attract. This even occurs on the physical plane.

One company for whom I was working had a director of engineering who was six feet four inches tall. He weighed over 300 pounds and sported a head of curly red hair and a bushy auburn beard. I must have referred six or seven candidates to him, all of whom he found unsatisfactory for one reason or another. As far as I was concerned, however, all of them were perfectly well qualified. I decided to visit the manager in person and discuss the position with him in greater detail, hoping to learn why I was off the mark.

As soon as I stepped into the engineering area, the answers to all my questions immediately became clear. Each one of his four engineers was over six feet tall and each had facial hair. None of the candidates I referred to him had been tall or sported facial hair.

The urge to be positively disposed toward those with whom the interviewer shares a similarity is often referred to as the *halo effect*. Here is how it works. In the process of your discussion with the candidate, you uncover an element in the candidate's background that matches one in your own. Perhaps you learn that your employment history is similar; maybe the candidate comes from the same part of the country that you do. Whatever that similarity is, it causes you to sprinkle a little gold dust over the entire interview. Then, when negative information surfaces, your inclination is to dismiss its importance: "Well, she may be a little unethical, but she's also a graduate of Learnwel University. She can't be all that bad. After all, I'm a Learnwel grad myself."

Another side to the issue of personal preferences that bears mentioning concerns gut-level feelings. Every once in a while, a candidate who looks perfect on paper—with the appropriate skills, experience, qualifications, and background—will seat him- or herself in front of you. During the interviewing process, however, you develop a gut-level feeling that tells you, despite the apparent glorious background, this candidate is all wrong for the job. If someone were to ask you how you came to that conclusion, you probably would not be able to explain rationally why you feel that way. You just know. If this ever happened to you, and you made a conscious decision to ignore that gut-level message and hire the candidate anyway, I'll bet that the candidate did not work out.

It is important to listen to those gut-level messages. There is an abundance of information you pick up subconsciously from a candidate's body language. Moreover, if you have been working in a particular organization for a protracted length of time, you have accumulated a good deal of conceptual knowledge concerning the type of person who is likely to be successful in the organization. You can also distinguish what type of candidate is not apt to flourish in that environment. It is a sense of the corporate personality and whether the candidate fits the mold or conflicts with it.

Personality Traits of the Candidate

In previous years a myriad of tests were developed to assess such things as intelligence, initiative, drive, and loyalty ad nauseam. In 1971 the federal courts struck down the use of such tests as discriminatory in the landmark case *Griggs v Duke Power Company* (404 U.S. 424).

From that time on, any such test had to be validated before it could be used as part of the preemployment evaluation. Validating test materials turned out to be prohibitively expensive and unbelievably complicated. Eventually, validated tests for very specific candidate backgrounds (such as accounting, engineering, and sales) became commercially available in the marketplace. The vast majority of organizations, however, opted not to use such tests as part of the employment interview process.

A number of organizations, however, developed their own validated test materials by testing employees *after* they had been hired and *after* they had been in their respective jobs for six months or so. After several years the organizations had collected sufficient data to establish the validity of the test materials they had elected to use.

Educational Background of the Candidate

There was a time when organizations tried to staff every vacancy with college graduates. The result was overqualified people in underdemanding jobs. These new hires quickly became bored and quit. Today, because of the high cost of turnover, most organizations are very careful to match people and jobs based on something more than just educational level.

Many organizations put great stock in where candidates went to school, their GPA, and their nonacademic activities on campus. The belief is that a graduate from a state university could not have gotten as good an education as a graduate from an Ivy League school. Then, too, the higher the GPA, the better employee they would probably be. And participation in nonacademic campus activities, such as sports, glee club, and the like, could translate into superior human relations. It is essential that you always look beyond the superficial facts.

Suppose a candidate graduated from a state university with a 3.0 GPA and did not participate in sports or other extracurricular activities. During her four years, however, she held down a full-time job in order to finance her education. How can that record be compared to a graduate from an Ivy League school who also has a 3.0 GPA, was involved in all kinds of sports and campus activities, and did not have to work in order to finance his education? (See Chapter 3 for more information on how to assess candidates with little or no work experience.)

Formal education may prove that the candidate has the capacity to learn. It says nothing, however, about his or her ability to think, sort through various pieces of information, and generate a solution to a problem. After a few years of work experience, where the candidate went to school is no longer as important as what he or she has accomplished in the workplace.

Behavioral Skills of the Candidate

In its simplest form, assessing the behavioral skills of a candidate is like giving a typist a typing test. These kinds of tests have always been considered legal as long as they mirror exactly what the candidate would be doing on the job. In other words, if you were hiring an accounting clerk who was supposed to post figures to columns, you could give the candidates a posting test but you could not test them on addition and subtraction. If the candidate would be using a calculator at the job, you would have to furnish the candidate with a calculator in the test situation.

If it is at all possible to test an applicant, do so. There is no other way to be certain that the candidate can do what he or she alleges to be able to do. Candidates will tell you anything to protect their candidacy. It isn't a case of purposefully lying. There is something going on at a much deeper psychological level. They want your approval, and the only way they know they have that approval is if you offer them the job.

Most candidates are astute listeners. They will analyze every question you put to them, searching for any hint of the response you want to hear. Their intent is to give you the right answer. Most candidates have learned that, if they can get away with it, a safe answer to almost any question is "yes."

I have a number of clients in the high technology industry who are involved in the manufacture of computer hardware equipment. Their ads in the newspaper read as follows:

Assemblers: No experience required; we will train.
No specific educational level necessary.

They are interested in only one thing: Is the candidate dexterous? The candidate comes into my office, and I ask, "Are you dexterous?" The candidate has no idea what I'm talking about but smiles and says, "Yes!" How do my clients have me test that out? They give me a small subassembly from the plant. I place it in front of the candidate and say, "Play with it; show me how you would start to put this thing together." In five minutes I have the answer as to whether the candidate is dexterous.

I once had a client who owned a chain of gas stations. He used to have frequent job openings for night manager. He would ask these candidates, "Can you make change?" and they would always enthusiastically respond, "Yes!" One new hire cost my client $4,000 the first month he was on the job. If my client had only said to the candidate, "The machine says ten dollars and thirty-five cents; the customer gives you a twenty dollar bill. What's the change you give back to him?" he would have known instantly that this applicant could not make change.

All of this seems quite simple if you are interviewing secretaries, gas-station attendants, and accounting clerks. Those jobs require skills that are easy to test. Most of the people you interview, however, are professionals with highly specialized backgrounds. For these candidates such things as analytical thinking, problem solving, team leadership, creativity, and communication are the critical skills. How do you go about testing candidates for those kinds of competencies?

■ VERBALLY TESTING THE BEHAVIORAL SKILLS OF THE CANDIDATE

Here is the strategy to test a candidate's behavioral skills. Generate 10 good questions and use them during the interview as your test. There are two reasons why you should use at least 10 questions First, you want to plumb the depth, breadth, and width of the candidate's knowledge, experience, and skills. You cannot possibly do that with just four or five questions. The second reason is more complicated.

In its traditional process, the design of the interview is to encourage candidates to clarify their skills, experience, qualifications, knowledge, and background. Then you make some sort of assessment as to how a particular candidate and his or her package of qualities will perform in your environment.

What this new strategy will do is encourage candidates to delineate their skills, experience, qualifications, knowledge, and background and then tell you how they might use them in *your* environment. This takes some complex analysis, creative synthesis, and mental grappling on the part of the candidate. You want to see the candidate do that effectively with more than four or five questions. Besides, 10 is a nice round number.

There are two keys in generating these questions:

1. They must be framed in such a way that the candidate has no idea as to what the right answer might be.

2. You know the answer you are looking for *before* you ask the question.

Some of the best such questions are framed as follows:

- Problem-oriented or puzzle questions that begin with the words "What if . . ."
- Questions that begin with the words "What has been your experience with . . ."
- Questions that ask, "What has been the most-challenging (or difficult or rewarding) situation you've faced as a manager (or team leader or engineer)?"

"What If" Questions

"What if" questions can be fashioned to reflect actual events or problems that already exist in your organization. This way, you create a situation that forces the candidate to mentally transpose his or her package of skills into your environment. Because these questions reflect actual events, you already know which answers will solve the problem and which ones will not. If you describe an actual situation that has not yet been resolved, the candidate may provide you with some new approaches to solving the problem. Such questions totally engage the candidate mentally and provide an excellent opportunity to observe his or her body language. Most important, you have the opportunity to track the candidate's thinking process, the most crucial resource a professional-level candidate will bring to your organization. You want to be certain that the person you hire can think.

Many interviewers believe that these "what if" questions are far superior to any other interviewing strategy. In truth, they are an excellent tool to have in the kit. It is a mistake, however, to rely on only one technique. It would be like a football team that only utilized one play. You will see many other questioning techniques in Chapters 5 and 7. Here are two examples for engaging the candidate with "what if" questions:

Manager: Suppose you discovered that your employees were pilfering office supplies. How would you address that problem?

Candidate: I am not familiar with the rules and policies in your organization for handling that sort of thing. [*The candidate is declining to answer the question.*]

Manager: I realize that. However, I am not interested in the nitty-gritty details of your answer. I would just like to know what your general approach to this problem might be. [*The manager insists the candidate answer the question.*]

Manager: What if you were put in charge of a work team where morale was low, productivity poor, and interpersonal hostility high. What would you do to get the group back on track?

Candidate: Perhaps the best solution might be to disband the group.

Manager: Suppose that were not an option. What would you do to get the group back on track? [*The manager insists that the candidate think about how to resolve the problem.*]

There is one big drawback to "what if" questions. You cannot create them on the spur of the moment. They must be designed ahead of time and completely written out. Unless you can actually read the question word-for-word, you are likely to telegraph the answer, usually by laundry listing a variety of possible responses:

Manager: What if a peer stopped you in the hallway and said that he and his team had run into big problems with some project? He and his team all agreed that you have the expertise to rescue the situation, so they promised the general manager, who is two levels above you, that you would take care of everything. He says that the general manager wants you to have a report ready by tomorrow's 9:00 A.M. managers' meeting. What would you do? Would you ask the peer to set up a meeting with his team so you could review the project? Would you suggest that if he needs your expertise so desperately, he should ask your boss to assign you this task? Would you call the general manager and try to get yourself off the hook? Or would you tell this person that only you and your boss can commit your time, wish him luck with the project, and walk away?

Candidate: That last choice is very appealing. I think I would do that and then contact my boss to learn if she knows anything about this project and if she wants me involved in it.

The more appropriate way of setting up this question would be as follows:

Manager: What would you do if a peer stopped you in the hallway and said that he and his team had run into big problems with their current project? They all agreed you have the expertise to rescue the situation, so they promised the general manager, who is two levels above you, that you would take care of everything and have a report ready by tomorrow's 9:00 A.M. managers' meeting.

Candidate: Do I know what their project is all about and am I familiar with these problems they've run into?

Manager: No, on both counts.

Candidate: And you want to know what I would do?

Manager: Yes.

If your "what if" question is to be a true exploration of the candidate's problem-solving strategy, then you must allow him or her to create the structure for responding to the issue.

"What Has Been Your Experience with" Questions

Beginning a questioning sequence with "What has been your experience with" will help you avoid a commonly used questioning pattern (known as leading the witness) that consistently provides totally useless information on which to base a hiring decision. Here are some examples.

Manager: This job requires some travel. How do you feel about travel?

Candidate: Oh, I like to travel. I traveled quite a bit on my last job.

Manager: So travel won't pose a problem for you?

Candidate: No. No problem.

Suppose this particular candidate is coming from a job where he was on the road about 30% of the time, and the position you have will require him to be on the road 80% of the time. You may have a bad fit, and with this line of questioning, you will never uncover that fact. It would be much more effective if you went after the travel information with the following questioning sequence:

Manager: What has been your experience with job-related travel?

Candidate: At my previous job I traveled about 30% of the time. And frankly, if a month went by and I wasn't out on the road at least twice, I felt something was missing.

Manager: What I hear you saying is that 30% travel is just the right amount to make life interesting.

Candidate: I wouldn't even mind 35 to 40% travel. Even at that level, I could keep my family happy and my paperwork up-to-date.

Willingness and availability to work overtime is another important topic that is covered in many interviews. Here again, unprepared interviewers learn nothing if they approach the questioning process in a haphazard way:

Manager: Overtime is a big part of our work ethic around here. Will overtime cause any problems for you?

Candidate: Oh no. No problem. At this level, I would expect to work some overtime.

Manager: Good. It sounds as if you'll fit right in here.

As a result of this ridiculous exchange, I hired a candidate who, when I mentioned "overtime," was thinking about working until 6:00 P.M. or 6:30 P.M. maybe one or two days a week. My company, however, expected its professional and managerial staff to work every night until at least 6:30 P.M. and 12 or more hours over the weekend—every weekend. If I had approached the overtime question in a more thoughtful manner, I never would have hired this particular candidate:

Manager: What has been your experience with overtime?

Candidate: Once in a while I would stay until 5:50 P.M.—especially if I had something I wanted to finish. But I've always believed that if you are well organized and stay on top of things, there's never a need to work overtime except in very, very unusual circumstances.

Manager: I'd like to hear about those unusual circumstances.

Stress is a big component of secretarial jobs. It comes from having to answer to multiple bosses who have a variety of priorities. Unfortunately, the question regarding stress is generally framed in a way that provides no useful information:

Manager: This job has a lot of stress to it. How are you at handling stress?

Candidate: I'm very good with stress. In fact, I think I do my best work when I'm under stress.

What is a stressful situation for one person may not be stressful for someone else. It would have been more constructive for you to word the question in such a way that the candidate tells you what creates a stressful situation for him or her. A more effective way to ask about the candidate's tolerance for stress is as follows:

Manager: What has been your experience with stress on the job? (*or* What for you creates stress on a job?)

For some secretaries, a dull day is stressful. They like to have hundreds of different things going on all at once so that the day goes by quickly. For other secretaries, dealing with more than three people is a strain, and interruptions destroy their effectiveness. If you are familiar with the environment of the job vacancy, you know if the type of stress prevalent at this particular job would be unsuitable or acceptable for a particular candidate.

"What Has Been the Most Challenging Situation?" Questions

When you go out into the marketplace in search of experienced candidates, it is because you are seeking a person who can just walk into the job and do it. Maybe you tell yourself that you need someone who can operate in the position with very little supervision. You want someone who can think on his or her feet; someone who is a good problem solver in that particular area because of experience. Unless you have prepared your questions ahead of time, however, you are likely to fall into an unproductive questioning pattern that will not provide you with the information you need to make an appropriate hiring decision.

Manager: This job requires someone who is a creative problem solver—a person who can think on their feet. How are you at creative problem solving?

Candidate: I'm very good!

Manager: Good, because that's just what we need around here.

With adequate preparation, the exchange can be very different. Moreover, you would obtain the information needed to make an accurate evaluation of the candidate:

Manager:	What has been the most-challenging situation you faced as an executive?
Candidate:	On my last job I was asked to take over the accounting function. The comptroller was let go because of his illegal manipulation of the accounting statements. Records were a mess and employee morale was at an all-time low. In addition to which I had the IRS and the SEC looking over my shoulder. It was an absolute nightmare.
Manager:	Sounds awful! How come you were given this particular assignment?
Candidate:	Originally, I was hired to take over the company's purchasing function. It had been performing poorly. I was able to turn things around rather quickly. I guess they thought I would be able to do the same in the accounting area.
Manager:	Were you?
Candidate:	Well, things are pretty well straightened out now, but it took a great deal of time, effort, negotiation, and creative problem solving. I can tell you there were days when it seemed as if I was trying to stop the Titanic from sinking with a canteen spoon.
Manager:	I'd really like to hear exactly what you did to get things back on track.

Never ask candidates if they've had problems with anything. Substituting any other word will do just fine, but the word *problems* stops the interaction dead in its tracks even when the question is a good one:

Manager:	Supervision often involves being able to solve difficult people problems. What kind of people problems have you had as a supervisor?
Candidate:	I've never had any serious problems. I've always tried to be fair and honest with my people, and I think when a boss does that, people will respond positively.

Here's what you get using a word other than *problems:*

Manager: What has been the most-difficult employee *situation* you faced as a supervisor?

Candidate: I had this one employee who came to us from a local immigrant resettlement agency. Apparently, in his country of origin, it was customary for people to use threats of violence to get their way. We discovered that this young man carried a large switchblade on his person and would not hesitate to threaten other employees over the simplest of things. The company expected me to "reeducate him." My staff and I wanted him terminated.

Manager: So what did you do?

Remember, in designing a verbal test of 10 questions to be asked during the interview, you should rely on queries that begin with the following words:

- What if?
- What has been your experience with?
- What has been the most-challenging (or difficult or rewarding) situation you've faced as a manager (or team leader or engineer)?

None of these questions provide the candidate with information as to what the right answer might be.

■ BEHAVIORAL QUESTIONS VERSUS PUZZLE QUESTIONS

There is an enormous difference between "What would you do if" questions and questions that ask "What has been your experience with" or "What has been the most-challenging situation." The first question is known as a puzzle or problem-solving question. It is designed to discover how the candidate thinks. Imbedded in the question is the assumption that if the candidate has read enough books on management, he or she can probably come up with a suitable response. The last two questions reach for the candidate's actual, real-life response to a situation. That type of question is known as a behavioral question. Most hiring mistakes are made because the interviewer has relied on too many puzzle-type questions and not enough behavioral questions.

Behavioral questions ask candidates to discuss their actual reactions to specific past situations. Most have an easily identifiable format, such as the following:

Tell me about a situation where you were presented with a project that had no history, guidelines, or structure other than a due date. How did you start?

Describe a time when you were supervising a mediocre performer. What strategies did you use to motivate the person and increase his or her effectiveness?

In the past, how have you ensured that your staff trusts and respects you?

Describe a situation where you dealt successfully with unwanted changes that your boss or the organization had thrust upon you.

Describe the circumstances under which you have supervised most effectively.

Tell me about a time when you successfully coached an employee. I'd be interested in hearing what the performance problem was and how you assisted the person to correct it.

Please describe a common type of conflict situation *you experienced in your previous job.* What process did you use to resolve such situations?

Tell me about a decision you made where things did not turn out as well as you had anticipated.

Relate an incident in which your integrity was challenged.

Behavioral questions target the belief that past performance is the best predictor of future performance. In other words, whatever actions the candidate took in the past situation are probably what he or she would do if faced with a similar situation in the future. These questions can bring forth a good deal of valuable information—about the past. Such questions, however, should be followed up with exploration concerning what the candidate learned from the experience and which he or she will carry forward to future situations:

Manager:	Tell me about a time when you and your staff had a great deal of work to accomplish within an insufficient time frame. How did you handle that?
Candidate:	I just made it mandatory that everyone work overtime until the project was completed.
Manager:	Mandatory?
Candidate:	Well, I gave them the old team speech and told them we all had to pitch in. Of course, I did the overtime with my people. That helped the motivation.
Manager:	And everyone just went along?
Candidate:	Well . . . mostly. . . . There are always one or two who protest.
Manager:	What did you do about the protestors?
Candidate:	I just ignored their excuses and insisted that they go along with the rest of the team.
Manager:	What have you learned from handling such situations in this manner?
Candidate:	I've learned that I'm not very popular with my employees. However, I know that my bosses are always going to leave stuff for the last minute and then push me to get it done right away. The only way to deal with these kinds of situations is to put that pressure on to my people.
Manager:	So you just pass the pressure along.
Candidate:	Right. My bosses certainly aren't going to change their ways. I had to find some method of coping with the problems my bosses created. I figured the best way was to copy them.
Manager:	What have you learned about yourself as a result of operating in this manner?
Candidate:	I've learned that it doesn't take a lot of effort to be a difficult boss. That makes me a little sad. I've always wanted to be a manager who handles everything with patience, understanding, and respect.

Puzzle or problem-solving questions ask what the candidate *would do* in such-and-such a situation. Behavioral questions ask for what the candidate *actually did* in past situations. Behavioral questions are about how candidates use what they know or how they react (in spite of what they know) in specific, real-life situations. Here are some examples of behavioral questions juxtaposed with puzzle questions that ask for similar information but from a different angle:

Behavioral: What strategies have you used to control interruptions?

Puzzle: Suppose you had an important project to do and you kept getting interrupted. How would you handle that?

Behavioral: Describe how you typically go about learning a new skill.

Puzzle: If you were told you had to learn a new skill, how and where would you start?

Behavioral: I'd like to hear about the most-challenging communication you have ever come up against. What made it challenging? How did you handle it?

Puzzle: What do you think are the characteristics of an effective communicator?

Behavioral: Tell me about a situation where the customer's expectation of how their issue should be resolved was clearly impossible. How did you solve that problem?

Puzzle: What if you had a customer who wanted their problem resolved in a way that was totally against company policy? How would you handle that?

Behavioral: What have you done to ensure the full sharing of information among your individual staff members?

Puzzle: Suppose your staff members were not sharing crucial information with one another, and the unit's effectiveness was suffering. How would you turn that situation around?

Behavioral questions are grounded in the belief that the candidate will be faced with situations in the future that will be quite similar to those he or she faced in the past. In addition, behavioral questions assume that the resolution strategies that the candidate used in the past will be available to use in the future. That is not necessarily true. In most cases those future situations will be quite different. If the candidate does face similar situations, the resolution strategies available will be different.

Knowing what the candidate did in the past, therefore, is not sufficient. You also want to know how the candidate thinks and processes information. This is why it is vital that you ask what the candidate has learned from past experience and how that learning is likely to influence future decisions. It is also why you should vary your use of behavioral questions with puzzle questions. You want to challenge the candidate's reasoning ability and judgment concerning situations he or she may not have experienced. A good interviewing strategy is made up of 75% behavioral questions and 25% puzzle questions.

Once you have your 10 test questions designed, you may want to sit down with those employees in your organization whom you consider to be superstars. Let them hear the questions. See how they answer them. This will provide you with additional information regarding what the answers should sound like when they come from a viable candidate.

■ THE FIFTH CRITERION: SELECTION BY OBJECTIVES

Selection by objectives is a new criterion that you should add to the previously discussed four criteria traditionally used as the foundation of the evaluation strategy: personal preferences of the interviewer, personality traits of the candidate, educational background of the candidate, and behavioral skills of the candidate. Selection by objectives assumes that people who have succeeded previously at meeting important objectives—in school or on previous jobs—can do so again, in this job. Alternatively, it assumes that if this candidate has botched and bungled on previous jobs, the chances are excellent that he or she will do so again on this job.

A surprising 80% of the candidates who present themselves for employment consideration live their lives in a remarkably consistent pattern.[1] Of that 80%, only 20% will ever be able to change their pattern. For the remaining 60%, the same issues will recur. All you need to do is look at their paperwork and/or listen to them describe their work history and that pattern will emerge.

If you are like most hiring managers, you probably do see those patterns, but you talk yourself out of their negative implications. Perhaps you tell yourself, "This is a terrific place to work. I'm a great developmental boss. I just know this opportunity will make a crucial difference in the candidate's life. Here he will finally achieve success."

The substantiation of behavior patterns is visible in every aspect of employment. For example, someone who hires bank tellers will tell you that a candidate who stole money from the cash drawer at First Town Bank will probably do the same thing at Second Village Bank. If you were to question a longtime sales manager, he or she would tell you that the sales candidate who cheated on her expense account at Smith Manufacturing is sure to cheat on her expense account at Jones Fabrication. As a department manager, you might have the following exchange with a peer:

You: Don't ask Marie to handle that for you.

Peer: Why not?

You: Because she'll cut corners on your project.

Peer: Perhaps if I explain the importance . . .

You: Believe me, it won't help. Marie cuts corners on everything she does.

People carry this stuff around with them like a sack of potatoes. It goes with them throughout their entire life. They do the same things over and over; no matter what the environment or the circumstances, the same problems occur again and again.

For example, a particular candidate sounded very good on the telephone, so you invited him in for an interview. He presented you with an application that indicated under "Reason for

Leaving," *difficult supervisor.* In his prior position, "Reason for Leaving" was given as *dispute with manager.* The position prior to that one, the "Reason for Leaving" was *disagreement with management.* So you said to the candidate:

Manager: I'd be interested to learn more about this discord and friction which drove you to change jobs.

Candidate: Well, it isn't possible for one person to get along with *everyone* in this world.

You thought to yourself, "He's right. Even I don't get along with everyone around here." So you hired him for the position, and guess what? He couldn't get along with anyone in your organization, either.

Then there was the candidate who had series of highly responsible senior management positions. She was an impressive candidate. At least you were impressed. As she related the history of her various jobs, you learned that within each one people seemed to have conspired against her to "make me look bad" and eventually force her to leave the organization. In one job it was her boss who feared her ability would outshine his, and so he set her up to fail. At another company, it was her peers and subordinates who withheld important information from her. At a third company, it was the comptroller who cut her budget, making it impossible for her to achieve the department's goals. Every explanation was logical. Because she had all the knowledge and experience required for your vacancy, you hired her.

Sixty days later, her supervisor came into your office and presented you with her first probationary report. It recommended that she be terminated. "She refuses to accept responsibility for her mistakes and errors in judgment. She is especially quick to place the blame on others whenever anything goes wrong in her area."

You suddenly remember that she had actually told you that in her employment interview. Obviously, you hadn't been listening to the pattern of what she had been saying. You had gotten lost in the details of her stories.

When you interview, you need to look for people who have succeeded in meeting important objectives before—in school, on other jobs—because then you can be reasonably certain that they will also be able to meet objectives for you. Even when the staff is overworked and the department understaffed, they will reach their goals. They will work until the job is done because that's the way they have always done it. In other words, *past performance is the best predictor of future success.*

If you are going to utilize what the candidate has (or has not) accomplished at previous jobs as a yardstick for determining his or her potential to achieve for you, however, you will need something more than a simple job description from which to work. You will need a set of job objectives.

■ JOB DESCRIPTION VERSUS JOB OBJECTIVES

A job description lists tasks and activities. It is not a sufficient foundation on which to base an interview. You should also have a statement of job objectives: a statement of the achievements, outputs, and results to be expected from the person hired into the position. Using tasks and activities as the basis for your expectations can be a big mistake. A specialized task today may well be archaic tomorrow. Changing technology, computers, and the Internet are continually altering the content and context of every job these days. By hiring people on the basis of skills and tasks they mastered last year you may be judging ability by a yardstick that is already obsolete. A candidate's ability to achieve objectives, produce good results, and think logically and perceptively are characteristics that no amount of change can make obsolete. These are the items you should look for.

For example, suppose you are looking to hire a geewiz machine operator. A candidate comes through your door who proves to you that he is the absolutely very best geewiz machine operator in the entire United States. You hire him, knowing that the geewiz department is going to outfit the plant with a whole new generation of computer-assisted machines—geewiz-LS400 machines—within 12 to 18 months. Your company has a six-month probation period followed by regular six-month performance review periods. You new hire is, of course, spectacular according to his first two performance reports. He should be. After all, he is the best geewiz machine operator the world has ever seen. Then, in his 14th month, the new geewiz-LS400s are installed. Your new hire can't get the hang of how these machines operate. In frustration his supervisor comes into your office and says, "You've got to help me get rid of this bozo. He can't do anything right. He doesn't learn, no matter how many times we go over things."

When you look up the bozo's performance records, you find two performance reports that state he's the best the department has ever seen. You point to the very reports that the supervisor created and say, "I'm sorry, but until you create some appropriate documentation, we have to keep him. He's past his probationary period, and there's nothing in his file to indicate he's anything other than marvelous."

This kind of thing happens every day in businesses when people do not consider what is needed in a candidate to produce the desired results and outputs. It would have been wiser to question your geewiz candidate on such topics as how long it took him to learn a new piece of equipment, rather than his skill at using a piece of equipment. He should have been asked how many pieces of equipment he knew how to use and whether he ever taught anyone how to operate a piece of equipment. In other words, what should have been explored was his depth of knowledge, ability to learn, and flexibility. Because the focus was only on the task of operating the geewiz machine, the person hired was someone incapable of growing with the job because his learning curve had gone into retirement.

Setting Up the Position Description

There is one question that targets job objectives (and which should be at the top of every request for an additional staff member): *What expectations fulfilled within the next 12 months will you regard as satisfactory performance from the person hired into this position?* (see Table 2.1).

As an astute interviewer, you must evaluate, examine, and explore the job thoroughly before speaking with a single candidate. You may have no experience doing that. You may identify with the candidate and think about the days when you sat out in a hallway with sweaty palms, waiting to be interviewed. You are now, however, a buyer of services and as such, you must change your thinking.

Perhaps it is a cold way of looking at things but as an interviewer, you are actually buying a human unit of production for

Table 2.1 Position (Description) Objectives

Position / Vacancy / Job Title			
What Expectations Fulfilled Will I Regard as Satisfactory Performance?			
Key Responsibilities [usually five items]	*Performance Expected* [quality, quantity, time, cost]	*Method of Measurement* [How will you know it when you see it?]	*Competency Required*

the organization. If that human unit doesn't work out, you will be forced to take some time-consuming and unpleasant steps to eliminate it from the organization. It is best, therefore, to hire the right person the first time, thus saving a lot of grief later on. This means it is essential that you think and talk in terms of what you want in the way of achievements, output, and results rather than tasks, activities, knowledge, and skills.

Once you have clarified your expectations, you can consider what knowledge, skills, experience, education, and so on (the competencies) a candidate needs to have in order to meet those expectations.

Most jobs include five key responsibilities and many additional less-important duties. You want to focus on the five key responsibilities. It is helpful to go through the mechanical process of writing down the duties, preferably in priority order. Just putting them down on paper helps you focus on exactly what you need to be looking for in a candidate. For each responsibility, consider the performance expected, the method of measuring the performance, and the competency required to obtain satisfactory performance (see Table 2.1).

For example, suppose you are looking to add a salesperson to your staff. A key responsibility may be to increase sales by 10% in the coming year. When you consider "Performance Expected," you realize that writing "Increase sales by 10%" does not really take in the entire picture. Let's say your organization sells oak trees and radishes. Oak trees require a customization process and a long sales cycle. Oak trees are so costly that customers are obliged to involve a team of people to make the purchasing decision. These sales add considerably to your profit margin. The radishes, on the other hand, are easy to sell. They are not a customized product; they are a commodity. Your organization has priced its radishes far below the price of radishes charged by your competitors. Radish sales, although profitable, really add very little to your bottom line. What they do is get you in the door.

Your "Performance Expected" of the new salesperson must therefore indicate both sales of oak trees and sales of radishes. Even though you would like to establish a parameter of 90% sales of oak trees and 10% sales of radishes, it is not practical. Oak-tree sales are time consuming, and your salesperson needs to be generating some sales of radishes while working on the oak-tree sales. Maybe you decide that a ratio of 30% oak-tree sales to 70% radish sales is equitable.

"Method of Measurement" takes place at the point in the sales process where the commission is declared "earned." You are then ready to look at "Competency Required." If you only consider the competency needs of radish sales, a trainee with minimal industry experience might be sufficient. Oak-tree sales, however, require someone who has experience dealing with senior-level executives. Such salespeople need polished presentation skills, facilitation, and consulting skills, as well as in-depth technical knowledge.

Suppose the second "Key Responsibility" on your list reads "Service our existing customers." Once again, you see that the word *service* doesn't cover the issue. Does it mean phone them once a month to ask, "How's it going?" Does it mean encouraging the customer to increase their level of acquisition of your products or service? In examining the issue of "Performance Expected" you might want to consider putting in something about converting 5% of your radish-purchasing customers into oak-tree customers. Perhaps you want your new salesperson to encourage the oak-tree customers to increase by 10% the level of consulting assistance your company can provide.

Maybe your company is about to release a new product into the marketplace. Every one of your customers are potential buyers of this breakthrough product. The new product, however, represents a totally innovative technology. Customers will have to be educated and convinced of the value of this new technology. In your mind, therefore, *service* may mean introducing all existing customers to this new technology. Perhaps your expectation of actual sales of this new product is secondary. When you consider "Method of Measurement," you have to determine how you will judge whether your salesperson has educated all your customers about this new product. Is distributing literature sufficient, or will you require some level of actual sales? Depending on what you require under "Method of Measurement," you may write in the "Competencies Required" column "Ability to influence others" or "Ability to explain complex technical information with clarity."

Now you can understand why a meticulous evaluation, examination and exploration of the position must be done *before* speaking with a single candidate. It is the key to a successful placement.

■ NOTES

1. These percentages are based on the reported experience of my clients. See also Martin Seligman. *What You Can Change and What You Can't.* New York: Knopf, 1994.

Chapter 3

Designing
and Using the
Master Match Matrix™

■ SETTING UP THE MASTER MATCH MATRIX™ (MMM)

There is a fairy tale that out there somewhere in the marketplace exists the perfect candidate. It only requires looking long enough and hard enough to eventually find him or her. Wrong! The perfect candidate does not exist. Some candidates are very strong in some areas and very weak in others. What you need is some sort of tool that will enable you to see what your trade-offs are. The Master Match Matrix™ (MMM), which I developed, is a tool that will not only show you those trade-offs with great clarity, but it will also provide you with an effective, objective evaluation process. The MMM strategy allows you to evaluate any number of candidates against a list of distinct requirements for a specific job.

The MMM is illustrated in Table 3.1. You simply list the requirements for the position horizontally across the top and then record the names of the candidates down the left-hand side of the document. The MMM compels you to focus on the specific requirements of a particular job against which the attributes of each individual candidate can be measured and judged. In addition, it allows you to think about both the short-term and long-term requirements of the job. This piece of paper essentially becomes the document that controls your search.

It is generally easy for someone to be precise about the qualities they do *not* want in an employee and generally diffi-

Table 3.1 Manager's Master Match Matrix™

Position: _____

Candidate's Name	Needs						Wants	
	First-Priority Competency	Second-Priority Competency	Third-Priority Competency	Fourth-Priority Competency	Fifth-Priority Competency	Sixth-Priority Competency		

cult to get a real handle on the qualities one *does* want. The MMM demands that you examine specifically what it is you want.

Every matrix must be job specific in order to be at all useful. Once you have developed an MMM for a particular position, however, you can use that same MMM over again, every time that position opens up. The relative importance of the various requirements may change, but the requirements themselves will not. Designing an MMM is not a complicated process, but it does take thought. It is actually a three-step process.

Step One

Step one in creating an MMM is to sketch in broad brush strokes what the candidate needs to have in terms of knowledge, background, experience, skills, attitude, and so on in order to achieve the stated objectives for that job. These descriptive items are written along the top of the MMM in priority order, with the most important one on the left and going in decreasing importance to the right (see Table 3.2). Each item is then given a score that decreases by one. If you have eight items that you are looking for in a candidate, the first one has a total possible score of 8, the second item has a total possible score of 7, and so on. If the candidate fulfills that first item to your satisfaction, he or she receives the full score of 8. If the candidate did not completely satisfy that requirement, he or she would get some score less than 8.

If the candidate completely satisfies the second requirement, the best score you could give him or her would be 7. If not, the candidate would get some score less than 7. At the end of interviewing any number of candidates for that one position, you add up the total scores for each candidate and theoretically hire (or recommend for hire) the candidate with the highest total score (see Table 3.3).

You can also use the MMM score as a guide for the discussion when you ask your top-scoring candidates to return for a second interview. The scores will indicate where you should concentrate your second interview: on those areas where the candidate received a discounted score because of a perceived weakness or lack of required attributes.

Table 3.2 Sample Manager's Master Match Matrix™ for Administrative Manager

Position: Administrative Manager

Candidate's Name	Needs					Wants		
	Two Years Experience Supervising	*Delegation and Coaching Skills*	*Participative Leadership Style*	*Conflict-Managing Skills*	*Goal-Setting Managing Strategy*	*Superior Communication Skills*	*College Graduate*	*Professional Appearance*
Agnes Jones								
Phil Aline								
Joseph Potter								
Hannah Spolling								
Louise Baker								
Connie DeLessie								
Oscar Lemoninen								

Table 3.3 Sample Completed Manager's Master Match Matrix™ for Administrative Manager

Position: Administrative Manager

| | Needs | | | | | | Wants | | | |
Candidate's Name	Two Years Experience Supervising	Delegation and Coaching Skills	Participative Leadership Style	Conflict-Managing Skills	Goal-Setting Managing Strategy	Superior Communication Skills	College Graduate	Professional Appearance	Total Score
Agnes Jones	8	3	2	1	0	1	0	0	15
Phil Aline	7.5	5	6	5	2	2	1	1	29.5
Joseph Potter	8	6	6	5	2	1	2	1	31
Hannah Spolling	8	3	5	5	2	3	1	0	27
Louise Baker	4	7	6	3	2	3	2	1	28
Connie DeLessie	7.5	7	6	5	4	3	2	0	34.5
Oscar Lemoninen	4	7	3	2	0	1	2	1	20

Recommendation: Second interviews for DeLessie (34.5) and Potter (31).

It is possible that, at the conclusion of the process, you may not hire the person with the highest total score. There may be other issues that tempt you to hire a candidate who seemed extremely smart over one who had a little more experience, for example. Nevertheless, the MMM will still clearly show you your trade-offs. It also displays the strengths and weaknesses you would be getting with each candidate.

Using the MMM strategy gives you an unexpected gift. All interviewers have their particular biases. Perhaps you prefer candidates who are neatly dressed (i.e., appropriately dressed for the particular job). If a person comes to the interview dressed in a slovenly manner, you may assume he or she will be sloppy and careless in their work. Such an assumption may be wrong, but the thoughts are there. If the department where the particular vacancy is located is staffed with people in their early 20s and your candidate is in their 40s, you would probably have a concern about age. Age discrimination is against the law, but the thoughts are still there. If you are drawn to the more verbal, personable types, you may be uncomfortable with shy and quiet candidates who have difficulty making good eye contact. None of these concerns have anything to do with the candidate's ability to handle the job. Nevertheless, the thoughts are there.

It is impossible to give a candidate your full attention if you are busy reminding yourself every 10 seconds to ignore that the candidate is inappropriately dressed, not think about the candidate's age, remember that verbal facility isn't a requirement for this job, and so on. It is difficult to battle one's biases and listen to the candidate at the same time. If you are busy pushing certain mental considerations aside, your attention will be on that and not on the candidate. Put those issues at the low end of your MMM, where they will receive a minimal score of 1 or 2. That way, you are mentally free to concentrate on the items that are of critical importance to the job.

Even though the MMM shown in Table 3.2 only has a total of 8 items against which the candidates are being judged, it is easily possible for your MMM to have as many as 15 or 20 items. Just place the most important on the far left and the least important on the far right, with a scoring pattern that decreases by one as you go from left to right.

Step Two

The second step in designing your MMM is to ensure complete clarity about what is actually meant by each of the broadly written items placed at the top of the chart. You may tell yourself, for example, that what you really need for this vacancy is someone who can think on his or her feet and be a creative problem solver. Before you write "ability to think on their feet" and "creative problem solver" on your MMM, ask yourself what you really mean by those phrases. You could mean, for example, any of the following:

- What I really need is a self-starter—someone who can work with a minimum of supervision.
- What I really need is someone who is not afraid to use their initiative—someone who is willing to step outside the parameters of the job and assume significant responsibility beyond their designated function.
- What I really need is someone I don't have to train. We're so busy right now, there's just no time for training. I must have someone with a good deal of experience in this area.

The point is that broad brush-stroke terms have many different meanings. In order to make an suitable match between the candidate and your job vacancy, you must go beyond generic terms because they are not precise enough to be useful.

Suppose, for example, you are hiring a supervisor to add to your staff. You tell yourself that you need a person who is a "good communicator." Do you mean verbally or in writing? Are you talking about communicating with various levels of the organization or with customers, clients, vendors, and suppliers? Are you thinking about communicating internationally with people of different cultures or immigrants with little knowledge of the English language? Do you mean communicating face-to-face or on the telephone? Once you are clear on the meaning of these larger concepts, you are ready to proceed to the third and final step in setting up the MMM, which is question generation.

The more definitive you can make the items at the top of the MMM, the more effective and precise the process of question generation will be. Some items will be easy to score. For example, if one of the attributes on the MMM is "college graduate," all you have to do is ask candidates to submit a copy of their transcript. "Five years supervising experience" can be verified by checking with previous employers. Other items, such as "motivated," "dependable," and "good human relations" are much more difficult to score. Keep in mind, however, that you can put anything across the top of the MMM. All you have to do thereafter is obtain enough data to satisfy yourself as to whether the candidate has that specific quality. Well-thought-out questions are the key to your success.

Step Three

Set a fundamental requirement for yourself to develop 25 to 30 on-target questions from which you will select and use 10 during the actual interview. Armed with those preselected questions and a 40-minute time frame, you should be able to conduct an interview that provides you with accurate, reliable results. At the end of 40 minutes, you should not only make a decision to hire or not to hire, but you should also know exactly what the candidate would be bringing to your organization in terms of strengths and weaknesses if you decide to hire him or her.

Because the design and selection of the questions occur prior to encountering a single resume or candidate, it is worthwhile to have a variety of appropriate questions available from which to choose the final 10. First, the candidate's paperwork may supply some of the answers to your preselected questions. Second, your initial conversation with the candidate may also satisfy some of those questions. Third, the candidate's experience or lack thereof in a particular area may make the asking of some of the questions irrelevant. Obviously, you are going to need more questions at the ready than you will actually use.

In addition, in answering one of your questions, the candidate may well provide you with enough data to score a number of items on the MMM. For example, the position might require initiative taking, creativity, and analytical skills. You ask the question, "Tell me about the most innovative approach you have ever taken to solving a problem." The candidate responds, giving you data on all three issues. From a practical point of view, therefore have 25 to 30 preselected questions ready, at least three for each of the attribute categories on the MMM.

■ PUTTING STEPS ONE, TWO, AND THREE TOGETHER: SUCCESSFUL QUESTION GENERATION

Suppose one of your supervisors comes to you and says, "We need a sharp technical person on our Alpha team, a scientific type who is a good team player." Before you write "good team player" on an MMM, you need to get some clarification on what the supervisor means by "good team player."

You: "Good team player" is a little too generic. Could you give me a little more detail about that requirement?

Supervisor: What I really need is a person who:

- Interacts well with others.
- Exhibits excellent listening and communication skills.
- Is willing to do more than their fair share.
- Knows how and when to compromise and negotiate.
- Is able to resolve conflicts without my intervention.

Now, instead of just putting "good team player" on the MMM, you will use four or five additional attribute spaces with more specific captions: "human relations skills, experience on teams, listening and communication skills, negotiation skills, and conflict management skills."

What specifically should you ask a candidate in order to ascertain whether he or she is truly capable of participating effectively on a team, that is, whether he or she has the qualities listed above? You already know that working with others in a team setting requires outstanding skills in human relations. People without such skills can cause all kinds of problems that eventually affect the group's productivity. Additionally, experience on a team as a team member does not automatically qualify a candidate as a *good* team player. The candidate may well have destroyed the team of which they were a member. Here are some of the questions you might consider using:

What has been your experience working on a team as a team member?

What was the most difficult situation you faced as a team member?

What role did you play in that situation?

Describe the circumstances under which you would work most effectively on a team.

What is your idea of a good team player?

What are the major differences between being an effective employee and being an effective team member?

Suppose you need to add another supervisor to your staff. You know you want someone with at least three years of experience who has good leadership skills. Before you write "good leadership skills" on your MMM, have a conversation with yourself. What do you consider constitutes good leadership skills? After a bit of thinking, perhaps you come up with the following list.

What I really need is someone who can:

- Build and maintain collaborative working relationships with his or her staff.
- Build and maintain an atmosphere of trust.
- Manage conflict effectively.
- Use goal setting as a motivational and productivity strategy.
- Inspire each employee to stretch their capabilities.
- Use delegation as a means of developing the staff's potential.
- Provide an effective coaching and performance-feedback process.

Getting work done through other people requires superb human relations skills and a good deal of old-fashioned common sense. Supervisors who do not understand how their behavior can impact the staff can cause dissatisfaction, a low level of productivity, and the loss of talented personnel. You thoughtfully remind yourself that experience at managing others does not automatically qualify a candidate as a good leader. Because leadership is such a complicated topic, you decide to add three additional attributes to your MMM: delegation effectiveness, goal setting, and staff development. Once that's done, you can quickly put together a list of appropriate questions, such as these:

For Leadership

What have you done to maintain a strong relationship between yourself and each individual staff member?

What role do you typically play in managing conflicts that arise between staff members?

What techniques have you used to encourage your people to give you the bad news when they screw things up?

For Delegation Effectiveness

Tell me about a time when you influenced one of your people to assume more responsibility or to take on a task that you knew would be difficult for them.

What do you believe are the keys to successful delegation?

I'd be interested to learn how you determine which tasks get delegated to whom.

For Staff Development

How have you ensured objectivity when evaluating the performance of one of your staff?

Tell me about a time when you knew that one of your employees was having a performance problem. What kind of assistance did you provide them?

What techniques have you used to encourage employees to develop their own capabilities?

How would you motivate an employee who is afraid to make decisions?

How often and under what circumstances do you involve your staff in your decision-making and problem-solving efforts?

For Goal Setting

What role has goal setting played in your leadership strategy?

What role do you play in the goal-setting activities of your employees?

Suppose you had an employee who sets easily achieved goals. How would you encourage him or her to set more challenging goals?

■ CONSTRUCTING A MATRIX FOR CANDIDATES WITH LITTLE OR NO WORK EXPERIENCE

It may seem like a waste of time to design a MMM when the position is entry level and for which the candidates will have little or no work experience. It is not a waste of time. The task is made much easier if you consider school as if it were a job. There are goals to be achieved, problems to be solved, interpersonal issues to be resolved, deadlines to be met, and decisions to be made. It is just that the environment in which these things take place is a bit different from the standard work environment.

When I ask clients why they are interested in hiring a recent college graduate to staff a particular position, they speak about potential. I put "potential" on the MMM and ask, "Potential for what?" I am told:

Potential for growth.

Potential for learning.

Potential for eventually managing others (leadership).

The traditional method for looking for evidence of these qualities is to explore extracurricular activities. Did the candidate participate in team sports? What role did he or she play—member or team captain? If on the yearbook staff, did the candidate coordinate various activities or was he or she out in the community selling advertising space? Did the person run for a class office or was he or she appointed to the honor society because of GPA? Did the candidate assist in earning tuition and if so what kind of work did he or she do to earn funds? All of these issues are valuable because they do provide some useful information about the candidate. There are, however, two items that will provide you with critical data: decision making and time management.

Each year during a person's college career, there is a four-month period known as summer break, which the person can structure any way they wish. (Can you remember the last time you had four months of unstructured time to do with exactly what you wanted?) You want to investigate exactly what they did with that time. Presumably, your preference is that the candidate worked during that period of time. Because every decision must contain a solution objective in order to be meaningful, you should always ask what type of work the candidate did. Some candidates will say they selected a physically difficult, back-breaking job in order to earn enough to help fund their education. Others will say they took a position, at low pay, in order to gain some experience in the area of their anticipated career, believing it would give them a leg up on the competition after graduation.

It is not important which type of work they did. What is critical is that they knew there was a decision to make and that they made it. What you do not want to hear is that the candidate did not consciously make a decision about this four-month resource. At the end of a four-year college career, he or she would have squandered one full year without any goals, self-direction, or objectives. If you translate this behavior into the work setting, perhaps this is a candidate who can only function well with close supervision, who is not a self-starter, and who has difficulty recognizing decision opportunities.

It is a customary expectation at work that time plus effort will equal results. Although it isn't always true, most people function under that assumption. It is common to hear at work, "If I can just put in a little more time on this thing, I'm sure I'll figure it out." There is an opportunity cost, however. Putting more time into one thing means taking it away from something else; time is inelastic. You want to see that this recent graduate has some understanding of time management and is already functioning with this model in mind.

A popular line of questioning in any interview is to explore job likes and dislikes. In the case of the recent college graduate, you should explore what courses they liked and which ones they disliked. Usually those they disliked were the ones with which they had problems. Problem courses in school are serious issues that must be resolved quickly. You want to know how the candidate went about dealing with those issues.

Manager: When you realized you might fail calculus, what did you do?

Candidate: I thought that if I could put in another five hours a week of extra study, maybe with the assistance of a tutor, I could pull out a pretty good grade. But it meant that I had to give up glee club.

It should bother you to hear comments like this:

Manager: When you realized you might fail calculus, what did you do?

Candidate: I changed my major so that I could drop calculus altogether.

Here is a person who, when faced with a problem, walks away from it. If you hire this candidate, will he or she be likely to do the same thing when faced with a difficult problem on the job? It is said that one can test the caliber of people by the size of the problems they are willing to handle. Here is a person who is not willing to tackle his or her problem and who, instead, takes the easy way out.

■ INCLUDING THE ISSUE OF MOTIVATION IN THE MMM

You should make the issue of motivation a key item on every MMM you design: The candidate must be interested in *this* particular vacancy. Of course, it is important to hire people who are well-rounded and who have interests in their lives other than work. You should always keep in mind, however, that you are hiring an accountant or an engineering manager, not a skier or a sailing enthusiast. You want to be certain that the candidate's interests lie strongly in the career that he or she has chosen. That means the candidate:

- Has made some determined, specific efforts at self-development.
- Sees a future for him- or herself in this type of endeavor (i.e., is goal oriented).

- Experiences joy and excitement as a result of meeting job challenges successfully.

When people are interested in what they do, they make efforts to get better at it. No job is performed in a static situation. You should question candidates on how they have taken advantage of changes in their environment to explore new ways of honing their skills and expanding their knowledge. Here are some questions to assist you:

> What have you done recently to become more effective on your present job?
>
> What typically gives you the most satisfaction on a job?
>
> Describe a situation when you went beyond the limits of your job. What motivated you to make that extra effort?
>
> What kinds of circumstances or events have influenced you to learn something totally new?
>
> What goals have you set for yourself in the past three years? Why those particular goals?

Goal orientation can be a stale topic. Never address it by asking, "What do you expect to be doing in 20 years?" Instead, ask the following:

> What do you hope to find at this company that you haven't found at your previous company?
>
> What turns you on about this type of work?
>
> What would you say is the most critical element you are looking for in a job? Why?
>
> Why are you looking at our company?

Something the candidate wants very badly is missing in his or her present employment situation, and you want to know what it is. If he or she were thoroughly and completely satisfied there, this person would not be sitting in front of you. Some crucial goal that has no chance of being achieved in his or her present job situation has driven this person to engage in this agonizing activity called job hunting. If your vacancy can support and further the candidate's goal, and the candidate is qualified for the position, you may have a good match. There is a more detailed discussion of the importance of the candidates goals in Chapter 4.

During the first 20 minutes of the interview, you will be asking the candidate, "What's the most interesting (challenging, exciting, rewarding) situation you faced as a team leader (customer-service representative, supervisor, engineer, analyst)?" You want the candidate to make a mental picture of a difficult challenge he or she faced at work and then mentally reexperience the joy of conquering that challenge successfully. When people are interested in what they are talking about, the pupils of their eyes get larger, they lean forward in the chair closing the distance between you, the speed of their language increases, and some even get their hands into the conversation by making all kinds of illustrative gestures. You can see the excitement and interest physically displayed right there in front of you. (For additional information on reading body language, see Chapter 6.)

During the last five minutes of the interview, you will probably ask about the candidate's spare-time hobbies and/or activities. You want to see more energy and excitement in their body language when the candidate talks about successes at work than when describing leisure-time activities. If you see more excitement in the person's body language when he or she talks about skiing or sailing, you can guess that, when the weather conditions are right, this candidate may well call in sick in order to pursue this other activity. More important, however, this candidate is not mentally captivated by the work in this occupation, even in instances where he or she has experienced significant success.

■ NOTE TAKING AND SCORING THE MMM

Some interviewers take copious notes all through the interview; others take very few. Then there is the group that takes no notes at all. How that third group is able to recall anything that went on in the interview without note taking is a mystery. Realize, however, that, every time you break eye contact with the candidate to make a note, you draw attention to the fact that whatever the candidate has just said is of particular importance to you. You may not want that to happen. In addition, breaking eye contact for any reason in the interview can be interpreted by the candidate as a negative.

In order to solve this problem, you should devise your own form of shorthand and doodles where you can just write down a single key word that will bring the entire segment of conversation back to you with great clarity. Use a sheet of paper that is about four-by-six inches. At the beginning of the interview, tell the candidate, "I may be taking notes while we talk so that I can remember what we said here"—"may" meaning that you may not take notes. The size of the paper indicates that you don't expect to be taking very many if you do take notes.

At the start of the interview, therefore, you will have three pieces of paper on your desk: the candidate's application and/or resume, your single sheet of paper for note taking, and your sheet of 25 to 30 prepared questions. Your MMM is in the desk, where the candidate cannot see it.

As soon as the candidate departs, you, armed with your four-by-six-inch piece of paper with your shorthand comments, open the desk drawer and score the MMM. Thus the evaluation process begins immediately after the candidate walks out of your office. What the MMM strategy has done for you is allow you to separate your information-gathering process (listening) from the evaluation process. For this to be most effective, however, it is crucial that you do the scoring as soon after the interview as possible. You want to capture that information while it is fresh. You went through a lot of preparation to get quality data, and with the passage of time, it will surely get stale.

If the candidate will be interviewing with others in the organization, the only marks you should put on the candidate's application and/or resume are the words "interviewed by" along with your initials and the date. It is possible that the candidate may see this paperwork at some point, and you do not want anything on it that might present a legal complication later on. Any written observations or facts that could negatively influence others in their evaluation of the candidate should be put on a separate paper that becomes part of your personal files. You can, however, share your observations verbally with others in your organization if asked.

To ensure that your organization gets the best possible person for the job, you should encourage your staff to participate with you in the development of the MMM, especially if the vacancy involved is vital to your group. If you intend to involve others on your staff in the interviewing process, make sure you divide up the MMM issues so that the candidate gets a totally different set of questions from each of the people participating in the interviewing exercise. For example, you might want to handle the work experience and leave the education and technical portions to your technical person.

■ HIDDEN BENEFITS TO USING THE MMM STRATEGY

Using the MMM strategy will make the entire interviewing-selection process quicker and more accurate in eight specific areas: (1) more appropriate matches, (2) more competent listening and evaluation, (3) more effective recall, (4) preventing the buying of unneeded skills, (5) identifying the elements that determine success, (6) a focus on what the job actually needs, (7) more objective process, and (8) better recruitment assistance from human resources.

More Appropriate Candidate-Job Matches

Using the MMM forces you to analyze the job before you analyze a single candidate. You will therefore be able to make a better match between your requirements for the position and the candidate's skills. The requirements will not fluctuate according to the attractiveness of the candidate seated in front of you. Candidate attractiveness is dependent on the following factors:

- The mood of the interviewer.
- The number of interviews already conducted that day.
- The time of day of the interview.
- The quality of the previous candidate.

The MMM strategy requires that you be adequately prepared so that candidate attractiveness does not affect your evaluation process. This means that you have to determine ahead of time what questions you are going to ask—independent of any particular candidate.

The traditional strategy for conducting an interview by a person who is untrained or inexperienced is to look at the candidate's paperwork first. Then, based on the information contained in the resume or application, he or she will create some off-the-cuff questions that elucidate some of that resume data. Once the interviewer has the candidate's resume information well delineated, a determination is made as to whether that information is relevant to the job requirements. Such an approach creates a lot of unnecessary extra steps in the evaluation process.

Not everything on the candidate's resume needs to be clarified—only those things that pertain to the requirements for that particular job. By making the desired attributes (as shown on the MMM) the foundation of the interview, rather than the candidate's paperwork, you can save yourself one whole step in analysis. But you must be adequately prepared with a preselected number of questions, the answers to which will enable you to score the MMM.

One of my clients searches the marketplace for bright people with five to seven years of experience in the general field of computer software programming and analysis. When such candidates present themselves to be interviewed, the human resources department hires them on the spot for no specific position. What would previously follow was a lengthy series of interviews between the candidate and managers from various departments around the company. This process continued until some manager decided that he or she had a specific slot that matched the candidate's specific skill set. In other words, the management team spent its precious time functioning as a career placement service for the candidates. A single candidate may have interviewed with as many as 15 different managers before locating an appropriate job.

By utilizing the MMM strategy, the interviewing and placement process that these promising candidates were forced to endure was cut to three interviews. Moreover, the company was able to gain the use of the candidates' talents more quickly while at the same time freeing up the managers for more relevant efforts.

More Competent Listening and Evaluation

Once you begin preselecting your questions, you will discover that your listening skills improve immensely. Interviewing forces a person to listen and evaluate at the same time. The human mind cannot do them simultaneously and do an effective job at both; one is going to suffer. Most of the time what suffers in the interviewing process is the listening. An untrained interviewer will ask a wonderful question. While the candidate is responding, however, instead of listening to the candidate's answer, the interviewer is mentally busy trying to devise another fantastic question to spring on the candidate just as soon as he or she stops talking. Untrained interviewers get really proficient at delivering salvos of great questions. Because they rarely hear the candidate's answers, however, they can never follow up appropriately. Without listening, an interviewer will miss out on many possibilities for gaining significant information, as shown in these examples:

Manager: Under what circumstances would you seek assistance from your manager?

Candidate: She was not the easiest person to deal with, so I rarely asked her for anything. I guess it's fair to say that I went off on my own more often that I should. [*Follow-up is needed to explore "more often than I should."*]

Manager: What pressures have you faced that would enable you to do well in a management role?

Candidate: As a team leader in a cross-functional group of peers, I had to get agreement on priorities from a group of diverse folks whose individual priorities were in direct opposition to the team's mission. I was pretty successful most of the time, but there were other times when I got nowhere. [*Follow-up is needed to explore "other times when I got nowhere" and how the candidate brought "diverse folks" into agreement on priorities.*]

Manager: What modifications or changes have you made with regard to your job? Which ones would you consider risky, and why? Why did you make those changes?

Candidate: I made changes when it seemed to me that things would operate more effectively with a different approach. [*Candidate answers the question most recently asked, which is "why did you make changes" and does not respond to "what changes" or "what made them risky."*]

Manager: If you join us, what kind of assistance would you like to have from those of us on the management team to get you off to a good start?

Candidate: Hmmmm. First, I'd want clear expectations from my manager. [*Traditional answer*] More important, I'd want some detailed information about the internal politics. Not knowing that stuff can get a new person into serious difficulty. [*Follow-up is needed to clarify "politics" and the candidate's obvious "serious difficulty" experienced on previous jobs.*]

More Effective Recall

One of the benefits of the MMM strategy is that it allows you to recall every single candidate with meticulous clarity. If you are like most managers, any interviewing you do is done sporadically—for example, two candidates last week, one candidate this week, and three candidates the next week. How do you remember everyone when it comes to make a hiring decision two months later? Did you write "yellow shirt, green tie" or something equally clever in the corner of the application and then discover that you actually interviewed three candidates who wore that color combination? Maybe you noted "looks like Aunt Mary 20 years ago" but forgot you have two Aunt Marys?

For a manager, effective hiring means that you must also have an effective recall system if you are ever going to get to closure on a candidate. After two weeks, every candidate in your memory looks alike and sounds alike. In order to come to closure on someone—anyone—you are forced into a series of phone calls or second interviews to the various candidates for the sole purpose of reacquainting yourself with them. What a waste of time, and what an impression you make on the candidates: early Alzheimer's.

No Buying of Unnecessary Skills

The MMM strategy will prevent you from hiring (and paying for) skills you don't need. For example, perhaps you had a good deal of difficulty in school with foreign languages. One day a candidate walks into your office and tells you during the course of the interview that he can speak eight languages fluently:

You: Eight languages fluently??? That's fantastic!!! [*Halo effect*]

So you hire him. Of course, nowhere on the job description/ requisition does it say that you need someone who speaks eight languages fluently. Of course, you had to pay top dollar to get him. Three months later, he comes into your office and says, "You don't use my eight languages here and I'm getting rusty." You say, "Right. We only speak one here." You have a very expensive, unhappy employee who will shortly add to the company's turnover rate, and you will find yourself back in the interviewing game—again.

The MMM strategy brought one teaching hospital a significant salary savings by solving a seemingly intractable problem. The hospital had an extensive medical laboratory, which it staffed with medical-school hopefuls and graduate biology students. There was an enormous amount of work every day and a great deal of pressure to run the tests and report the results as quickly as possible. Every three months or so, one particular position in the lab, prep bench, would open up. Whenever that happened, the work in the lab would become severely backlogged.

"Prep bench" was considered to be the worst job in the lab. This was where the specimens to be tested were received, cataloged, and set up for the appropriate tests. Traditionally, this position was staffed with a biology major from a local college who was trying to earn enough money for graduate school. The student was promised the opportunity to learn all the jobs in the lab. The work pressures in the lab were so great, however, that no one could ever find time to train the student in anything except prep bench. After a few months of excuses, most students became aggravated and quit. So, periodically, the lab became embroiled in an incredible backlog until a replacement for the prep bench could be hired and trained.

In order to solve the problem, the entire lab staff was involved in creating an MMM for the prep-bench position. Once everyone was focused on the specific requirements of the job, it quickly became obvious that the job of prep bench was nothing more than a medically oriented clerical function. Prep bench did *not* need someone with a medical or biological studies background; a simple interest in health care was all that was required.

Capturing of the Unique Elements That Determine Success

The MMM strategy also allows you to add in things that you know from experience truly make a difference when it comes to the candidate's success in the job. Sometimes these factors defy logic. In other instances, even if these factors made sense, no one would have ever considered putting them on paper or adding them into the requirements of the job description.

For example, my client who owns the series of gas stations put on his MMM "must live in the neighborhood." When I told him that "in the neighborhood" was not definitive enough, he changed it to "must live within five miles of the station." So I asked him, "Does it ever happen that on a cold, snowy winter evening, the employee will call up and tell you he can't get into work because his car won't start?" "Oh, all the time," was the reply. Now he puts on his matrix "must live within five miles of the station and have DieHard battery in car."

Many years ago, I consulted with a firm that provided custom-designed hardware and software to the printing industry. My client wanted help in designing a list of requirements against which he could judge sales candidates. Because his products were quite expensive, his salespeople generally dealt with fairly senior executives in the customers' hierarchy. Many of the most lucrative deals were made over dinner or on the golf course. The more senior the managers, the more time they could spend on the golf course. The MMM I designed for him included the following item: golf handicap.

Focuses on What the Job Needs,
Not on What the Candidate Lacks

This item is perhaps the most important of all: The MMM strategy allows you to take an objective look at the candidate's strengths, skills, knowledge, and abilities and evaluate that package against the specific requirements of a particular position.

An inexperienced or untrained interviewer generally hires by elimination. This candidate doesn't have the appropriate experience; toss him out. That candidate doesn't have a particular skill; toss her out. These two other candidates haven't had the required education; toss them out, too. The interviewer then ends up with the least-objectionable candidate (similar to how many people vote at election time!).

It really doesn't matter what the candidate does not have because you are not going to hire him or her on that basis. You are only going to hire the candidate for what that person does have—if you can use what he or she has. Consider this ridiculous exchange:

Interviewer: Your resume indicates you don't have a background in sales and marketing.

Candidate: That's true. But the position advertised did not ask for that.

Interviewer: I see that you don't have any experience managing large projects either.

Candidate: Right. But your ad asks for experience managing small projects.

Interviewer: I also see that you don't have a master's degree.

Candidate: And I don't have three heads either.

The MMM will clearly indicate that it doesn't matter what wonderful qualities the candidate brings to the job if you cannot use them. The only thing that matters is if the candidate has what you need.

More Objective Process

The MMM strategy gives you a stable foundation from which to launch the evaluation process. Starting the interview process by asking the candidate to clarify various issues on his or her resume (the usual strategy) means that each interview will be covering different items. Because every resume is different, each candidate's evaluation will be based on a moving target rather than on anything grounded and solid. With the MMM strategy, you can be more objective in evaluating each individual candidate because you are comparing each candidate to the same list of requirements.

Superior Recruitment Assistance from Human Resources

In most organizations today, a manager who needs to add a person to his or her staff approaches the human resources department with a requisition and a basic job description listing tasks and responsibilities and asks them to begin a recruitment process. Human resources will screen numbers of applicants and refer a short list of possible candidates to the manager. Many of those referred by human resources as viable candidates the manager will probably find unacceptable. A good deal of time is thus wasted by both the manager and the human resources department.

Although the human resources department is staffed with highly perceptive people, they do not know your business as intimately as you do. No matter what you tell them, there is much more hidden information that only you have. The problem is getting that information to human resources in some sort of format that will make sense to them. The MMM strategy will do that for you.

Once the MMM strategy becomes a solid part of your approach for employment selection, the time involved between the decision to add a person and the offer of employment to a candidate will be dramatically shortened. When you share your completed MMM with human resources, they will know exactly what attributes, skills, abilities, knowledge, experience, and so on you are looking for, as well as the relative importance of each. With the MMM in hand, every candidate on the human resources short list will be a truly viable candidate.

Chapter 4

Structuring the Interview

■ PREPARING TO BEGIN THE INTERVIEW PROCESS

As an astute interviewer you will need only a well-thought-out MMM, 10 good questions, and 40 minutes to conduct an effective interview. At the end of that time period, you may not necessarily make a hiring decision, but you will surely know the candidate's strengths and weaknesses as they relate to the requirements of the vacancy. If you do make a decision to hire after 40 minutes of conversation, you will know exactly what you are buying in terms of skills, competence, expertise, strengths, and weaknesses.

Perhaps you think your interviews go on much too long, especially on occasions when you and the candidate develop a strong rapport. These run-on interviews may occur because someone told you that the way to begin the exercise is to discuss something unrelated to the specific job—like hobbies.

This sounds like good advice, but it is not. Starting the interview on a non-job-related basis leads the conversation into nonproductive areas and wastes both yours and the candidate's time. The candidate came to discuss his or her capabilities and how he or she could fit in with your organization. Talking about his or her hobby of refinishing antique furniture is actually a bit inconsiderate. Moreover, as one candidate told me many years ago, "The longer such conversations go on, the more anxious and apprehensive I become. Best to get to the point right away.

87

Job interviewing is stressful enough without having to deal with the interviewer's insincere attempt to immediately become my very good friend."

Structured Format

To be an astute interviewer, you want to develop a structured format for every interview. A structured format involves making a decision—prior to the actual interview—regarding the areas in the candidate's background that you want to explore. It also involves planning a specific time frame for discussing each of those designated areas. In order to ascertain which areas in the candidate's employment history you need to investigate, you should begin by examining your statement of job objectives, performance expectations (see Chapter 2), and list of competencies required, along with your prepared MMM. Then look at the candidate's submitted paperwork (resume and/or application).

Suppose, for example, the candidate is a recent college graduate with summer work experience every year since he was a junior in high school. His major area of concentration was basic business accounting. The vacancy requirements include a working knowledge of computers, some programming experience, and some background in accounting methods. You are the hiring manager and the head of MIS (management information services). You intend to put your department through a computer conversion in the next six months. You have staff members willing to train a new employee, but you insist that any viable candidate be bright, show an aptitude for logic and numbers, and enjoy working with the computer. Because you have no serious concern about human relations, team activity, or potential for growth into a supervisory role, you determine that for this candidate you will concentrate on the following areas:

Summer employment.	10 minutes
His college accounting and computer-related projects.	10 minutes
Extracurricular activities.	5 minutes
Future career goals and educational plans.	5 minutes

That leaves you 10 minutes to sell the job if you found the candidate viable.

One of the most-sensitive positions to fill is that of a secretary to a senior-level person. Many such secretaries have said that they almost have to become the boss in spirit in order to be effective. Much of what they are expected to do and how they are supposed to do it is unsaid; they have to be intuitive regarding the true significance and expectations that are hidden behind the words. Because the relationship is one of partnership, the issues of human relations and personality fit make up a critical facet of matching the right candidate to the position.

Suppose you were the executive vice president of a major multinational corporation and needed a secretary. Let's say this is the fifth secretary to be placed in this position in the past 18 months. You claim that the last five secretaries were deficient skillwise. The information from those who left your employ indicate that you are a slave driver with the personality of Attila the Hun, the manners of a Neanderthal, and the language of a Hollywood gangster. Two of the secretaries left the position as a result of their doctors' recommendations; another filed a workers' compensation claim for stress; the other two quit at the insistence of their spouses, who objected to their working every night until 9:00 P.M. and being called in to work on the weekends.

The position requires someone who is able to work independently because you travel a good deal. Moreover, the secretary would be interacting with employees and customers from other countries, so a working knowledge of other cultures is necessary. Fluency in one or two foreign languages is definitely a plus but not a requirement. What is required is a person with patience, tact, superior organizational skills, and a commitment to accuracy. Because you manage to aggravate almost everyone with whom you come in contact, your secretary has to be a diplomat, able to clean up the emotional debris you invariably leave in your wake.

The present candidate is a woman with 25 years of secretarial experience as the executive assistant to a number of CEOs. Her most-recent position has been as the secretary to the owner of a large giftware-importing business. She was with him for the last four years and left because he sold the business. Based on the recent history of this position, you decide to focus on the following areas:

Actual tasks and responsibilities at her last two jobs.	10 minutes
Rapport maintenance issues with all former bosses.	10 minutes
Task likes, dislikes, and interests.	5 minutes
Hobbies and nonwork activities.	5 minutes

As with the MIS position that leaves you with 10 minutes to sell the job if you found the candidate viable.

The point is that 40 minutes is not a great deal of time. You will therefore find it helpful to plan a structured format that delineates the specific areas to be explored and the number of minutes you intend to spend on each one. Such a strategy helps you remain focused on what you need to learn about the candidate. It also gives you tight control over how the time is used.

The goal for the first 20 minutes of conversation should be to furnish you with sufficient information to make a "go/no-go" decision. It is therefore critical to concentrate on the areas that are most likely to provide you with the best, most-complete picture of the candidate's abilities.

Although the best area of information may vary from candidate to candidate, most often you will find yourself focusing on their most-recent job or jobs. This is because whatever a candidate has been doing over the last six months is a better indicator of what he or she could accomplish for you over the next six months than is a job held four years ago.

Recently, I was interviewing an engineer for a position in a research-and-development think tank. The candidate had about six years of what sounded like excellent experience working on very innovative projects. We then had this exchange:

Interviewer: Sounds like you've been working on some very advanced research. What would you say has been the most-rewarding project you've been involved with to date?

Candidate: My eighth-grade science project for which I won the National Science Foundation award. Would you like to see it? [*Before I could respond, the candidate dove into his briefcase and pulled out a sheaf of papers.*]

Perhaps this was the ideal candidate for the position. Perhaps his eighth-grade science project was so advanced that even now, 20 years later, the scientific world had not yet equaled its knowledge. I'll never know. With that kind of response, I felt I could not recommend him for the job.

The Structuring Statement

Once you have planned out how you intend to structure the 40-minute interview, you should tell the candidate what that plan is so that he or she is fully prepared to participate in the exercise. This can be done with a simple structuring statement. Here is a sample:

> In this company, we make every effort to match people with jobs that draw on their best abilities. We want you to be happy here. We'd like you to gain skills and face challenges that will advance your career goals as well as provide you with appropriate compensation for your efforts. Now, in order for me to do that, I need to know some things about you. For example, I need to know something about your previous job experience, maybe something about any self-development efforts in which you have been involved, and maybe something about what you do in your spare time. Now, suppose you start by telling me about your previous job here with Crunch & Munch Industries.

A good structuring statement accomplishes two things: It tells candidates (1) why you will be asking them questions, and (2) it lets them know the three areas from which you want them to develop their answers. In other words, with the structuring statement you have essentially told the candidate that there is no hidden agenda of trick questions.

In much of the literature on the subject of interviewing, there are numerous allusions to the fact that candidates will be apprehensive, nervous, and stressed. The first task of the interviewer, therefore, must be to calm the candidate down. I have never felt that part of a manager's interviewing responsibility is to play psychiatrist to job candidates. Candidates experience anxiety because they want to do this thing right, but they are ignorant about the interviewer's strategy. When you tell them how you intend to manage the interaction, candidates immediately relax. Now they know what to expect.

There is another reason to use a structuring statement, and that is to help you retain control of the interaction. An untrained interviewer will invariably lose control of the process. He or she probably never even figures out how it happened, how to prevent it from happening in the future, or how to regain control when it does happen. The structuring statement tells candidates, in a nice way, that the first 20 minutes belongs to you. Here is an example of an interview in which the interviewer loses control:

Manager: Please tell me about your experience as a supervisor.

Candidate: Well, I've been supervising for about four years now. How many people would I be supervising in this job?

Manager: There are currently three on staff, with plans to hire at least one additional person by the end of the quarter. How many people did you typically supervise in your previous jobs?

Candidate: It varied anywhere between 4 and 12. What specifically are the responsibilities of these three people?

Manager: The department is responsible for determining shipping costs, insurance rates, and recovery on loss or damage on the various shipments we transport. The work is divided up geographically, East, Midwest, and West.

Candidate: Does that mean each employee only has to know how to calculate shipping rates, insurance premiums, and so forth for just one section of the country? Are any of them specially trained in a particular area such as loss and damage estimating?

[Now the candidate is interviewing the manager; the manager has lost control of the interaction.]

Manager: We want each employee to develop very strong relationships with the customers in their area. Many customers have told us that's one of the reasons they prefer to ship with us. . . .

With a structuring statement to set the stage, the interaction is more likely to remain within the manager's control:

Manager: Please tell me about your experience as a supervisor.

Candidate: Well, I've been supervising for about four years now. How many people would I be supervising in this job?

Manager: I am delighted that you want to know more about the position, and we'll get to those details in a few minutes. First, however, I need to learn about your background so that I can determine if there is a good match between your experience and the requirements of the position. Please tell me about your experience as a supervisor.

The strategy is to thank the candidate for their question, *not* answer their question. Then paraphrase the initial structuring statement and ask your question again.

If you use the recommended postponement strategy when the candidate interrupts your flow of questions, it is possible that 20 minutes later, because you determine the person is not a viable candidate, he or she will then leave without getting their queries answered. However, you will have saved yourself some time. Moreover, because you have stayed with your strategy, you will know exactly why the person is inappropriate for the vacancy. If you had answered the candidate's questions when they were asked, you might have found the exchange moving far afield from the issues targeted on your MMM. The 20 minutes would have expired and you would have found out nothing of significance regarding the candidate's suitability for the position. A second interview would be necessary because the first one didn't get the job done.

You may have some concerns about the appropriateness of this strategy. The candidate had some pressing questions and you refused to answer them. The problem is, if you start out by answering all those questions, the candidate leaves the exchange having learned everything he or she thinks is important about the position but feeling that you were not really interested in his or her goals and career aspirations. Showing interest in a candidate means taking the time to hear about his or her career aspirations, employment preferences, and job concerns. You can only hear about those things if you ask the candidate to speak about them while you remain a silent but attentive listener.

A good structuring statement lays down the ground rules and gives the candidate a road map through the interview. It also provides you with tighter control over the direction and content of the interaction. A good structuring statement should take only about 30 seconds. If it goes on any longer, it's overkill.

Operant Conditioning

Today's candidates are resourceful enough to carefully assess everything in the immediate environment to determine how to do this interviewing thing right. If in the first 10 minutes of the interview, you do all the talking, you have taught the candidate that the way to do interviewing right—at least with you—is to listen while you talk. You certainly do not want candidates to learn that. You want them to learn that, in order to interview right, they have to talk while you listen. Experience at interviewing will teach you that it is absolutely crucial for you to limit the amount of verbiage that comes out of your mouth during the first 10 minutes of the interaction. After that, it doesn't seem to matter as much; but in that first 10 minutes, it is critical.

The most-effective interviewing strategy is to have the candidate speak 80% of the time while the interviewer speaks only 20% of the time. In addition, the substantive quality of the interaction should be provided by the candidate. The interviewer's function is relegated to keeping the conversation going by providing neutral but encouraging comments such as the following:

> Yes . . .
>
> Do go on . . .
>
> Really?
>
> And then what happened?
>
> Can you give me an example?

In effect, the only way you can condition the candidate to do most of the talking is by refraining from speaking. You have to put the pressure on the candidate to fill the silence. If it appears to you that every candidate you interview seems to be a clam, then the problem is you. You are talking too much. The candidates are just trying to be polite.

Perhaps you are so delighted about what is happening in your own career that you want to share your excitement with the candidate. Maybe you think that by sharing your enthusiasm you will awaken the candidate's. What actually happens, however, is that, after the interview is over, you will attribute all the elation and spirited language used as the candidate's. This will happen even though you may be aware that the candidate did not say anything substantive. Your hit rate, in turn, will be abysmal.

Untrained interviewers assume that it is important to tell the candidate all about the job at the very beginning of the interview. The problem is that once they get started they just won't stop. The operant conditioning will kick in, and the candidate will assume that all they have to do is listen. The poor candidate will never have a chance to tell the interviewer what is important to him or her in a work situation. Remember that, although it is essential to *eventually* tell the candidate about the job, it isn't necessary to begin the interaction there.

The purpose of the interviewing exercise is for you to ask questions that elicit relevant employment information on which future performance can be accurately predicted. The most-important skill in interviewing is listening. You can only listen to the candidate while he or she is physically there seated before you. Moreover, you can't learn anything about the candidate if you're doing all the talking. Remember that the second phase of the interview—the time period allotted for selling the job—is intentionally designated as the time for answering the candidate's questions. The issue for the astute interviewer is whether the candidate should be made to wait 20 minutes to get his or her questions answered.

It may not seem appropriate to make candidates wait to get their questions answered. You probably agree, however, that it is important for you to accomplish the interviewing exercise in as short a time as possible. You can also see the value of putting the pressure for talking off of you and on the candidate.

There are two good solutions that will preserve your time while satisfying the candidate's desire for information without creating a situation in which you would be conditioning the candidate to refrain from speaking. The first is to have another person speak informally to the candidate before you do so formally. This can take place while you are going over the candidate's paperwork one last time. It could be someone from human resources or even another employee in your area. Ask the person to introduce him- or herself to the candidate and offer to answer a few preliminary questions, for example; "Hi. My name is Allen. Ms. Mouthy will see you in just a minute or so. She asked if I would welcome you and make myself available to answer a few basic questions about what it's like to work here and what she's like as a boss."

The second strategy is to provide the candidate with something to read about the department or company. Do not use the annual report or similar tome. Put together a simple page or two of information that can be read while you are going over the candidate's paperwork one last time. Both strategies provide the candidate with a little information concerning some initial questions. More important, however, both strategies will preserve the operant conditioning and save you time.

■ THE FIRST 20 MINUTES

You can regard the first 20 minutes of an interview as a courtesy interview. At the end of that time period, you should be able to make a decision regarding whether the candidate is suitable or unsuitable. If you conclude that the candidate is not appropriate for the job, you should terminate the interview at that point.

Even though the first 20 minutes is the courtesy interview, it does not always take 20 minutes to discern that a particular individual is inappropriate for the job. That determination can often be made within the first three minutes. Concentrate hard on *not* allowing that to happen. The danger is that, when that initial impression is very strong (either good or bad), you could find yourself using the entire 20 minutes to validate that first impression. The interview then has a preprogrammed conclusion. As a result, you could miss valuable information. The following example illustrates the assumptions people make on the basis of initial impressions.

Many years ago one of my clients conducted a revealing study of management (untrained in interviewing) professionals and their legendary ability to evaluate candidates quickly. My client videotaped a series of individuals walking into an office setting. Each person was instructed to go over to the desk and extend their arm as if to shake the hand of the person standing behind the desk. Instead of a person standing behind the desk, however, there was a camera poised at the approximate height at which an interviewer's face might be if he or she were standing to greet a candidate. Each person was videotaped for a total of 40 seconds: opening the door, entering the office, walking over to the desk, and extending their arm as if to greet the interviewer. At this point the image would fade out. Interviewers were then asked to evaluate each candidate based on what they had seen.

From just 40 seconds of observation, without hearing the candidate say one word, a plethora of comments and evaluations were made regarding personality, mood, behavior patterns, financial background, hobbies, political leaning, age, state of health, birthplace, social status, educational attainment, motivation, eating habits, exercise preferences, ethnic, racial, and religious background, leadership capabilities, integrity, honesty, sociability, loyalty, dedication, detail orientation, open-mindedness, obsessive-compulsive behavior, marital status, trustworthiness, and ethics!

The purpose of the interview is to get relevant information about the candidate regarding a number of issues:

- Competencies required for handling the work.
- Interest in doing the job.
- Ability to adjust to the work environment.
- Likelihood of being accepted by peers and superiors.
- Probability of remaining with the organization.
- Potential for growth and development.
- Ability to articulate well.
- Factors that might interfere with performance.
- Level of maturity.
- Clarity of judgment.
- Sense of self-management and control.

None of this can be accomplished if you have already allowed yourself to be programmed into an initial decision made on 40 seconds of observation. Use that first 20 minutes to listen actively. Encourage the candidate to provide you with as much quality information as possible. Any evaluation of what you hear must wait until the 20 minutes are complete. At the end of the 20-minute time frame, you make a decision to continue the interview, if you believe that the candidate is viable, or to terminate the interview, if you think that the candidate and the job are not appropriate for one another.

If you determine that the candidate is viable, then you continue the interview for an additional 20 minutes (see Figure 4.1). An efficient and productive interview of a suitable candidate, therefore, should take approximately 40 minutes. By the end of 40 minutes, you may not make a hiring decision, but you know with certainty what the candidate would bring to the organization in terms of strengths and weaknesses if he or she were hired.

Although a 40-minute interview should be sufficient to evaluate a professional, technical, or executive candidate, it may well be overkill in terms of evaluating a clerical person. At that level, you might consider a 15-minute courtesy interview and 30 minutes for the total interview.

The First Segment: 20 minutes

Courtesy Interview
- Explore the area of best information.
- Make a "go" / "no-go" decision.
- Examine the candidate's goals.

The Second Segment: 10 minutes	*The Third Segment: 5 minutes*
For Viable Candidates ■ Sell the organization and the job. ■ Answer the candidate's questions.	■ Explore the next area of information. ■ Cover self-development efforts and attempts to avoid professional obsolescence.
	The Fourth Segment: 5 minutes
	■ Explore the next area of information. ■ Perhaps look into nonwork activities.

Figure 4.1 Structuring the Interview.

Suppose that you determine a candidate does not have the skills needed for the job before the initial 20 minutes is over. Why should you prolong the discussion? There are two good reasons. The first has to do with public relations. An organization has a reputation to uphold in the community; it is important that potential candidates leave the interaction feeling that they were treated with respect and consideration.

The second reason has to do with expanding the channels of recruitment. It may be true that this candidate does not have the skills and experience you require. People who work in the same type of occupation, however, know one another. If a candidate leaves the interview with a good feeling about you and your organization, he or she may say to a friend, "They couldn't use me at Dynamerica because I do not have gizmohoochi skills; but you do, and I know you are unhappy where you are. Why don't you go talk to them; they seem like very nice folks." The idea is not to close off any potential avenues of good talent. In truth, good people are hard to find.

If you are like most managers who find themselves in the interviewer role, you have difficulty terminating the 20-minute courtesy interview graciously. Even though you know you have no interest in the candidate, you continue to talk, describing all the wonderful challenges and benefits working for the organization will provide. Why do that? You are only tantalizing the person and wasting both your time.

By dramatically altering your body language, you can end the interview gracefully and with dispatch. Here is how to do that. During the initial 20 minutes, make certain you give the candidate your complete attention, with good, strong, and direct eye contact. At the end of the 20 minutes, lower your eyes to their paperwork, turning the pages over a few times while keeping your eyes on the papers. Then stand up (your eyes still on the candidate's paperwork) and extend your right hand preparatory to a good-bye handshake while saying, "Well, I guess I have all the information I need." Then raise your eyes to look at the candidate and say: "Thank you very much for coming in to see us. It was a pleasure to meet you. We have a number of other candidates to interview and should be ready to make a decision within the next several weeks. We will contact you at that time." With such body language and speech, there is no question in the candidate's mind that the interview has reached its conclusion.

■ THE IMPORTANCE OF THE CANDIDATE'S GOALS

If the proposed work relationship is to be successful, both parties must gain support for their respective goals from it. Otherwise you are building in turnover. It is not enough that the candidate seems perfect for the job in terms of knowledge, experience, and talent; the job must also seem ideal to the candidate in terms of augmenting his or her career.

An excellent time to cover the issue of goals is when, during the first 20 minutes, you are exploring all the details of the candidate's most recent job. If you decide this candidate is an excellent match for the vacancy, and you make him or her a job offer, you want to be sure that your offer will be accepted. This is why it is essential that you discover something about the candidate's plans for the future and about the type of work environment in which the candidate feels fulfilled. The candidate has the answers to these issues; you don't. In this area, it is important not to make any assumptions, as the following example illustrates:

A very large investment corporation was losing its corporate human resources vice president to a federally inspired and funded community program. After an extensive search the company finally found the ideal candidate. The vice president extolled the candidate's virtues, accomplishments, skills, and knowledge: "Even though we've had to offer a higher level of compensation than we anticipated, he's well worth it in terms of background. I feel we're lucky to have been able to get him to join us."

A scant three months later, this prized candidate quit the job.

Consultant:	What happened?
Vice president:	He felt he wasn't being given the latitude he wanted in terms of running his own shop. He said we gave him an empty title with no authority behind it.
Consultant:	His desire for power should have been picked up in your interviewing process.
Vice president:	What makes you say that?
Consultant:	You made certain that he met your goals, but evidently you neglected to make sure that

your organization would simultaneously
meet his goals.

You may see the perfect candidate for a particular vacancy
and tell yourself, "Don't let this one get away." Your impulse is
to sell, sell, sell. You may know that the job in question cannot
possibly satisfy the candidate's expectations, but your department really needs those skills. If you mislead the candidate into
accepting your position, you have given yourself a ticking time
bomb. It is not a question of *if* the person will quit the job, only
when. In addition, you can be sure that, when this person dis-
covers he or she has been manipulated, you will be confronted
by one very angry human being.

Here's one example of what can happen in such a situation.
An engineering candidate was quite clear when he explained to
the department manager that his sole purpose for changing
jobs was financial. His second child was going to be quadru-
plets. The department manager was desperate to have the candidate's skill set and so promised him a substantial raise after a
successful six-month probationary period. The salary figure already in play was far in excess of what had been budgeted for
the position. The department manager knew that further increases would be impossible for at least two years.

One year later the engineer brought his manager a proto-
type of what he had invented to solve the problem of a key customer:

Manager: This is wonderful! How soon will the blueprints be
ready for manufacturing?

Engineer: They are ready now. Here they are.

Manager: There are no measurements on these drawings.
The shop can't make anything with these. Go put
the numbers on the drawings.

Engineer: Not until you give me a 30% salary increase.

Manager: That's blackmail!

Engineer: I left a good job based on your financial assurances.
You never had any intention of giving me what you
promised. I think that kind of dishonesty is worse
than what I'm doing. By the way, if you decide not

to give me that raise, I will resign, and you will
have to explain things to the client.

Reluctantly, the manager gave the engineer the 30% increase,
retroactive six months. The engineer accepted the raise and
two weeks later, when he received his retroactive salary check,
he quit the job. The client never did get his invention, and the
company lost a good customer.

An unskilled interviewer will spend far too much time selling candidates on what the interviewer assumes are the most
attractive elements of the job. When this happens, candidates
leave the interview with the impression that the interviewer
(and therefore the company, as well) is not truly interested in
their personal career aspirations. After all, the interviewer
never asked what was attractive or important to them.

When you ask about a candidate's goals, he or she will leave
the interview feeling that you are sincerely interested in his or
her plans for the future. That being the case, you immediately
increase your chances 10-fold that any offer you make will be
accepted. This is true even if the candidate has received an
offer from another organization at a somewhat higher salary
figure.

With all the downsizing, right sizing, reengineering and
other assorted euphemisms for laying people off, candidates
today recognize that they must be their own career coaches. A
person will spend 11,000 days of their life between the ages of
21 and 65 at work. That is a staggering amount of time to spend
at one single activity for organizations that evidence a decided
lack of concern for an individual's personal goals. As an astute
interviewer you want to be certain that all candidates you
spend time with understand that you (and thus your organization) have a personal stake in their career success. The unspoken message that you want every candidate to go away with is
that you (and your organization) understand that corporate success rests in part on the personal success of the individual employees in the company's employ.

Here are some questions that will help you to uncover the
candidate's career goals:

What do you expect to be doing in five years?

In what way do you think this job will prepare you for that?

What kind of experience or training are you looking for? Why?

How will you know that we could provide you with that kind of experience?

How would you know that this organization could make a real difference in your career by helping you reach your personal goals?

The following questions will assist you in discovering the kind of environment in which the candidate feels fulfilled:

What are you looking for in a job?

What would it look like if this organization could give you that kind of challenge?

What kinds of efforts did you make to try to get those opportunities at prior jobs?

What are the typical obstacles that have prevented other organizations from offering you those kinds of opportunities?

If you could construct this job exactly the way you wanted it, what would it look like?

How would you determine if this was the right job for you?

■ SELLING THE JOB AND THE ORGANIZATION

The first 20 minutes is concluded, and you have determined that this candidate is a potential hire. You decide, therefore, to continue the interview. You should devote the next 10 minutes to selling the job and the company (see Figure 4.1). If you have obtained sufficient information about the candidate's goals in the first 20 minutes, your sell phase will be easy because you know exactly what the candidate is looking for (or looking to avoid) in a job situation.

It is important that you sell what is appropriate to the candidate. If the person is 22 years old, do *not* tell him or her about the terrific retirement plan the firm has. At 22, a candidate isn't thinking about getting old, let alone retiring. A 22-year-old may however, be interested in tuition reimbursement. On the other hand, a 42-year-old will probably be curious about the company's retirement plan.

I once had a client who had been searching for someone with a very specific technical skill set whose responsibilities would include some minor supervisory duties. The supervision requirement was not a pivotal issue; the technical skill set, however, was critical. In fact, my client was paying an exorbitant price for contract labor to fill the technical portion of the position while he was searching for an appropriate candidate.

Then one day the ideal candidate—skills, experience, education, background—was referred to him by human resources. My client was so excited after reading the resume that he ran out into the hall, seized the candidate's hand, and pumped it up and down saying, "Am I glad to meet you! How soon can you start?" The startled candidate responded. "This vacancy you have here . . . umm . . . does it involve supervision?" My client answered enthusiastically, "Yes, and your people are young, bright, and eager!" Whereupon the candidate said, crossing his arms tightly over his chest, "The place I'm working now I have to supervise and I hate it. Thank you very much for the interview." The candidate then turned and walked out.

During the 10-minute sell phase of the interview, you want to tell the candidate about the *personal,* career-related benefits that will be gained if he or she joins the organization. You also want to answer any questions the candidate may have about the position and the organization. Both the company and the candidate must feel reasonably certain that the requirements and conditions of the job and the skills and expectations of the person complement one another.

You can gain some very useful information about this area of complementary interests when the candidate asks questions about the company. The appropriate follow-up to any of the candidate's questions should be about why that particular piece of information is important to him or her. Here are two examples of this type of follow-up:

Candidate: You said I'd be part of an eight-member engineering team in a department of several other engineering groups.

Director of engineering: Yes. That's right.

Candidate:	How many engineering teams are there, and do they get involved with each other's work?
Director of engineering:	I'm curious: Why is that important to you?
Candidate:	It's difficult enough working on one team without having to coordinate your work activities with those of other teams. Each team thinks their priorities are the most important. There's a lot of time wasted trying to coordinate everyone's priorities. Then, whatever the decision, no one is completely satisfied. It makes for a lot of bad feelings. I hate that.

Upon hearing that, the director of engineering concluded that this candidate was not the right person for this job.

Candidate:	As I understand it, overtime is expected at the end of each month and all during the month of October for the year-end closing of the books.
Accounting manager:	Yes.
Candidate:	How extensive would that overtime be?
Accounting manager:	Very extensive. Why is that a particular concern?
Candidate:	Currently I'm taking a full load of courses to complete a master's degree in finance. Excessive overtime would impact my studying, and it will certainly conflict with my classes.

Upon further discussion, the accounting manager confirmed that completing her degree was the candidate's top priority. If the company could not accommodate her, she would not be interested in the position. Now the accounting manager had to decide whether to make such an accommodation for this candidate or seek someone else who could consent to the overtime.

■ THE RELEVANCE OF SELF-DEVELOPMENT

Following the 10-minute sell phase, you want to take 5 minutes to delve into the next area that is likely to give you worthwhile information. Perhaps you want to explore the issue of education and training. This is not about having the candidate repeat the educational information described on the resume, but rather a discussion of any self-development efforts in which the candidate has been involved.

Today, occupational requirements change rapidly. The last thing your organization needs are employees who have relaxed themselves into professional or technical obsolescence. This is the point at which you want to ask such questions as these:

What criteria do you use to evaluate your effectiveness?

When there are additional responsibilities available and you have to pitch in, how do you decide which extra assignment to adopt?

What job experiences have added most to your development? How?

In what areas would you like to become more effective?

What are you doing to develop those skills?

Sometimes the candidate will respond. "The company doesn't provide any training; there's no opportunity for growth; the job is no longer challenging. That's the reason I want to leave." Ultimately, each person is responsible for his or her own development no matter what their organization may or may not be doing. Should a candidate say those things, you should follow up with these questions:

How much of your own personal time have you devoted to developing yourself and for what specific purposes?

What have you been doing on your own to increase your knowledge and capability?

■ THE RELEVANCE OF
SPARE-TIME/NONWORK ACTIVITIES

With the last five minutes, you may want to ask about outside interests and hobbies. A candidate's response to such questions can sometimes lead into illegal areas, so this line of questioning can be risky. For example:

Manager: Do you hold membership in any professional or social groups or associations?

Candidate: I am the president of the Over-Fifty-but-We're-Nifty professional association, so a lot of my spare time is involved with those responsibilities.

Many years ago, I was working in an employment agency that was engaged in placing former felons into jobs so that they could rejoin society. All of these candidates had completed serving their sentences. We were told by the local criminal justice system that under no circumstances were we to ask the candidates anything about their crimes. The person seated in front of me had a strong background in landscape design and horticulture. In fact, according to his paperwork, he had at one time owned a small gardening and lawn business. Because I am a gardening buff, I could not resist delving into that side of his history (halo effect).

Manager: With such a strong background in gardening, I assume that you spend your spare time involved in activities related to that.

Candidate: Well, no, I don't. I have to attend all kinds of group therapy sessions for domestic violence. See, I nearly killed my wife two years ago. . . .

In spite of the possible legal danger involved, asking candidates about their non-work-time activities can provide you with information regarding their preference for solitary pursuits versus more collegial situations. People's time at work is structured for them by their bosses and responsibilities. Spare-time activities, however, are self-selected and may therefore tell you how a person would choose to structure his or her time at work given the choice. In other words, a person who chooses to organize his or her spare time with solitary pursuits would probably prefer—if allowed—to work alone rather than in a team. In answer to a simple, open-ended question, you can often obtain significant information, especially if you manage a team-based organization:

Manager:	What do you do in your spare time?
Candidate number one:	I have an extensive stamp collection, and now, with Internet capability, I can buy and sell stamps without ever leaving the house. It's wonderful.
Candidate number two:	My spouse and I are members of a semiprofessional folk-dancing troupe. On weekends, we are either involved in competition or busy practicing with the team. Last year our team won the Eastern States Competition and we all got to go—all expenses paid—for a week in Bermuda.

It is obvious from their responses that candidate number one prefers loner activities whereas candidate number two prefers situations that allow interaction with other people. Moreover, for candidate number two, there is a focus on the achievement of a group goal as the purpose for the activity. In other words, it's more than purely a social activity. Be aware, however, that whether a candidate is a loner or group oriented is not always reflected in spare-time activities. Sometimes a candidate will say, "On weekends I take the boat out into the middle of the lake so no one can get to me because, frankly, by the end of the week, I am peopled out."

Another reason to ask candidates about spare-time activities is to discover where they like to put their energies. It is a well-recognized fact that rest, relaxation, rejuvenation, and a well-rounded life are the best defenses against burnout, while also making for a more congenial and productive employee. When someone spends *all* his or her time working, that person may have other, perhaps unspoken, goals that are more important to him or her than a career with your organization.

Manager:	What interests occupy your time outside of work?
Candidate number one:	I have a real estate broker's license, and I've been actively involved in

selling real estate on weekends for the last 10 years.

Manager:	What interests occupy your time outside of work?
Candidate number two:	My spouse is in her own business, and basically I help by keeping the books and running the office.

If you are looking for a candidate who can put in a fair amount of overtime, these two will not fit the bill. Moreover, you should have a real concern about their long-term career plans. It looks like both candidates are interested in self-employment rather than a career with your organization.

Spare-time activities can also tell you something about a person's values:

Manager:	What do you do when you're not working?
Candidate number one:	I like reading mystery stories and historical novels.
Candidate number two:	I read and record books for the blind.
Candidate number three:	I work out at the gym, jog, bike ride; you know, stay active and keep in shape.
Candidate number four:	I work with a local group rehabbing old buildings into shelters for the homeless.

■ CLOSING THE INTERVIEW

You and the candidate have now concluded 40 minutes of mutual investigation. A good standard close is to thank the candidate for taking the time to explore the opportunity. You should also express how much you enjoyed speaking with him or her. Then try to provide the candidate with some sense of what is to follow:

Interviewer: I expect to complete the preliminary interviews by the end of the week. If there is to be a second interview, you will hear from me within two weeks. In any event, if you have any questions, please do not hesitate to call. [*Give the candidate your business card.*]

If you have determined that the candidate is not an appropriate match for the job, then a letter should go out (probably from human resources) the following day telling the candidate of that decision. Even in cases in which both you and the candidate realize that he or she and the job are not right for one another, send a letter.

Chapter 5

The Primary Tool of the Interview: Questioning

There are four basic kinds of questions used in the interview process: direct, open-ended, clarifying, and self-appraisal. There are also behavioral questions and problem-solving or puzzle questions, which are forms of the open-ended question. Each type of question plays a useful role in the interviewing process. If you maintain a strong focus on listening, then selecting the appropriate questioning technique at any point in the conversation will become an instinctive process.

■ DIRECT QUESTIONS

Direct questions are designed to focus the candidate's attention onto a specific piece of information. Such questions require a specific answer; they narrow the range of possible responses to a very few words—usually "yes" or "no." They are also used to gather minute data, such as a date or the number of something:

Manager: Did you like that job?
Candidate: Yes.

Manager: How many people did you supervise?
Candidate: Seven.

Manager: Was the project successful?

Candidate: Yes.

Manager: When did the reorganization occur?
Candidate: Last March.

■ THE JACK WEBB TECHNIQUE

Although direct questions furnish the candidate with an exceptionally clear idea of what you want to know, they often provide
you with very little useful information for assessing the candidate's suitability for the job. They do not give you any idea at all
of how the candidate thinks, makes decisions, understands
him- or herself, or perceives his or her environment. Also, if
you use direct questions back-to-back, you condition the candidate to give you one- or two-word responses, regardless of the
type of question you ask. When this happens, the interview
takes on the quality of an interrogation. This is because, when
used back-to-back, direct questions seem accusatory and threatening. The interview does not flow but rather moves along in
fits and starts.

For example, here is a manager whose overuse of direct
questions causes the candidate to respond even to open-ended
questions such as "why" with one or two words:

Manager: How many jobs have you had in the past five
years? [*Direct*]

Candidate: Four

Manager: Do you like changing jobs so often? [*Direct*]
Candidate: No.

Manager: Do you always look for similar work? [*Direct*]
Candidate: Yes.

Manager: Why? [*Open-ended*]
Candidate: I'm good at it.

Manager: Tell me about your job with Grabitt & Runn.
[*Open-ended*]

Candidate: There's not much to tell.

Manager: How long were you with them? [*Direct*]
Candidate: Eighteen months.

Manager: What did you do there? [*Open-ended*]
Candidate: Software development.
Manager: Do you like that kind of work? [*Direct*]
Candidate: It's okay.
Manager: Why did you leave there? [*Open-ended*]
Candidate: Layoff.
Manager: You were laid off? [*Direct*]
Candidate: Yes.
Manager: Is that when you went to Sockett Toome? [*Direct*]
Candidate: Yes.
Manager: You were there for only six months? [*Direct*]
Candidate: Yes.
Manager: How come you left there so quickly? [*Open-ended*]
Candidate: Boredom.
Manager: Did you ask for something more challenging? [*Direct*]
Candidate: Yes.
Manager: What happened? [*Open-ended*]
Candidate: They said "no."
Manager: Is that why you left for Bynther & Dunthatt? [*Direct*]
Candidate: Yes.
Manager: What happened there? [*Open-ended*]
Candidate: Boss problems.
Manager: Did you like the work? [*Direct*]
Candidate: Yes.
Manager: Tell me about the "boss problems." [*Open-ended*]
Candidate: He was a control freak.
Manager: A control freak? [*Open-ended*]
Candidate: Yes.

In terms of interviewing etiquette and conversational protocol, all the candidate has to do is answer the question. When you ask a direct question, you cheat yourself out of a wealth of significant and sometimes unexpected information that you get when you use open-ended questions. In addition, with an open-ended question, there are choices for follow-up questions that are not available when direct questions are used. Compare these scenarios:

Direct question:	Can you work well without supervision?
Candidate:	Yes.
Open-ended question:	What kind of relationship do you like to structure with your manager?
Candidate:	I appreciate a boss who will tell me clearly what the goals and expectations are for my performance. And, I work best with a boss who treats me as a competent professional, one who allows me to negotiate some of the critical details of my work such as time frame, additional resources, and priorities. I also want a boss who is willing to leave me on my own to get the job done.
Follow-up (a):	Suppose your manager was unable to give you that kind of clarity; what would you do to force the issue?
Follow-up (b):	Please explain what you mean by "negotiation of critical details."
Follow-up (c):	When working on your own, at what point might you make the judgment that you need your boss's input?
Direct question:	Did you like that job?
Candidate:	Yes.
Open-ended question:	What three things did you like most about that job?
Candidate:	Well . . . I liked the variety of tasks, the people I worked with, and the fact that the boss gave me a lot of latitude.

Follow-up (a): I'd like to hear more about the variety of tasks you were involved with.

Follow-up (b): I'm not clear I understand what you mean by "latitude." Could you say more about that?

Follow-up (c): What types of people were you working with?

When someone is new to interviewing, he or she will invariably telegraph the right answer (i.e., the answer the interviewer wants to hear) with the use of a direct question preceded by an explanatory sentence. This technique is known as *leading the witness*. It is a dumb strategy because you cannot learn anything about the candidate this way. For example:

Direct question: This job has a lot of pressure to it. Do you work well under pressure?

Candidate: Yes.

Direct question: You may have to put in a lot of overtime on this job. Will that be a problem?

Candidate: No, no problem.

Direct question: Around here everyone has to be very flexible because priorities are changing all the time. How flexible are you?

Candidate: Oh, I'm very flexible.

There are instances, however, when you need a piece of specific data and a direct question is the most effective way of getting it. In those situations, there are two strategies that you can use. The first is to use direct questions like salt and pepper—sprinkled throughout the interview and never back-to-back. This strategy is known as the *one-two approach*. The second strategy is to use an introductory phrase so that the direct question is somewhat disguised. Here are some examples of the first strategy:

Direct question: Do you have any experience dealing with angry customers?

Candidate: Yes.

Open-ended question: What specific techniques do you use for handling such situations?

Direct question: How many people were there on your team?

Candidate: Seven.

Open-ended question: What specific role did you play?

Direct question: Are you the kind of person who likes challenges?

Candidate: Yes.

Open-ended question: How do you like to be challenged?

Now, compare the following direct questions with ones that are disguised by the use of an introductory phrase:

Direct question: How many jobs have you had in the past five years?

Introductory phrase: *I'd be interested to learn* how many jobs you've held over the past several years.

Direct question: How often did you to get together with your boss to set goals?

Introductory phrase: *In your working experience,* how often did you and your boss get together to set goals?

Direct question: When did you get your last salary increase?

Introductory phrase: *I wonder, do you recall* the date of your last salary increase?

Suppose, because her company was not doing well, the candidate has had no raise for two years. As soon as you ask, "When did you get your last salary increase?" the candidate exhibits some defensive body language. She crosses her arms over her chest and leans back in the chair, lengthening the distance between you. She is thinking that, if she admits to no raise for two years, you will assume there was something unsatisfactory about her performance at her previous job. On the other hand, if you say, "I wonder if you recall the date of your last salary increase?" you are much more likely to get a nondefensive, informational response such as the following:

Candidate: Actually, I haven't had a raise in two years. The company was doing poorly in terms of sales. We were told that, in order to avoid a layoff, there would be no raises for one year. After that, everything was to go back to normal. Because things were no better two years later, I decided to look for another job.

Direct questions have yet another use. It is true that a candidate will be nervous in the interview until he or she starts speaking. You therefore want to force the candidate to talk as early on in the process as possible. Direct questions are superbly effective for accomplishing exactly that. Here are the most popular:

Did you have any trouble finding us?

Nice weather we're having, isn't it?

Would you care for a cup of coffee?

Realize, however, that, even though you have succeeded in getting the candidate to speak through your use of a few direct questions, you have not influenced the person to say anything useful in terms of the evaluation process.

■ OPEN-ENDED QUESTIONS

Open-ended questions do not require a specific answer to a particular question. Instead, they allow for a wide range of answers. When you use them effectively, open-ended questions compel the candidate to use many words in order to create a sufficient response.

Open-ended questions ask for opinions, the reasoning behind some action or decision, or the explanation of a procedure. They are never perceived as threatening. In fact, they help develop rapport. Best of all, they frequently uncover unanticipated information. Here are a few samples:

What is your opinion about . . . ?

What do you feel were the contributing factors to . . . ?

Under what circumstances would you . . . ?

How did you go about handling that situation?

What were your reasons for making that decision?

Then what happened?

How did you determine what the real problem was?

Many untrained interviewers do not like to use open-ended questions because they can be very time consuming. In addition, open-ended questions momentarily put the control of the direction of the interview into the hands of the candidate. You should not consider these reasons to be drawbacks, however. In exchange for the extra time involved, and a little flexibility on your timing plans, you will obtain better-quality information. You will get some insight as to how candidates think, perceive, and process their experiences. You will also get some indication of their personalities and beliefs about themselves.

Suppose your time plan is to spend 8 to 10 minutes discussing the candidate's supervisory experience on his or her most-recent job. Then, in answer to one of your open-ended questions, the candidate gives you what is known as *free information.* Free information occurs when the candidate says or does something that hints there is more to the story. It may be a hesitation in his or her delivery, it could be a sigh, it could be an offhand remark. (For more on *free information,* see Chapter 7.) The candidate's unexpected free information comment entices you to ask an unplanned question. If you decide to explore that free-information comment, not only have you set your time plan aside, you may have also altered the direction of the interview. The process is called *branching,* and it often provides some of the most valuable information in the entire interview.

In the following example, by branching, you discover that this candidate blames his people for the failure of his project and seems unwilling to use this negative situation as a learning experience for both himself and his staff:

Manager: That sounds like a very challenging project and an extremely important one for the corporation. How did you go about organizing it?

Candidate: Organizing it? You mean like dividing up the various tasks among my staff so that my people could pull it together?

Manager: Yes, so that the project would be successful.

Candidate: I did all of that but . . . well . . . frankly . . . things didn't work out as well as I had hoped. [*Free information*]

Manager: What results were you hoping for? [*Unplanned open-ended question*]

Candidate: I thought my staff would feel honored that we were selected for the project. I expected they would pitch in and work together as a team. But they didn't.

Manager: Why do you think that happened? [*Unplanned open-ended question*]

Candidate: I guess I overestimated my people's aptitude for teamwork and their willingness to assume responsibilities that were outside their individual job descriptions. Everyone griped about the extra work. There were endless squabbles about who was supposed to be doing what. The whining and complaining about them having to juggle regular work priorities along with their project tasks never stopped. Drove me nuts.

Manager: At what point did you realize there was a problem? [*Unplanned open-ended question*]

Candidate: Almost immediately—about three days into the project.

Manager: Once you identified the problem, what did you do?

Candidate: I sent everyone a memo reminding them that this was a team effort and I expected them to pitch in. I also held a staff meeting and gave them a good pep talk. But nothing seemed to help.

Manager: What else did you consider doing?

Candidate: That was about it. After all, they aren't children, even though they behave that way. They knew

> what they were supposed to do. They just didn't want to do it. Just plain lazy, I guess.

Manager: If you were faced with the same situation today, what would you do?

Candidate: I would ask my boss to select another group—one that already had a history of working together cooperatively on tough projects—people who were not afraid of a little extra work.

Many television interviewers are masters at using open-ended questions. Some can ask one short question and their interviewee talks nonstop for 15 minutes. There is one television interviewer, however, who uses a very unusual strategy—Barbara Walters.

■ THE BARBARA WALTERS TECHNIQUE

The interviewing technique that Barbara Walters uses seems to work well as she questions people about their personal lives. When used in the employment interview, however, it not only confuses the candidate, it also cuts down on the quality of the information received.

Here's how it works. Barbara Walters will ask her guest one question—usually an open-ended one. Before the person has a chance to respond, she immediately clarifies that question by revising it with several additional, related questions—usually direct or closed-ended questions. The result of all this verbal revision is that, by the time Barbara Walters stops speaking (because she has run out of breath?), there are several questions awaiting answers from the guest. Most people will answer the question most recently asked. One person in 10 will pick the question he or she likes best and answer that one. On one memorable occasion one of her guests caught Barbara Walters on her technique. He said, "Barbara, in answer to your questions: Yes. Yes. No. No. No."

This is not a useful strategy in employment interviewing because the more you revise the original question, the narrower you tend to make the area from which the candidates will select their possible responses. It is always best to ask one question at a time. Usually the first question in the series will be the best (and the most open-ended) one.

Manager: What were the evening courses you took recently? Was it your boss's idea to take them? Were they work related or for self-development? Have you always taken courses at night? Do you just enjoy learning?

Candidate: Yes. I do enjoy learning.

Manager: How do you like to be supervised? That is, what kind of supervisor brings out the best in you? Did you like your last supervisor? Did you get along well with her?

Candidate: Our relationship was pretty good.

Manager: What are your career plans? Would you like to be doing similar work in five years? Are you interested in continuing on in this field? Are you willing to take additional course work and training in order to move ahead?

Candidate: I am very interested in continuing on in this field.

If you use the Barbara Walters technique, it means that you have not thought through clearly what it is you wish to ask. If you have not worded your question in a clear manner, however, avoid the temptation of trying to clarify it by asking more questions. Being verbally precise in the interview is important, but not critical. Understand that listening is a critical part of communication. No matter what the position, whenever you interview you should be concerned about a candidate's communication and listening skills. In fact, the greater the responsibilities, the more critical it is that the candidate for that job be competent in both listening and speaking.

The best strategy for you is to simply ask *one* question and leave it there unrevised. Let the candidate struggle with it. Candidates are very capable of asking for clarification. Some will say, "What?" Others will ask, "Do you mean in terms of my work in general or with regard to this specific situation?" Still others will ask, "Could you repeat the question, please?"

No matter how confusing you may have made the question, there will always be an opportunity to clarify it after you have heard the candidate's response to it. In the meantime, however, you are learning something about the candidate's listening skills firsthand. It is the acid test.

Suppose you ask the candidate a perfectly clear and reasonable question but the response is completely off the mark. You then restate the question using different words and continue on. Now suppose this happens several times during the interview. You should begin to wonder if there is something wrong with the candidate's listening skills. If you hired the person to join your staff, gave them an assignment, and then left the area for several minutes, could you be sure that they would do as you had asked?

■ CLARIFYING QUESTIONS

Clarifying questions ask for more information or for a more-complete explanation than what the candidate has just provided. You should use these when you believe that what the candidate has just said is unclear or incomplete.

In most interviewing circumstances here is what happens. You have just asked a perfectly clear and reasonable question. The candidate has made a perfectly clear and reasonable response. You immediately make three assumptions.

1. The candidate means exactly what he or she has said.
2. The candidate is using words in the same way and with the same meanings as you do.
3. Whatever the candidate has responded represents all the data he or she has on that topic.

None of these assumptions may be true. Following up with a clarifying question will clear up all those assumptions.

There are two basic types of clarifying questions:

1. One asks for a definition.
2. The other asks for an illustration.

Asking for a definition is a great way of getting past those old cliches that candidates love to toss around in the interview:

Manager: What are you looking for in a job?

Candidate: What I'm really looking for is growth.

Manager: Tell me what you mean by "growth." [*Clarifying question*]

Candidate: I'm tired of working with a boss who doesn't allow me to make any decisions about what I'm doing. I want a job where I can work on my own.

Manager: You have an prominent position at Gotcha, Inc. I'm curious as to why you have decided to leave them.

Candidate: It's time I went to a higher level in my career.

Manager: What specifically do you mean by "higher level"? [*Clarifying question*]

Candidate: I should be doing more important work at this stage in my career.

Manager: I'm not sure I understand what you mean by "more important work." Could you say a little more about that? [*Clarifying question*]

Candidate: I want a better title.

Manager: What made you decide to apply for a position with our company?

Candidate: I've heard this is a great place to work.

Manager: What specifically have you heard that would make this a great place to work for you? [*Clarifying question*]

Candidate: Umm . . . well, you have this brand-new facility and great benefits.

Often you will see resumes that state the candidate left a particular position for a "better opportunity." However, when you examine the situation at their succeeding job, you find that the candidate was actually given less responsibility and earned a lower rate of pay. It is time, therefore, to ask the clarifying question: "What specifically did you mean by 'better opportunity'?"

As an astute interviewer, you already know that candidates do not use words the same way you do. When you ask a candidate to clarify the meaning of what they said, you avoid making assumptions about what the candidate means. In some instances, rather than asking for a definition, you can ask for an illustration of what the candidate is talking about. This tactic is especially useful when the candidate is attempting to superficially slide past an important issue. Consider these exchanges:

Manager: What has been your experience managing or coaching a team?

Candidate: I've done quite a bit of that. My teams were always successful, and I've always found the experience very rewarding.

Manager: I'd be interested to learn more specifically how you went about ensuring that your teams were successful.

Candidate: Apparently, this position requires some expertise at team management. That is no problem for me because I have a lot of experience in that area.

Manager: Could you give me some specific examples of the strategies you have actually utilized in managing teams? [*Clarifying question*]

Manager: Others in the position have described this as a high-stress job.

Candidate: Stress never bothers me. I'm very organized.

Manager: I'm not completely sure I understand what you're saying. Could you say a little more about that? [*Clarifying question*]

Candidate: Good time management prevents job stress, and I am a great manager of my time.

Manager: Please give me some examples of the specific techniques you use in managing your time and how those techniques prevent stress. [*Clarifying question*]

Manager: What's the most-challenging situation you faced as a foreman?

Candidate: Dealing with the union, especially when I needed to discipline a worker. No matter how I approached the situation, it was always a problem.

Manager: I'd like to hear more about that.

Candidate: You know how it is. The contract sets management and labor against one another. It's just difficult.

Manager: I imagine it is not easy. Can you give me some examples of the types of problems you faced and the specific techniques you used in attempting to resolve those problems? [*Clarifying question*]

The question always comes up: "How do I know if the candidate is telling me the truth?" Well, you don't. However, when you start hearing those old cliches, you should suspect that you might just be hearing a distortion of the facts or a complete fabrication of the truth.

Suppose you are interviewing a candidate for the position of admitting clerk in the emergency ward of a large inner-city hospital. Because your series of clarifying questions does not produce anything except more cliches, you ask for an illustration of what the candidate is talking about:

Interviewer: Why are you interested in this type of work?

Candidate: Well, I like people.

Interviewer: Perhaps you'd better tell me what you mean by "liking people" and how that relates to being an admitting clerk in a medical emergency environment. [*Clarifying question*]

Candidate: I really enjoy meeting people, so I thought I'd be terrific as an admitting clerk.

Interviewer: Please tell me what you mean by "meeting people" and how you would accomplish that in a health emergency situation. [*Clarifying question*]

Candidate: Well, I get along well. People seem to like me.

Interviewer: Can you give me some examples from your recent job? [*Clarifying question*]

Let's say you were inquiring into the candidate's interpersonal skill and comfort level for a cooperative endeavor in a team setting and that person responded to your questions with vague cliches. Asking for an illustration will help you get the information you are after:

Manager: If I were to ask your previous manager about your ability as a team player, what do you think she would say?

Candidate: She would tell you I am a good team player who works hard, produces superior results, and who knows how to mind their own business.

Manager: Could you tell me more about what you mean by "minding your own business"? [*Clarifying question*]

Candidate: Well, I keep to myself most of the time—you know, nose to the grindstone and all that.

Manager: I'm still not sure I understand what you mean by "keep to myself most of the time" and how that works in a team setting. [*Clarifying question*]

Candidate: Well, I have more experience and knowledge than the others in the area, so I didn't ever need their help. I can do what I have to do completely on my own.

Manager: Can you give me an example of your interactions as a team player? [*Clarifying question*]

Cliches hold a certain appeal for candidates. They allow people to answer a question without really saying anything of substance. It is a safe way of responding to a hazardous question that, if answered honestly, might provide enough information to disqualify them from further consideration. Delving into a candidate's superficial response with a few clarifying questions generally produces very worthwhile information. Moreover, after the first few such questions, the candidate realizes that shallow responses are unacceptable:

Manager: What experiences on your last job added most to your development?

Candidate: I guess taking over as supervisor in the quality control area.

Manager: How did that role develop you?

Candidate: It was quite a challenge.

Manager: Tell me what you mean by "quite a challenge." [*Clarifying question*]

Candidate: Well, . . . things are never as simple or clear-cut as they seem on the surface. A person can get in over their head right away and not know it.

Manager: I'm not sure I understand what you mean by "get in over your head." Could you explain that a little for me? [*Clarifying question*]

Candidate: Nobody warns you about the sticky stuff; you have to learn that all on your own.

Manager: Can you give me an example of what you had to learn about on your own that was "sticky stuff." [*Clarifying question*]

Candidate: It was all the politics. I never knew there was so much politics in that place until I tried to get something done.

Manager: Tell me what you mean by "politics." [*Clarifying question*]

Candidate: I could not make any decisions on my own. No matter how trivial the issue, everything had to be approved of by the general foreman, the operations coordinator, and the plant manager. Going through all those levels took up too much of my time, so I went around them. Got done what had to be done and got in trouble for it.

Manager: Got in trouble for it?

Candidate: Yeah. They said I was breaking their stupid rules.

Manager: So what happened?

Candidate: I got fired.

■ THE PARROT

The strategy known as the *parrot* works the same way as the clarifying question. It is a request for more information or a more complete explanation of what has just been said. You can use it in situations in which you believe that whatever the candidate has just said is unclear or incomplete. It is an easy technique to use. Simply repeat, in a questioning tone, the last word or phrase that the candidate has said. For example:

Manager: What would you like to have on this job that you didn't have on your last job?

Candidate: I'd like some freedom and latitude.

Manager: Some freedom and latitude? [*Parrot*]

Candidate: Yes. I'd like the authority to make decisions on those issues that affect my job.

Manager: What rules and regulations did your previous employer have regarding lateness and absenteeism?

Candidate: Oh, they were pretty liberal.

Manager: Liberal? [*Parrot*]

Candidate: Management didn't care what hours you kept as long as the work got done. So some people worked at night, others came in at 11:00 A.M. and worked until 7:00 P.M. Everyone kept different hours.

Manager: What do you think is the single most important quality for a manager to have?

Candidate: First and foremost, the person should be a good listener.

Manager: A good listener? [*Parrot*]

Candidate: Yeh. The best boss I ever had always took the time to hear our ideas. The worst boss I ever had wouldn't listen to anybody.

■ SELF-APPRAISAL QUESTIONS

Self-appraisal questions ask candidates to analyze and evaluate themselves and/or their actions and skills. Undoubtedly the most-popular self-appraisal question of all is, "What do you consider your greatest strengths to be?" Here are a few more:

What kinds of things do you do best?

Which skills and personal resources would you say have been the major contributors to your success up to now?

Why do you feel you would be effective in this particular position?

What special skills and abilities would you bring to this job that other candidates would not have?

Each of these questions invites the candidate to boast about him- or herself. Every question says, "Please tell me the good things about yourself." Nowhere do you ask for any problems or weaknesses.

Many untrained and inexperienced interviewers love to ask some form of the question, "We all have strengths and weaknesses; tell me about your weaknesses." You should *never* ask that question. It is bad interviewing technique. It is asking candidates to furnish you with a reason for *not* hiring them. A candidate would have to be a fool to do that. When untrained or inexperienced interviewers are asked why they use this question, they explain that this technique allows them to find out if the candidate possesses some level of self-awareness. Others will say that it is a quick method of uncovering any factors or pieces of information that immediately eliminate the candidate from further consideration. Neither reason makes any sense.

If you were to ask such a question, you would most likely to get two kinds of responses. One type of candidate will select a positive quality and turn it into a negative:

Manager: We all have strengths and weaknesses. Tell me about your weaknesses.

Candidate: I've been told I'm overdedicated.

Another type of candidate will insist that his or her work history has been very positive in terms of matching his or her strengths with job requirements:

Manager: We all have strengths and weaknesses. Tell me about your weaknesses.

Candidate: Weaknesses? Every job I've ever had has gone so well that I don't really have any data to give you in response to that question.

Both candidates are telling you that they absolutely refuse to disclose anything that could jeopardize their candidacy. Nevertheless, as an astute interviewer, you know that candidates come to the interview prepared with two lists. One is an "A" list, which details all the relevant and favorable facts and attributes they want to tell you about—the glorious reasons why you should ask them to become part of your staff. They are terrific at organizational skills, wonderful with people, marvelous at team leadership, and not bad at strategic planning either.

There is a "B" list, however, which you are certain exists and about which you are exceedingly interested. These are the negative issues that the candidate has sworn will not be dragged from her lips, even under severe and painful torture. First of all, she has just been fired from her most recent job because of a $350,000 cost overrun on an important project that she was managing. Second, she has a history of authority problems and has never had a good working relationship with any boss. Third, even though her resume indicates a college degree, that is not true; she lied.

This B list of items is just as foremost in a candidate's mind as is the A list. In all probability, the candidate has cautioned him- or herself to be careful not to go anywhere near these topics in framing responses to any of your questions. By asking, "We all have strengths and weaknesses; tell me about your weaknesses," do you actually expect that the candidate will come right out and say:

> Actually, I've never been able to get along with any boss I've ever had; it's difficult for me to take orders from other people. In addition, I'm really not very responsible when it comes to numbers. As a matter of fact, I got fired from my last job because the project I was managing incurred a $350,000 cost overrun. Your opening here sounded really good, and I knew you wouldn't see me unless I had a college degree, so I lied on my resume. I never went beyond high school.

There is no way you can get the candidate to tell you these B-list items by asking for them directly. What you must do is create a positive and accepting atmosphere in which these negatives don't seem so important. By so doing, those B-list items simply slide into the conversation. It doesn't take much effort for this to happen because the B list is already foremost in the candidate's mind. All you need to do is use positive self-appraisal questions in combination with silence.

■ USING SILENCE

It is nearly impossible in an interview situation for two people to sit there looking at one another in stone silence. In fact, according to a Harvard Business School study on communication, the maximum amount of time two people can sit in absolute silence is 21 seconds. In the 22nd second someone will speak.[1] It should not be the interviewer.

There are two times in the interviewing process when it is vital to use silence. The first is after you ask the question. It is critical that you keep quiet and allow the candidate to construct his or her response. The worst thing you can do is try to be helpful by either coaching the candidate, rephrasing your original question, or providing a laundry list of response choices. When you do that, you have effectively derailed the candidate's train of thought.

Self-appraisal questions especially cause candidates to become very busy mentally. First, they have to figure out what the question meant: What is it that you are looking for and how does that relate to the job requirements? Second, they have to decide how to answer the question so they sound qualified. Third, they have to put their responses together in words and phrases and with the proper syntax so that they sound convincing and competent. They also want to skirt any issue on their B list in presenting their response. All of that takes time. Twenty-two seconds is not a lot of time. It only seems interminable because you are sitting there doing nothing but waiting for the candidate's response. Remind yourself to be patient. Eventually the answer will come.

The second time you want to use silence is *after* the candidate responds to your self-appraisal question. This time you will not have to wait 21 seconds. All it takes is an extra five seconds of silence, and an additional flood of words will follow. After the initial 21 seconds of silence, you get the candidate's well-prepared, well-designed, well-worded, and well-screened response containing only items from the A list. After the second silence of five seconds, you will hear items from the candidate's

B list. So, with just a little patience and silence you will see many candidates talk themselves right into or right out of a job.

Manager: Which of your many skills and abilities do you think we could use best on this job? [*Self-appraisal question*]

21 seconds of silence

Candidate: It sounds as if this position really needs someone who has the ability to sell their ideas to higher management. Also, you need a person with an in-depth understanding of the marketplace. Not only do I have such knowledge, I also have a strong background in business planning. I understand business strategy and marketplace pressures on profit margins. I've had a good amount of successful experience dealing with all of those issues at both Flyby-Nite Manufacturing and Major Misfitt Corporation.

5 seconds of silence

Candidate: Hollin-Wall Limited was another story. My ideas were sound—perhaps a bit risky and unorthodox—but sound. It was just the wrong time in terms of what was going on in the marketplace.

Manager: On your last job, what do you consider was your greatest strength? [*Self-appraisal question*]

21 seconds of silence

Candidate: Obviously my organizational skills. I consistently impressed the staff with my ability to manage multiple priorities for numbers of people. Everyone depended on me to keep track of their paperwork, project due dates, appointments, and so on. My manager counted on me to control interruptions by limiting the staff's access to her, restricting the number of phone calls she had to handle, and by helping her to take better control of her time.

5 seconds of silence

Candidate: Of course, I couldn't make everyone happy. In fact, generally no one was entirely happy. I was the least-popular person in the entire department. If you ask my manager for a reference, you'll probably hear that I was hard-nosed and controlling and stubborn, but really I was only doing my job.

Manager: What special skills or strengths would you be bringing to this job that other candidates would not? [*Self-appraisal question*]

21 seconds of silence

Candidate: I am a real people person. It's more than just having good human relations. I like to think of myself as the departmental morale builder. I know that people work better when their environment is caring and friendly. I would make sure that people's birthdays and anniversaries were remembered. If a staff member had a death in the family, I would start a collection for flowers. I was always available if a coworker needed help with something or wanted to talk over a personal problem. That's the kind of thing that builds a real team feeling among people. People need something more than a continuous insistence by management for productivity, results, output, or "deliverables," as my last boss used to call it.

5 seconds of silence

Candidate: According to him, I didn't have enough deliverables. I guess he really didn't understand the importance of what I was doing.

The use of silence is effective in these instances because both the A and B list are salient in the candidate's mind. By asking self-appraisal questions that seek only positive information, the candidate becomes less concerned about the items on his or her B list. Perhaps the candidate assumes the requests for positives indicates that you have been sufficiently and favorably impressed with his or her capabilities. Therefore, there's no harm in sharing a little negative information. After all, making mistakes is part of being human.

■ ENCOURAGEMENTS

Sometimes candidates will give you their well-formulated response to your positive self-appraisal question and then, even though you respond with 5 to 10 seconds of silence, you are not rewarded with an additional rush of words. There you are, leaning forward in the chair, hands open in the receiving posture, grinning expectantly like an idiot, and the candidate says nothing. Should that happen, follow your 5 seconds of silence with "encouragements."

There are three kinds of encouragements you can use: one- or two-word comments, which are the most effective; direct requests to elaborate on what was already said; and various body-language cues:

1. One- and two-word comments:

   Yes.

   Good.

   Hmmm.

   Uh-huh.

   Interesting.

2. Direct requests to elaborate on what was already said:

   I'd like to hear more.

   Do go on.

   Please continue.

3. Use of body-language cues:

   Nod your head "yes" periodically.

   Make a small sweeping motion toward yourself with your hand.

■ BEHAVIORAL QUESTIONS

Behavioral questions are a specialized category of open-ended questions, which is why they are mentioned here. See Chapter 2 for complete discussion of this style of question.

■ A FINAL CAUTION ABOUT QUESTIONS

A great deal of this book is about questioning technique and types of questions. There is even a section (Appendix B) devoted entirely to sample questions to assist you with question generation. The truth is, however, that, no matter how targeted or insightful your questions may be, if you do not know how to follow up with additional queries after the candidate responds, your superior questions will gain you nothing. Follow-up is pivotal to your success at interviewing.

A useful strategy to assist you with spur-of-the-moment question generation during the interview is called the *hooking principle.* This works by fashioning a question out of the last remark made by the candidate, using some of the candidate's words. Here are a few samples:

Candidate: Until that happened, I really hadn't given much thought to the *importance* of individual goal setting for my staff.

Manager: So why do you think that's *important* now?

Candidate: I just felt that her *expectations* for my performance were never that *clear.*

Manager: What attempts did you make to *clarify* those *expectations?*

Candidate: I was the first person in that job. There was no *procedure* or *process* of what to do or how to do it. It was difficult.

Manager: How did you go about establishing the *processes* and *procedures* needed?

■ NOTES

1. See Herb Cohen, *You Can Negotiate Anything* (New York: Bantam Books, 1981); Howard Raiffa, *The Art and Science of* Negotiation (Cambridge, MA: Harvard University Press, 1982).

■ REFERENCE

Nierenberg, Gerard. *Fundamentals of Negotiating.* New York: Hawthorne Books, 1973.

Chapter

Listening Visually: Body-Language Cues in the Interview

■ WHEN THE CANDIDATE'S BODY LANGUAGE IS SIGNIFICANT AND WHEN IT IS NOT

There is one time, and one time only, when the candidate's body language is significant, and that is immediately after you ask a question. At that moment you will see before you the candidate's psychological response to that question reflected in the body language.[1] Immediately after the body-language reaction, the candidate's verbal response quickly follows. All during the interview, the candidate will be moving around somewhat, perhaps making various hand gestures as he or she speaks, squirming or making adjustments in the chair, and looking around the room. You will be making similar gestures and movements as well. All of that movement is perfectly normal and irrelevant in terms of hidden meanings. The single moment in which the body language of the candidate is important comes as your question floats off into the air. It is only a brief moment, barely a 10th of a second.

Two categories of body-language cues are significant in the interview situation: (1) the size of the physical distance between you and the candidate (the part that is controlled by the candidate) and (2) the amount of continuous eye contact the candidate maintains with you. People lean toward the things they like and away from the things they don't like. The astute interviewer, therefore, will notice exactly when in the conversation the candidate leans forward in the chair, closing the distance between the parties. Alternatively, an astute interviewer will scrutinize what is happening in the dialogue when the candidate leans away, or pushes back against the chair, increasing the physical distance between the parties. When the candidate comes forward, you should anticipate hearing something positive. When the candidate appears to move away, you should assume you will now hear something that the candidate believes might effect his or her candidacy unfavorably.

The second cue involves candidates' eye movements. Candidates should be giving you fairly uninterrupted direct eye contact all through the interview. At some point in the interaction, candidates may avert their eyes, suddenly becoming very absorbed in looking out the window, or examining their hands, or watching themselves pick lint off their jacket. This is evidence that they would like to get away from your question. The physical constraints of the situation do not allow them to do that. So they escape as much as they can by increasing the distance between themselves and you or by directing their visual attention somewhere else.

What you want to look for immediately after you ask a question is gross changes in body language followed quickly by a verbal response. As mentioned previously, if you see positive body language, anticipate hearing a positive response; if you see negative body language, anticipate hearing a negative response. The problem comes when you see negative body language but the response is positive. Then you know the candidate is lying.

You could spring forward in the chair, point your finger accusingly at the candidate, and bellow, "Aha! You're lying!" Instead, ask a clarifying question such as, "Can you give me an example from your recent job?" (both a behavioral and a clarifying question).

Interviewer: I was curious as to the reason for the lack of job information between May of 1994 and July of 1996. Please fill in that gap for me.

Candidate: [*Eyes avert to lap; fingers twisting rapidly in lap; back is pressed against the chair; eyes look up to the ceiling then back at interviewer; voice lowers to a whisper.*] I actually had a series of odd jobs that had no relationship to my skills and career objectives.

Interviewer: Can you give me some examples? [*Clarifying question*]

Candidate: [*Hands making small flailing gestures; squirms in chair, eyes moving around the room rapidly; vocal strength is more normal.*] Well, you know, just odd jobs. . . . Driving a taxi, store clerk . . . stuff like that.

Interviewer: Could you tell me more about why you were involved with "stuff like that"? [*Clarifying question*]

Candidate: [*Shoulders slump; eyes avert to floor; fingers twisting slowly; words are mumbled.*] I was just trying to keep myself busy and put bread on the table. [*Sighs, reestablishes eye contact, straightens up in chair; voice is normal.*] I have a teenage son who was arrested for selling drugs. There was so much turmoil with the trial and all, I couldn't deal with anything else. Eventually I lost my job at the bank. Until things got sorted out with Jimmy, I really wasn't capable of doing anything significant. I guess that makes me a poor risk for this job, doesn't it?

Interviewer: Not at all. I can understand how difficult that situation must have been for you. Tell me how you've handled a difficult work-related situation that may have caused you a similar amount of stress. [*Behavioral question*]

There are a number of additional significant body-language cues. One of the most informative is fidgeting. It is not normal for an adult to fidget. Perhaps it is understandable in the very first few seconds of the interview due to nervousness, but certainly not after that. If your candidate starts to fidget, you know he or she is having problems with the direction of the conversation.

In the days when smoking was an accepted part of the American business scene, I always encouraged my candidates to smoke. It was interesting to me when and how they put the cigarette out. When smoking was no longer available to me as an inducement to telltale body language, I supplied my desk with a tray of fidget items that were within easy reach of my candidates. The tray held retractable ball point pens with noisy push-button tops, paper clips that could be threaded together, and colorful rubber bands that begged to be stretched.

For me, another revealing gesture was teeth grinding. So often in work situations, circumstances occur that cause a person a great deal of tension. If the candidate responded to that stressful situation by "gritting their teeth and bearing it," and if I said something in the interview that brought that situation to mind, the candidate would experience a similar level of discomfort. I might then see their jawline stiffen. Sometimes I noticed a grinding motion in the muscles just under their ears. At other times I would see a vein in their forehead suddenly become quite prominent.

Interviewers need to be attuned to such revealing body-language cues as a nervous laugh, reddening face, and inordinately long silences that come prior to a candidate's verbal response as signs of discomfort with the line of questioning. For example, sometimes candidates will open up and tell you things they later wish they had not said. Their conversation with themselves is, "You fool, you blew it. You shouldn't have said that." This thought is accompanied by a hand up to the mouth quickly followed by a crossing of arms across the chest in a defensive posture. It looks at first as if the candidate is attempting to push the words back into his or her mouth, which is something one often sees children do. It is not normal, however, for a adults to speak with their hands at their mouths. The arms crossed over the chest indicates the candidate is retreating into a more guarded position. When you see those two gestures in sequence, mentally replay what was recently said. Try to determine what it is that the candidate communicated that he or she now believes may have damaged his or her employment chances.

Of course, many gestures do not carry a significant message. The key is to concentrate on the *gross changes in body language that occur immediately after you ask a question.* In fact, it is essential to look for a family of gestures, not just one. For example, many candidates cross their arms over their chests. This may mean they are cold. It could also indicate that the chair in which they are seated is not very comfortable and that holding their arms in this manner puts their back in a better relation-ship to the chair. When combined with a tightened jawline and averted eye contact, however, a sudden crossing of the arms across the chest probably signifies defensiveness with regard to the question.

Body language varies from culture to culture as well. In the United States, we put a great deal of value on a straight look in the eye and a firm handshake as evidence of honesty, integrity, and forthrightness. A shy candidate, or one from a background in which looking at someone directly in the face is considered disrespectful, could well be discarded as a viable candidate by the unknowledgeable interviewer. Such a candidate will refrain from looking at the interviewer throughout the entire inter-view. The gross changes in body language that occur as a result of a distressing question, however, happen a little differently. As the disturbing question dies in the air, the candidate gives the interviewer a quick, hard look in the eye, sits up a little straighter, adjusts him- or herself in the chair, and then re-sumes looking away. The candidate's verbal response will quickly follow.

Of course, not all body-language cues are negative. As noted in Chapter 3, candidates who are interested and excited about what they are discussing reveal this in their body language: The pupils of their eyes get larger, they lean forward, they tend to speak faster, and they use illustrative hand gestures.

■ FOLLOWING UP ON BODY-LANGUAGE CUES

There are two methods for responding to body language. One strategy is to comment on it directly. The second is used if you think the candidate may be lying. In that case, ask for an illus-trative example of what he or she just said (a clarifying ques-tion). Understand, however, that in the interview process it is a big mistake to ignore the candidate's body language. Candi-dates' words may lie, but their body language always tells the truth.

Even though we may not be consciously aware of it, every-one reacts to blatantly negative body language by quickly mov-ing away from the topic that engendered it. We all like to think of ourselves as considerate people who do not intentionally cause others discomfort and embarrassment. An untrained interviewer may tell him- or herself, "This exercise is stressful enough without me adding to it." The astute interviewer, however, knows that, even though the candidate's body language is telegraphing discomfort, it is critical to pursue that particular topic vigorously.

An interviewer may determine that a particular candidate should be hired. However, if the interviewer did not examine some significant area of the candidate's background because of concern over the comfort level of the candidate, that interviewer has done a gross disservice to both the candidate and the organization. The area of discussion that the interviewer avoided may well be significant in terms of the vacancy. By avoiding it, the interviewer may have put the candidate into a position in which he or she may well fail. Moreover, the interviewer may have created a difficult and costly problem for the company.

When the candidate's body language tells you that there is more significant information available but he or she is reluctant about providing it, comment directly on what you see, as in the following example:

Interviewer: I'd be interested to learn why you decided to make a job change at this point in your career.

Candidate: [*Pushes back from the desk; leans back against the chair; crosses one leg over the other; crosses arms over chest; looks away into a far corner of the room; shrugs his shoulders, then looks back at you.*] It just seemed like it was a good time for me to move on.

Interviewer: I sense there was some difficulty around your leaving. [*Responding directly to the body language*]

Candidate: Well, frankly, my boss and I didn't always see eye to eye on things. He was new, and I'd been around for eight years. You know how those things are. Just better all around if I got out.

Interviewer: With so much strong experience in operations management, I am surprised that you decided to go into personnel work. Why the transition?

Candidate: [*Jaw tightens; eyes avert to window; right hand rubs back of neck; there is some slight leaning back* *against the chair.*] I was afraid I might be getting stagnant. I thought it might be time to try something new, something a little more challenging.

Interviewer: My guess is that this transition was not your choice. [*Responding directly to the body language*]

Candidate: [*Eyes open wider; leans forward in the chair; voice is louder.*] You're right! The company was taken over by a conglomerate. They brought in their own management team. I was given a choice between this personnel job and a miserly early-retirement package. I'm too young to retire. [*Moves back into the chair; eyes avert to the floor; voice level drops to just above a whisper.*] But I think I'm too aggressive for personnel work.

Interviewer: What I hear you telling me is that the personnel job isn't going well for you. [*Responding directly to the body language*]

If you believe that a candidate may not be telling the truth, continue with a clarifying question that asks for an example to illustrate what he or she has just told you—as if you just don't quite understand what the candidate is trying to say. Here are two examples:

Interviewer: What has been your experience working with teams?

Candidate: [*Head drops forward and down; eyes avert downward to the desk; hands are fiddling with a pen; looks up at you and smiles.*] I really enjoy working with other people on a team.

Interviewer: Can you give me an example from your recent job? [*Clarifying question*]

Interviewer: I don't want to give you impression that you will be working without supervision. However, at the present time, we are a little short staffed on the management side of the house, so a lot of what you'll be doing you'll be doing on your own.

Candidate: [*Pushes chair back and away from the desk; eyes move to the floor; arms cross over the chest; legs* *cross; looks at you, smiling weakly.*] Oh, I work very well by myself.

Interviewer: Great. Give me an example of some project that you did on your own at your last job. [*Clarifying question*]

■ THE INTERVIEWER'S BODY LANGUAGE

You want the candidate to understand that he or she is getting 100% of your attention during the interview. You also want to create a climate of positive acceptance—that you will value whatever it is the candidate wishes to tell you and that you are not going to judge or criticize his or her life and career choices. All of those messages are conveyed through your body language. Therefore, (1) give the candidate good, strong, direct eye contact; (2) do not sit back in your chair (remembering that people lean toward the things they like and away from those they don't like)—instead, lean slightly forward in your chair; (3) in order to demonstrate that you are receptive to whatever the candidate chooses to tell you, keep your hands in full view, palms slightly open; and (4) a smile or a nod "yes" now and then doesn't hurt either.

Many recent college graduates have taken classes in "How to Take an Interview." They have been told to mirror the body language of the interviewer. If your questions are dull, boring, and awful, the candidate will have no problem answering those questions, monitoring and imitating your body language, and at the same time mentally preparing a "to-do" list for when the interview is over. If your questions involve the candidate mentally and engage him or her emotionally, that candidate will be too busy developing responses to be able to monitor his or her own body language or notice yours.

Without intending to do so, unsophisticated interviewers can telegraph their reactions to candidates' responses through their body language. This tells candidates when they are on the right track and when they have given a "bad" answer. If you are not aware of your body language at every moment during the interview, you could easily give the whole show away. Once, a long time ago, for example, I was interviewing an engineering candidate who had just graduated from college:

Interviewer: What was your favorite course in college?

Candidate: Music appreciation.

Interviewer: [*Pushes back into the chair and away from the desk; eyes open very wide, with surprise in voice.*] Music appreciation??

Candidate: [*Leans forward in the chair toward the desk; makes erasing motion in the air at eye level with right hand and speaks quickly.*] I was kidding. I was just kidding!

Another situation in which interviewers must be aware of their body language is during the so-called round-robin process. The round-robin, or multiple-interview, process can be extremely valuable in selecting candidates. This is because each interviewer brings different skills, interests, and experience to the interaction. The problem of telegraphing the reaction to a candidate's response through body language, however, can totally ruin the value of the multiple-interview process. The following is an example of how that can happen.

Peter interviews the candidate at 9:00 A.M., Paul interviews that same candidate at 10:00 A.M., and Mary interviews the person at 11:00 A.M. Unfortunately, because they have not adequately planned, all three will be asking the same questions. This is a big mistake. All three should have met at 8:30 A.M. to reassess the information needed according to the MMM. Then they should have decided who would ask what in order to avoid duplication of queries.

At noon all three get together to discuss the candidate. Peter thinks the candidate is not capable of handling the job. Paul believes that with a little coaching the candidate will be relatively effective in the position. Mary thinks this is the best candidate she has ever seen for this particular vacancy and that an offer should go out immediately before some other firm grabs him. Because the "He's okay" score is two to one, the candidate will be hired and will bomb. Peter will rub it in by telling the others, "See, I told you so." The other two will wonder how they could have been so wrong about the candidate.

The answer is simple. As he went through the round-robin exercise, the candidate was learning what the expected answers were from the body language of the interviewers. By the time he got to the third interview, he was a genius at giving the right responses.

■ LISTENING SKILLS

When communicating in any situation, one person speaks to the other from his or her own context or particular mind-set of that moment (see Figure 6.1). For example, it may be 4:00 P.M. You are anxious to go home. Human resources has sent over three candidates for you to interview. They are seated outside your office—waiting, like crows on a clothesline. You look out your office door; groan inwardly, and say to yourself, "Well, let's get this over with as quickly as possible. Twenty minutes in and out for each one, and I'll be able to get out of here by five o'-clock". At this moment in time, your mind-set is very task oriented and focused on getting the interviews over as quickly as possible.

The candidates' mind-sets, however, are one of anxiety. They have convinced themselves that you are *the* decision

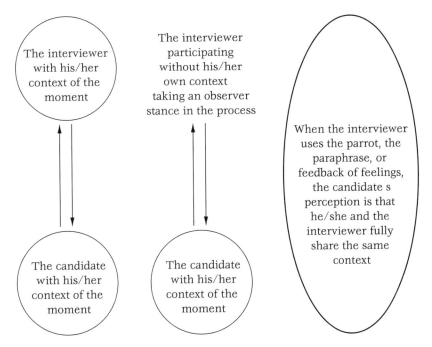

Figure 6.1   Active Listening.

maker and that this is the job they have always wanted. Each had hoped to make an extraordinary impression, but during lunch one slopped a little ketchup onto the front of his shirt. The candidate is thinking, "This is it. I'm meeting the decision maker, and here's this ketchup blob on my shirt. What am I going to do? I know, I'll hide it. Maybe if I button up the jacket and keep my arm pressed tightly against my side like this, it won't be noticed." So, with these mind-sets, you and the candidate are going to attempt a meaningful exchange.

Forget it! A meaningful exchange will never happen unless you give up your mind-set or mental context so that you can truly listen to the candidate and not the conversation going on in your own head. As a competent interviewer you must be able to participate in the interview by first recognizing the candidate's context or mind-set. Second, you must be able to communicate through the candidate's mind-set and *without* a mind-set of your own. This is quite difficult to do because every person is strongly affected by the presence of the other person with whom they are interacting at the time.

Suppose, for example, the candidate who seats him- or herself in front of you is wearing a hearing aid. You raise your voice 10 decibels. Why do you do that? Well, you're trying to help him hear. The candidate does not need you to shout, however. He is wearing a hearing aid.

Perhaps the candidate is a recent high-school graduate and this is his or her first interview ever. The candidate is nervous; beads of sweat are gathering on his brow and damp spots are beginning to show in the underarm area of the candidate's jacket. You probably have to fight the desire to lean across the desk and say, "Hey kid, the answer to that question is . . .", because you feel the candidate's discomfort and you want to eliminate it. You want to be helpful. Such behavior in the interview, however, is totally inappropriate.

What you must do is participate in the interview in two distinct capacities: as the questioner and also as an observer. While the interview is going on, you must do more than make appropriate verbal responses. You must also be cognizant of what the candidate is doing physically and what he or she is attempting to communicate (i.e., the message behind the words), so that you can shape the direction of the exchange.

Think of it this way: The candidate is playing tennis and you are the backboard—*not* another tennis player. It is as if you say to the candidate. "Here's the stage; I throw the spotlight on you. If you want to portray yourself as Frasier Crane, play Frasier Crane. If you want to portray yourself as Andy Sipowicz, play Andy Sipowicz. At the end of your performance (the interview), I will applaud, no matter what role you play."

In other words, you attempt to play the interviewer role as a facilitator for candidates, assisting them in disclosing their skills, experience, talents, abilities, and anything else they want to tell you. You accomplish this not by being neutral but rather by exhibiting body-language gestures and verbal comments that are positive, encouraging, nonjudgmental and nonintrusive to the candidate's thought process.

The positive messages are communicated through body language that is open and accepting. The messages of encouragement are accomplished verbally with words such as "yes," "good," and "please continue." The nonjudgmental messages are communicated through what is *not* said. It may be true that you would not have made the choices with your life that that particular candidate has made, but however he or she has done it, your body language must confirm to the candidate that these choices are acceptable to you. You just want to hear about them.

There are three techniques that make this observer, or backboard, position possible: (1) the parrot, (2) the paraphrase, and (3) feedback of feelings. Using any of these techniques sends the candidate the reassuring message that whatever that person's context of the moment is, you share it. These tools deliver the message, "We are on the same wavelength. I truly understand you."

For example, you may recognize that the nervous recent high-school graduate is about to have a panic attack. You adopt the observer position by responding to the candidate's feelings, saying: "You know, I used to hate to be interviewed, too, it drove me nuts. But all I'm going to do here is talk with you for about 20 minutes—ask you a few questions about your school courses and maybe a little bit about your extracurricular activities, and really that's it."

Immediately the kid calms down. With the words "I used to hate to be interviewed too," the kid thinks, "Gee, this person *really* understands how I feel." You are then perceived as a friend and resource rather than as a critic or judge. The kid relaxes a little and becomes somewhat more candid, open, and frank.

In truth, you may never have been as nervous as this candidate about anything in your life. By putting yourself into the observer position, however, you were able to assess what he or she was experiencing and then find something appropriate to say to move the interaction forward in a positive manner.

In the following example, the candidate, a 35-year-old man, has had a remarkably successful 10-year career at the same organization, where he attained a fairly high level management position. Now, suddenly he's looking for a new opportunity in a very different sort of business:

Interviewer: I'd be interested to learn why you've decided to make a job change at this point in your career.

Candidate: [*He pushes back in the chair, crosses his arms across his chest, his eyes avert to a side wall momentarily. When he looks back at you, his jaw seems tight; he speaks in a strained voice.*] You might say it was an issue of unfulfilled expectations.

As the interviewer, you are now faced with three choices in terms of how to respond. You can parrot, letting the candidate know that you do not quite understand what he is telling you; you can paraphrase, putting what you have heard into your own words and asking for clarification; or you can interpret and feed back to him what you think you picked up in his body language and tone of voice. Here are examples of each technique:

The Parrot Technique

Interviewer: I'd be interested to learn why you've decided to make a job change at this point in your career.

Candidate: You might say it was an issue of unfulfilled expectations.

Interviewer: Unfulfilled expectations?

Candidate: The executive vice president was retiring, and it was understood that I was being groomed to take his place. Then out of the blue, the chief executive officer hired someone from outside the company instead of promoting me.

Interviewer: What a disappointment! Why do you think that happened?

The Paraphrase Technique

Interviewer: I'd be interested to learn why you've decided to make a job change at this point in your career.

Candidate: You might say it was an issue of unfulfilled expectations.

Interviewer: What I hear you saying is that the company promised you something and then didn't follow through. Is that correct?

Candidate: Well, nothing was actually promised. . . . I mean, no one ever said anything officially, but all the signs were there.

Interviewer: What a disappointment! Why do you think that happened?

Feedback-of-Feelings Technique

Interviewer: I'd be interested to learn why you've decided to make a job change at this point in your career.

Candidate: You might say it was an issue of unfulfilled expectations.

Interviewer: Sounds like you're pretty angry and upset about what happened.

Candidate: [*He leans forward in the chair and flings a hand in your direction; his face reddens, his eyes bulge, and his words explode in a loud rush.*] Well, how would you feel? Ten years of loyal, hard work, an unspoken commitment of the top job in the division, and it all goes for naught. Frankly, I feel used.

Interviewer: What a disappointment! Why do you think that happened?

If your interpretation (paraphrase) of what the candidate has said is incorrect, or if you have misread the candidate's body language or tone of voice (feedback of feelings), the candidate will immediately correct you. Your attempt to understand him or her by sharing the same context will still be perceived as a positive action. If you have been correct in your interpretation with either the use of the paraphrase or the feedback of feelings, the candidates' body language will reflect that instantly. Candidates will come forward in the chair, their eyes will open wide, and the speed of their language will increase. They may even get their hands into the conversation. In short, they will become instantly more animated when they speak. In fact, their first words may be, "You're absolutely right!"

Once you have created this shared context with the candidate and you are perceived in a more positive light, the candidate becomes more candid and spontaneous. In fact, the candidate may tell you things he or she later wishes they had not said. If the candidate realizes that he or she has said something that might hurt the application process, you will see that reflected immediately in the person's body language: for example, crossing of arms across the chest, hands up to the mouth, and most certainly, pushing back in the chair. All of this body language reflects an internal conversation: "You fool, you blew it." The candidate will then retreat into carefully monitored and restricted conversation. You certainly do not want that. You want the spontaneity and frankness to continue.

The tool for making sure that such frankness continues is called the *support/confront statement,* a statement that lets candidates know that whatever they have just divulged will not hurt their candidacy. At the same time it allows you to quickly move the conversation along, preventing candidates from dwelling on what they now perceive as a serious error in judgment.

To use the support/confront technique, first make a supportive and accepting statement regarding what the candidate has just told you. Follow up quickly with a question that leads the conversation in a slightly different direction. The candidate's body language will signify whether your gambit is successful by returning to a more positive demeanor. For example, the arms will uncross, the candidate will become more relaxed, and he or she may close the distance between you by leaning slightly forward.

In the following example the candidate is a young woman applying for a customer-service position. You believe she is well suited for the position and have already taken the time (in the sell phrase of the interview) to tell her about the job. One of things you told her at that stage was, "Most of our customers are very nice, but we have a few—about 10%—who can get really nasty and abusive on the phone." You are now in the latter stages of the interview in which you are asking about job likes and dislikes:

Interviewer: What did you like least about that particular job?

Candidate: One of the things I really hate is dealing with nasty people on the phone. . . . [*Suddenly the candidate's hand goes to her mouth; she moves back in the chair, she then crosses her arms across her chest and looks at you with her lips pursed together in a thin line.*]

Interviewer: Everyone on the customer-service staff would agree with you that dealing with nasty people is far and away the toughest part of the job. Tell me about the worst customer you've ever had to deal with. [*Support-confront statement followed by a behavioral question*]

Candidate: [*Her arms uncross: she smiles at you and leans forward.*] There was this one time when shipping had really messed up this customer's order. . . .

In the following example, as a result of creating a shared context, the candidate has related quite a story in which he portrayed his former boss in a very negative light. He observes that you are making a few notations on his remarks. He suddenly remembers that it is unwise to criticize a former boss to a potential succeeding boss:

Candidate: [*He straightens up in the chair and pushes back; his arms cross over his chest; then one hand comes toward his mouth, stops midway, and points to your note pad.*] Can we . . . ahh . . . make that off the record? I probably shouldn't have said all that.

Interviewer: I can understand how difficult that situation must have been for you. What I don't understand is why you waited so long before deciding to leave. [*Support-confront statement*]

Candidate: [*The candidate visibly relaxes; his arms uncross and he leans forward toward you.*] I hated to just give up. Except for Brutal Bruce, it was a great opportunity for professional growth and challenge. Moreover, I loved what I was doing. . . .

There is so much more to interviewing than just asking the right questions. The astute interviewer can learn a great deal by watching the candidate and listening for such things as significant pauses, changes in tonal quality, adjustments in vocal pitch, alterations in verbal pace, and variations in breathing. In fact, it often seems as if the candidate's authentic response is communicated through the body language while the fabricated response is communicated verbally.

Research studies indicate that only 7% of the message is delivered through words while 93% is conveyed through body language and tone of voice (7% from the verbal content, 38% from the tone of voice, and 55% from the body language).[2] If these statistics are true, they reinforce the importance of watching the candidate's body language throughout the entire interview.

■ THE IMPORTANCE OF LISTENING

Both for children and adults, all learning has been structured around verbal skills, with very little, if any, focus on the act of listening. The emphasis is on *sending* messages, not on receiving them. Whatever the job vacancy, the issue of good communication skills will always occupy one of the priority slots on your matrix. You will probably evaluate the candidates' communication skills (i.e., ability to listen) based on how they respond to your questions. In truth, the interview is the judicious test regarding communication skills.

Suppose, for example, you ask the candidate a perfectly clear and reasonable question and the candidate's response is completely off the mark. You may attribute the mismatched response to the candidate's nerves or to your own lack of verbal clarity. Correction is easy. You simply restate the question using different words. Now suppose this kind of misunderstanding happens a number of times during the interview. You would probably begin to wonder if there is something wrong with the candidate's communication skills:

Interviewer: What kinds of contributions have you made outside your regular job function that were not specifically related to your job responsibilities? [*Behavioral question*]

Candidate: I really enjoyed meeting with the customers and hearing about what changes they wanted us to make in our software so that our product could accomplish more for them.

Interviewer: I understood that that activity was part of your job. [*Clarifying statement*]

Candidate: Well, it was, but I really enjoyed that part of it. It was very challenging.

Interviewer: I'd be interested to learn if there were specific activities you engaged in that were totally outside of your normal responsibilities. [*Restatement of the question*]

Candidate: I assisted the marketing guys with their ads and brochures when they were designing the publicity for the release of our new "Quick Draw Mc-Graw" software package.

Interviewer: Exactly what did you do for the marketing department? [*Clarifying question*]

Candidate: I developed code for the software based on input from our customers, the strategic planning committee, and my boss.

Interviewer: What kinds of things did you do when you assisted with the publicity for the marketing department? [*Restatement of the question*]

Candidate: A successful ad campaign has to address two audiences, the techies and those who don't really understand the technology but who are in charge of evaluating and purchasing it. I helped on the techie side of things.

Interviewer: And what did you do? [*Restatement of the question*]

Candidate: I wrote the technical specifications and designed some of the diagrams. I also went over any technical language used to ensure it would make sense to the technical people who read it.

■ MAINTAINING LISTENING EFFECTIVENESS

Listening in the interview situation is an active rather than a passive activity. Because people speak at 150 to 175 words per minute and listen at 800 words per minute, there is a lot of time available for the listener's mind to wander.[3] Good listening is a constant battle to stay alert and focused. An astute interviewer realizes, therefore, that it is critical to schedule no more than four interviews in a day. If you interview more than that, every candidate will begin to look and sound alike. You will confuse the candidates, muddling up who said what. Listening would also be much easier if you could speak with diverse candidates for an assortment of different positions rather than similar candidates for a single position. Unfortunately, for a hiring manager, that kind of candidate assortment would be a rare situation.

In order to listen more effectively, summarize and paraphrase often. That way, the candidate knows you are paying attention. More important, however, you will be making certain that you understand exactly what the candidate was attempting to convey. The following types of phrases will accomplish this for you:

> Let me be sure I've understood what you've said. You're saying that . . .
>
> Are you saying that . . .
>
> So in other words, . . .
>
> What I hear you telling me is . . .

It goes without saying that your interviews should take place where there are no external distractions such as noise, telephones, interruptions, and so on. You must also ensure that there are no internal distractions either. Your mind should not be occupied with anything other than the candidate seated before you.

You can also use your own body language to help support the listening process and give the candidate your undivided attention. There is a formal listening position: Face the candidate straight on so that you can establish and easily maintain eye contact; sit slightly forward in the chair in an attitude of encouragement and interest with your hands on the desk in plain view. As the candidate talks, it is helpful to visualize the information in motion, as if you are watching a movie.

You will find that the most difficult task in listening is to refrain from making assumptions and inferences based on partial information. Always check things out by paraphrasing and summarizing often. Try to keep your feelings in neutral in the observer stance while your words and body language indicate encouragement.

■ LISTENING THROUGH SILENCE

Sometimes an interviewer will ask a question, anticipating that the candidate will answer immediately. What happens instead is an uncomfortable silence. For the untrained interviewer the temptation to jump in and be helpful—perhaps with a laundry list of suggested responses—can be irresistible. Such interruptions, however, are destructive in terms of interviewing productiveness. During those moments of silence, the candidate is sorting through his or her experiences, attempting to put together an answer to the question. Breaking into the silence effectively derails the candidate's train of thought. The result of such interruptions is that the candidate will respond to the interviewer's interruption rather than to his or her own thought processes; thus the interviewer loses valuable information.

Silence is not a negative, nor does it have to be filled with anything. You should simply let the silence happen, using the time to watch the candidate's body language, taking mental note of the feelings and emotions that are being expressed physically. It is also a good time to consider the direction the conversation is going and what information needs to be clarified.

■ THE LISTENING OR LEARNING CHANNELS

There is one other intriguing technique that can help you remain focused on listening. It involves identifying the candidate's *listening channels* from the word patterns they use as they speak. There are three channels on which people receive and process information: auditory, visual, and kinesthetic. Although everyone has all three channels available to them, most people prefer one over the other two.

According to various studies 10 to 15% of the population prefer the auditory channel, 30 to 35% of the population prefer the kinesthetic channel, and 50 to 55% of the population prefer the visual channel.[4] By discovering how candidates perceive and process information, how they find meaning in the events of their life, and how they formulate decisions based on those perceptions, you have another tool to use in assessing how the candidate will function in the work setting.

The auditory channel relates to hearing. Candidates who are auditory usually did very well in school because teaching is predominantly accomplished through lecture. These are also the candidates who like to listen to audiotapes, especially while they are driving. As employees, they may do exactly what the boss said, even though they realize that was not what the boss meant. They enjoy working on the telephone. As managers, they have a preference for getting their information verbally and through meetings rather than by reading reports. In fact, they are more likely to file reports they are given and instead ask the author to explain it to them.

The visual channel relates to seeing. Candidates who are visual find it easy to make pictures in their minds of what another person is saying. They have no problem with driving instructions because they can actually see the directions in their mind's eye. When an interviewer describes the job, these candidates are able to ask specific operational questions because they can actually see the procedures in action. In explaining something about a previous job, they will often sketch out a diagram or show the interviewer something in writing as an illustration of that they are attempting to describe. As employees, they are likely to listen or read only one-fifth of the boss's instructions and jump right into doing the task because they can visualize the intended outcome. In a new job situation, these are the fastest learners even though they may not always follow the exact instructions.

The kinesthetic channel relates to the sense of touch. Candidates who are kinesthetic have difficulty with driving instructions because they cannot get a feel for where they are going. Lateness to the interview is commonplace with kinesthetic candidates. Kinesthetic candidates are more likely to have had difficulty in school. For these candidates, an explanation of the job responsibilities is often not sufficient for their understanding. Kinesthetic candidates learn best by doing; they actually have to try things out for themselves. In the interview these are the candidates who may take longer than others to put together a response to a question. Their process time is a bit slower than those candidates who are visual or auditory. For these candidates, a three-month probationary period is a good idea. It gives them a chance to get a handle on things and get comfortable with the job. Kinesthetic people rely on their emotions and intuition to make decisions. A common response to "How did you make that decision?" is, "I just felt this was the right way to go."

A candidate who prefers the visual channel may make comments such as these:

"This *looks* like the right job for me."

"I can *see* what you're telling me."

"*In view* of the facts, it was not a *clear-cut* situation."

"She and I certainly didn't *see eye to eye* on things."

"Can you give me a *clearer picture* of the responsibilities involved?"

A candidate who prefers the auditory channel may say these types of comments:

"This *sounds* like the right job for me."

"Your description *rings a bell;* it *sounds* so familiar."

"She *expressed* her dissatisfaction *loud and clear.*"

"I *described* the problem in detail, but obviously my *words fell on deaf ears.*"

"Can you *tell* me again about the responsibilities involved?"

A candidate who prefers the kinesthetic channel may make statements such as the following:

"This *feels like* the right job for me."

"I appreciate the fact that you *laid all the cards on the table.*"

"I'm usually as *sharp as a tack* but I was unable to *come to grips with* that situation."

"I'm not *following* you. Would you please *start* again *from scratch?*"

"She could really get a person *hot under the collar* with her *heavy-handedness.*"

Interviewing is so much more than simply asking questions. Listening and watching are every bit as critical to an effective outcome. Learning to listen visually increases the quantity of the information available for selection decisions by at least 100%.

■ NOTES

1. The best books on the topic of body-language cues are Ray Bird-whistell, *Kinesics and Context* (Philadelphia: University of Pennsylvania Press, 1970); and Gerard Nierenberg and Henry Calero, *How to Read a Person like a Book* (New York: Pocket Books, 1971).

2. Nierenberg and Calero, *How to Read a Person Like a Book;* Jim Dugger, *Listen Up: Hear What's Really Being Said* (Shawnee Mission, KS: National Press Publications, 1995), 53–56.

3. Robert Montgomery, *Listening Made Easy* (New York: AMACOM, 1981).

4. The original research on this was done by Richard Bandler and John Grinder in their breakthrough book *Frogs into Princes* (Moab, UT: Real People Press, 1979). Since then, many others have adapted and expanded their work, now known as neurolinguistic programming. The most useful of these are Genie Laborde, *Influencing with Integrity* (Palo Alto, CA: Syntony Publishing, 1987); and Joseph O'Conner and John Seymour, *Introducing NLP* (San Francisco, CA: Aquarian Press, 1990).

■ REFERENCE

Dimitrius, Jo-Ellan, and Mazzarella, Mark. *Reading People.* New York: Random House, 1998.

Chapter

Additional Tools and Techniques

■ MAKING QUESTIONS MORE PRODUCTIVE

A simple question to a candidate will most likely result in a simple answer. It is more useful for you to ask a multidimensional question, which is likely to result in a multidimensional answer; it is a better use of your interviewing time. As long as you are going to design your questions beforehand, it becomes fairly easy to rework a routine question into an exceptional one. There are four ways to accomplish this:

1. Use numbers to make the question more quantitative.
2. Ask the candidate to compare and contrast something.
3. Request the candidate to analyze and evaluate different methods or strategies.
4. Require the candidate to put him- or herself in someone else's shoes.

Here are some examples of reworked questions:

Routine question: What are you looking for in a job?

Better question: What are the three most important things you are looking for in a job?

Routine question: What valuable lesson have you learned from your most-recent position?

Better question: What are the three most valuable lessons you have learned from your most-recent position?

Routine question: How would you motivate an under-achiever to fulfill his or her potential?

Better question: What four strategies might you use to motivate an underachiever to fulfill his or her potential?

Routine question: If you were hired for this job, what would be your priorities?

Better question: What do you think would be the major differences between your priorities for this job as compared with the priorities from your previous job?

Routine question: What goals have you set for yourself for the next two years?

Better question: What were the goals you set for yourself at the start of your previous job, and how do they compare with the goals you have set for yourself now that you are seeking a new position?

Routine question: What did you like most about being a supervisor?

Better question: What did you think were the major satisfactions in being a supervisor at your previous job as compared with the major satisfactions involved in being a manager here?

Routine question: How did you feel about the effectiveness of the absentee and tardiness policies at your previous job?

Better question: If you could design an effective absentee and tardiness policy, what would it include and why?

Routine question: Please describe the evaluation process used at your previous job.

Better question: What were the strengths and weaknesses of the evaluation process utilized by your previous employer?

Routine question: If you had an employee whom you believed had filed a false sexual harassment complaint, what would you do?

Better question: Suppose you were a mailroom clerk who had been unjustly accused of sexual harassment by a coworker. What steps would you take to clear yourself?

Routine question: Everyone has times when they must miss work for one reason or other. As a fair-minded manager, how many absentee days do you feel are an appropriate number to allow each of your employees to have in a single year?

Better question: Everyone has times when they must miss work for some reason or other. As the employee of a fair-minded manager, how many absentee days do you feel are an appropriate number that your boss should allow you to take each year?

Routine question: What kind of skills do you think a customer-service person should have?

Better question: If you were a customer, what skills and qualities would you expect to encounter in a good customer-service person?

■ NONQUESTIONS: MAKING THE INTERVIEW MORE CONVERSATIONAL

In order to create the feeling of a cordial conversation rather than an interrogation, try to alternate your questions with a more conversational, nonquestioning approach. Such a strategy increases the comfort level of the candidate because it feels less like an inquisition. It should also gain you more information than you would glean from a straight question. Here are several introductory phrases that you can tack onto the beginning of a question that will change the query into a statement:

I'd be interested to learn . . .
Tell me about . . .
I'd like to hear about . . .
Please compare the difference between . . .
Describe for me . . .
Please identify . . .
Walk me through . . .
I'd appreciate it if you could pinpoint when . . .

Question: Why did you decide to refuse that promotion and transfer? [*Notice how judgmental this sounds.*]

Statement: I'd be interested to learn why you decided to refuse that promotion and transfer.

Question: What was your most-challenging experience as a supervisor?

Statement: I'd like to hear about your most-challenging experience as a supervisor.

Question: What happened to the subordinates who left your supervision?

Statement: Tell me about what happened to the subordinates who left your supervision.

Question: What were your most-significant achievements at your last job? How were they accomplished?

Statement: Please identify your most-significant achievements at your last job and tell me how they were accomplished.

Question: What is the process you have used for terminating an employee for cause?

Statement: Walk me through the process you have used for terminating an employee for cause.

Question: Which specific work experiences have shaped your present career objectives?

Statement: I'd appreciate it if you could pinpoint specific work experiences that have shaped your present career objectives.

■ EXTENDING THE CANDIDATE'S RESPONSES WITHOUT PUTTING YOUR PERSONAL SPIN ON THINGS

There are many situations for which you will find it better to encourage candidates to extend, expand, and continue their response rather than have them respond to a new question. Another question may nudge the conversation in a slightly different direction when what you really want to hear is more on the specific topic or situation the candidate is currently describing.

Reminding yourself of the way conversations work is a great help in these situations: People take turns speaking. Just remember that, when it is your turn to speak, say as little as possible—only enough to keep things going. That means that all you have to do is make an encouraging noise. There are several ways by which you can accomplish this (see also Chapter 5):

1. Encouraging comments.

   Yes.

   Good.

   Uh-huh.

   Hmmm.

2. Words that convey intense interest.

   Oh no!

   Unbelievable!

   Good heavens!

   Wow!

3. Starting sentences for the candidate to complete.

So what you realized was . . .

And then you . . .

So the implication was . . .

And in the end . . .

4. Direct requests for the candidate to elaborate on what he or she has just said.

I'd like to hear more about that.

Then what happened?

Please continue.

Then what did you do?

5. Use of body-language cues.

Nodding your head "yes" periodically.

Making a small "come on" sweeping motion with your hand.

Here are some examples of encouraging a longer response:

Candidate: Although it was never an easy job, I felt I handled it well. However, when the new manager took over, things really went into a tailspin for me.

Manager: What happened?

Candidate: It's not easy handling so much responsibility, especially when you're not prepared for it and you just feel that you are being dumped on.

Manager: [*Nodding "yes"*]

Candidate: You can't let an employee get away with behavior like that. It's insubordination. I felt it was important to teach him a lesson right then and there.

Manager: So you . . .

Candidate: Then when I got out to the parking lot, there was blood everywhere.

Manager: Oh no!

Candidate: Then when he told me that some of my staff were also involved with the gambling, I decided I had better do something quickly before my boss heard about it.

Manager: Please continue.

Candidate: I was careful to let her know that this was just a coaching session. I had no intention of firing her over this mistake, as terrible as it was. I just wanted to be certain that something like this would never happen again.

Manager: Hmmm.

■ THE TED KOPPEL STRATEGY: THE BROKEN RECORD

Sometimes in the process of interviewing, you come across candidates who will attempt to creatively slide out of answering a question. Perhaps the question is difficult for them to answer. Maybe they fear their answer will open the door on some issue that would render them inappropriate for the particular vacancy. Whatever the reason, your question goes unanswered. Instead, the candidate takes your words and fashions a different but related question out of them. Then he or she answers their manufactured question rather than the one you asked. If you are not listening attentively, you will miss the maneuver. If you grasp what is happening, simply repeat your question. Do not say, "You didn't answer the question." The candidate already knows that. It is not a revelation. Do not say, "Perhaps you didn't understand the question," and then restate it using different words. You already know the candidate understood your question very well; his or her body language tells you so. The candidate is attempting to squirrel out of answering. Simply repeat the question—over and over until you do get an answer.

One or two repetitions are all you will really need because with the first repetition, the candidate understands that you are not going to let him or her off the hook. Ted Koppel of the television news show *Nightline* is a master at this technique. Here is the type of exchange he might have with such a subject:

Koppel: Senator Jones, how do you intend to vote on this measure now before Congress?

Jones: This is a very important issue that will impact every American.

Koppel: I understand that, Senator Jones. How do you intend to vote on this measure now before Congress?

Jones: My colleagues and I have been caucusing on this issue for weeks.

Koppel: I realize that, Senator Jones. How do you intend to vote on this measure now before Congress?

Jones: The ramifications of this issue cannot be taken lightly. All of us are hard at work trying to sort them out. For one thing . . .

Koppel: We can explore the ramifications in a few minutes. How do you intend to vote on this measure now before Congress?

The following are some examples of how this strategy could work in an interviewing situation:

Manager: What responsibility have you had for managing the work of others? [*Behavioral question*]

Candidate: [*Candidate pushes back into the chair; twists hands; looks away, then looks at you.*] As my boss's second in command, I frequently had to take over the department in her absence.

Manager: That's interesting. So what responsibility have you had for managing the work of others?

Candidate: [*Candidate readjusts in chair while looking away; looks back at you.*] My position was critical to the operation of the department. My boss relied on me to keep things under control when she wasn't there.

Manager: I understand that. So what responsibility have you had for managing the work of others?

Candidate: You mean like actual supervision?

Manager: Yes.

Candidate: Well . . . technically speaking . . . I guess none, really.

Nursing manager: This job requires availability for Saturday and Sunday work.

Candidate: [*Candidate squirms in chair; looks away.*] I guess a weekend every once in a while would be okay. Harry won't like it though.

Nursing manager: This job requires availability *every* weekend for Saturday and Sunday work.

Candidate: [*Candidate looks away and squirms; looks back at you.*] Sometimes my husband and I take off on weekends. Now that the kids are gone, we are able to do that pretty often.

Nursing manager: Sounds great. However, this job requires availability for Saturday and Sunday work.

Candidate: Aren't there a lot of other people who can cover the floor?

Nursing manager: Yes, there are and all of them understand they must be available for Saturday and Sunday work.

Candidate: So, what you're telling me is that, if I want this job, I have to be able to work weekends. Is that right?

Nursing manager: Yes, because this job requires availability for Saturday and Sunday work.

Candidate: Maybe this isn't the job for me.

Manager: When I contact your previous employer for a reference, what do you think he or she is likely to tell me about you? [*Self-appraisal question*]

Candidate: [*Squirms in chair; eyes avert down; twists fingers.*] I don't think you'll be able to reach him. He retired.

Manager: Surely the company can locate him for me. When I do reach him and ask him for a reference, what do you think he is likely to tell me about you?

Candidate: [*More squirming, looking down, and finger twisting.*] I think he went out west to live with his daughter or something.

Manager:	So what will your previous boss tell me about you?
Candidate:	[*Looks down and mumbles.*] It won't be good. He and I never got along.

■ TELEVISION'S "HAPPY, HAPPY GOOD MORNING SHOW" TECHNIQUE: THE LAUNDRY LIST

Every television station offers its own version of the "let's-get-the-day-started-on-a-happy-positive-note" show. Typically there are two hosts—one male, one female—and a weatherperson. They offer you five minutes of real news, lots of advertisements, and a few sound bites of famous guests. Here's how those interviews go:

Television host:	You really had a tough time in that second set. Was it because you lost focus, or was it because you were exhausted from yesterday's match, or was it due to the fact that your back was bothering you again?
Tennis star:	A little of all three, I guess.
Television host:	After the tournament is over, what will you be doing? Will you be working with your coach at the tennis center in Florida? Do you plan on traveling to Australia to participate in the Australian Open, or will you just take a little vacation?
Tennis star:	You know, a vacation sounds like a good idea.

What the television host has done is structure the questions by including in them a laundry list of possible responses. All the interviewee has to do is pick one, and their task of answering the question has been completed. In the employment process this is akin to presenting the candidate with a multiple-choice question. If you do something like that, you must disregard whichever response the candidate picks. After all, it is your population of possible responses, not the candidate's. Moreover, when you utilize the laundry-list technique, you effectively remove any requirement of thinking from the equation. Because of this, you should avoid using the laundry-list technique altogether. Here are a few examples from employment interviewing, each followed by better-worded questions:

Laundry-list question: Would you describe yourself as an involved shirt-sleeve executive or as someone who manages from the sidelines, letting others carry the ball?

Better question: How would you describe yourself as a manager?

Laundry-list question: How do you typically motivate your staff: by modeling the appropriate behavior, by giving them goals and objectives, or by being there to provide lots of feedback and enthusiasm?

Better question: What methods have you used to motivate your staff?

Laundry-list question: Did you leave your job with Creative Chaos because the pay was insufficient for what you were doing, or was it because you had become bored, or was it because you found management overly intrusive with regard to your work?

Better question: I'd be interested to hear about the reasons why you decided to leave Creative Chaos.

There will be occasions when the candidate will pull you into offering a laundry-list question. Most often this happens when the candidate asks you to clarify a question you have just asked. In an attempt to make your question explicit, you provide a laundry list of possible responses. Just remember that, if you provide the candidate with such a list, you will have, in effect, answered your own question.

In most cases, however, the request for clarification is the candidate's ploy to gain more time and/or information so that he or she can give you the response you're looking for. Your best strategy is to ask the question again, using different words. Here are some examples:

Manager: What do you think is the responsibility of a manager with regard to staff development?

Candidate: Staff development? I'm not sure what you mean.

Manager: Do you think a manager should be responsible for making sure that his or her people develop job-related skills? Do you believe that a manager should just encourage people to take care of those things on their own? Is it your opinion that human resources should direct that issue by arranging workshops and such?

Better response: What role should a manager play in ensuring the growing effectiveness and competency of his or her staff?

Manager: What kind of people do you work with on a day-to-day basis?

Candidate: Do you mean job titles within the company or people outside the organization like customers and vendors?

Manager: Do you regularly interact with executives, engineers, programmers, secretaries, accounting types, and people from the manufacturing line or do you just interact with customer representatives, buyers, suppliers, and vendors?

Better response: Both.

Manager: How much decision-making authority do you have in your present job?

Candidate: Are you asking if I have to coordinate my decisions with others or get them approved before I can act on them?

Manager: What I want to know is, do you provide your boss with recommendations and he actually makes the final decision? Do you make the decision completely on your own? Do you

have to team with groups of individuals before you make any decisions? In other words,
how much independence are you allowed in
your decision making versus how much red
tape you have to go through.

Better response: Walk me through the process you utilize in
your present job for making job-related deci-
sions.

There is one additional problem with the laundry-list technique: It allows the candidate an opportunity to give you a totally useless two-way response. You can recover the situation by
quickly following up with a request for more specific information (i.e., a clarifying question).

Manager: Do you like doing everything yourself, or do you
look for opportunities to delegate?

Candidate: It all depends on the situation. Sometimes I like
doing things myself, and sometimes enjoy dele-
gating stuff to others. It just depends.

Manager: How do you differentiate when to do which? [*Recovery*]

Manager: Do you prefer to work by yourself as an individual
contributor, or would you rather work in a team-
based environment?

Candidate: Sometimes I prefer to work by myself, and at
other times I enjoy working as part of a group.

Manager: Please give me an example of each type of situation. I'd like to hear about the type of project involved and the role you played in each situation.
[*Recovery*]

Manager: Do you like the challenge of learning something
new, or would you rather concentrate on sharpen-
ing your present skill set?

Candidate: I always enjoy learning something new, and I also
like working on becoming better at what I already
do well.

Manager: In the last 12 months, what did you learn that was entirely new? What did you learn that improved your competency at something in which you are already proficient? [*Recovery*]

■ DUMB QUESTIONS

Dumb questions include those that have obvious correct answers as well as those whose only function is to take up space in the silence. They are asked because the interviewer is either inexperienced, unprepared, or both. Dumb questions happen because the interviewer can't think of anything astute to ask at the moment. Very often, these questions have nothing whatsoever to do with judging the validity of the candidate for the position.

There are four categories of dumb questions:

1. Questions that telegraph the desired response.
2. Questions for which the answers, although obvious, cannot be checked for truthfulness.
3. Questions that offer a false choice of answers—like the laundry-list question, except that there really is no sane choice (if the candidate wants the job).
4. Questions that serve no purpose except to give the interviewer a little mental time for question generation.

With proper preparation, these dumb questions should never make it into your interviewing strategy. The problem is that such questions have a tendency to sneak in anyway. Should you find dumb questions creeping into your interview, the best thing to do is stop for a moment and regroup your thoughts. Don't worry about the silence. Just take a few moments and consider what information you need to gather in order to make a decision. Then purposefully create several behavioral or clarifying questions beginning with the words "Tell me about a time when you" or "Please give me an example of."

The following sections present example sequences that illustrate dumb questions in each of the four categories, followed by more-appropriate alternatives.

Dumb Questions That Telegraph the Desired Response

Dumb question: This job requires someone who has superior organizational skills. How are you at keeping things organized?

Candidate: I have great organizational skills.

Better question: Tell me about a time when things were very hectic at work and your organizational skills were really put to the test.

Dumb question: Part of this job involves interacting with customers. Do you think you could do that?

Candidate: Oh, yes! I think I'd be very good with customers.

Better question: What has been your experience interacting with customers?

Dumb question: What we need is someone who can maintain confidentiality. It can cause terrible problems for us if a staff member leaks information about intended salary increases, promotions, terminations, and the like. Do you think you'd have problems with that?

Candidate: No, no problem.

Better question: Please describe a time when part of your responsibilities included maintaining the confidentiality of significant information.

Dumb Questions for which the Answers Are Obvious and Cannot Be Checked for Truthfulness

Dumb question: How do you feel about high absenteeism and tardiness?

Candidate: It's not a good thing. It sure plays havoc with productivity.

Better question: What techniques have you used to control high absenteeism and tardiness at your previous job?

Dumb question: Do you get along well with other people?

Candidate: Oh yes! I work well with everyone.

Better question: Please describe a difficult interpersonal situation you had to deal with on your previous job, and tell me how you resolved it.

Dumb question: What do you think about your communication skills?

Candidate: I think they're pretty good.

Better question: I'd be interested in hearing about the most-challenging communication situation you faced as an account executive.

Dumb question: How well do you accept constructive criticism?

Candidate: I think I accept it very well.

Better question: For what types of issues have you been criticized by previous bosses? What, if anything, did you do differently as a result of those comments?

Dumb Questions That Offer a False Choice

Dumb question: Would this job represent a career path for you or just a way of making a living?

Better question: How does this position fit into your career plans for the future?

Dumb question: Do you like to suggest new ways of doing things, or do you just stick to the old tried-and-true proven methods?

Better question: What has been the most radical idea you've introduced in the past three years? How did you persuade others to accept it?

Dumb question: Are you a high achiever, or do you have a 9-to-5 mentality?

Better question: In what way did you change the scope and challenge of your previous job?

**Dumb Questions That Serve No Purpose
(Except to Give the Interviewer Time
to Figure Out the Next Question)**

Manager:	The person in this position will have a staff of three.
Candidate:	I've supervised before.
Dumb question:	So supervision will not be a problem for you?
Candidate:	Oh no, not at all.
Dumb question:	And you're sure that your supervisory experience is strong enough to manage a group of scientific types?
Candidate:	Of course.
Dumb question:	So this will not present any difficulties for you?
Candidate:	No, not at all.
Better question:	Tell me about a time when you supervised a group of independent, bright people. I'd like to hear about the special challenges you faced and how you resolved them.
Manager:	Negotiating will be a big part of this job because every team is tasked differently with its own internal customers, time lines, and priorities.
Candidate:	I'm used to dealing with that sort of thing.
Dumb question:	And you understand how to juggle and negotiate with different teams and integrate their priorities?
Candidate:	Oh yes. I'm an old hand at that.
Dumb question:	So you feel comfortable negotiating with different groups?
Candidate:	Yes.
Dumb question:	So negotiation won't be a problem for you?
Candidate:	No, not at all.
Better question:	Give me an example from your previous job when you had to negotiate and integrate the priorities of several different teams around

the division of scarce resources. I'd like to hear specifically what you did to unite everyone around one set of priorities.

■ IDENTIFYING AND FOLLOWING UP ON FREE INFORMATION

As discussed in Chapter 5, sometimes in the process of answering your questions, the candidate may toss in an offhand remark that implies there is a great deal more information lurking just behind the candidate's words. Sometimes the signal for such free information is displayed through body language or verbal hesitancy. There may even be a change in the speed and/or volume in which the candidate has been speaking. It is very easy to ignore the invitation to follow up. If you go after the additional information, however, you will gain some very valuable data. Here is a list of the invitations for free information to look and listen for:

- Unusually long pauses before answering.
- Inappropriate use of humor.
- Nervous giggle.
- Overly complex answer to a very simple question.
- Blushing for no apparent reason.
- Abrupt loss of eye contact.
- Immediate, heavy perspiring.
- Quick and obvious changes in the candidate's body language.
- Sudden change to more formal vocabulary.
- Instant change in the tone quality of the candidate's voice (e.g., suddenly going lower).
- Body language that conflicts with the verbal messages.

The strategy for responding to the candidate's invitation to free information is the direct approach. Simply tell the candidate that you are aware there's more to the story and you want him or her to go on and tell you the whole thing.

Manager: Why have you decided to leave your present position?

Candidate: [*Abrupt loss of eye contact; sudden changes in body language; tonal change in voice.*] Well . . . ummm . . . I guess you might say for growth . . . yeah, for growth.

Manager: Sounds like there's a lot more to it than just growth.

Candidate: Well, as you can see from my resume, I've been there almost three years, and there's no sign that I will ever get what they promised me when I first joined the company.

Manager: And what had you been promised?

Manager: If you could design your own job, how would you change it from your current (or previous) position?

Candidate: That's an easy one. I would want the authority to hire and fire my own staff.

Manager: Why is that?

Candidate: At my last job I had an inherited staff and . . . [*Voice tone changes to a lower register; verbal pattern slows down; loss of eye contact.*] Well there were problems. [*Long pause*] I'd just like a chance to start fresh. You know, with a clean slate, so to speak.

Manager: I gather that the staff problems you were facing were pretty serious.

Candidate: I thought so.

Manager: I'd like to hear about those problems.

Manager: For what reasons do you think your career progress has been slower than you anticipated?

Candidate: First, there was the merger with all the reorganization nonsense . . . and . . . so on. [*Loss of eye contact; voice lowers; words come slower.*] It was . . . not a good situation. Difficult . . . very difficult.

Manager: I take it you had a lot invested in that job and that the merger really changed things for you substantially.

Candidate: I'll say. A tyrant for a boss, my big project dead in the water, several of my staff relocated to other areas, and of course my overall responsibilities were curtailed.

Manager: How did you happen to come across the idea of developing strategic alliances?

Candidate: Well, I had seen this happening in Europe with our foreign subsidiaries. There, of course, it was more a matter of securing the survival of a business whose roots were in the United States. But I was certain such partnerships here would give us access to markets we wouldn't have any other way. Now, of course, this is the way everyone in the industry does business.

Manager: So how was your proposal for strategic alliances received?

Candidate: [*Sighs.*] It got a . . . sort of . . . less-than-enthusiastic reception.

Manager: Sounds like there's more to the story.

Candidate: There is, but it's not really germane to our discussion.

Manager: I'd like to hear about it anyway.

Candidate: [*Squirms in the chair; looks at hands and sighs.*] I really wanted this to work. I thought if I could prove to top management that it did work, my future in mahogany row would be assured; so I went ahead and committed the company to one strategic alliance.

Manager: When did that occur?

Candidate: Just before I introduced the concept to senior management.

Manager: So what happened?

Candidate: Senior management was not happy. I was pressured to resign.

Even though following up on the candidate's invitation to free information may take you outside the investigative parameters of the interview, it can provide you with some interesting insights into the character of the candidate. For example, from the last exchange, it appears that this candidate is quite a risk taker who did not hesitate to go outside the boundaries of his or her position to prove the value of his idea. Whether you want a candidate with such attributes is not as important as the fact that, with the appropriate line of questioning, you can bring those attributes to light.

Chapter 8

Interviewing for Personality Fit

This book has so far been concerned with determining a candidate's skills, qualifications, background, and potential. There has been little mention of personality fit. The truth is, however, that, even when the skills, qualifications, and background are right, the candidate may fail in the new position due to a poor personality fit within the department or organization. This is what makes interviewing seem like a great guessing game. Like most untrained interviewers, because I did not originally have a way to assess a candidate's temperament, I hired quite a few folks who looked and sounded as if they were perfect for the job and then turned out to be departmental disasters.

The interview is a brief opportunity to get a glimpse, a fragile impression, of a complicated, multifaceted human being. What was needed was a tool that would provide a quick and accurate comprehension and assessment of the factors that drove the behavior of the candidate seated in front of me. Although there are many psychological instruments that divide people into various personality types, most require careful thought and analysis. This is time that is simply not available in the interview process. There is one strategy, however, that requires very little time to learn and almost no effort to apply. In addition, its ability to provide astoundingly accurate results makes it the ideal tool for the interview. This particular strategy is based on the work of Dr. David McClelland, and I call it *people reading.*

Many years ago, McClelland, in his book *The Achieving Society,* theorized that a person's relationship to his or her work is based on a sense of self-identity that incorporates three basic motivational needs:[1]

1. The need to achieve (task- or achievement-oriented person).
2. The need for affiliation, friendship, and acceptance (affiliation-oriented person).
3. The need to feel powerful by assuming a leadership or controlling role over others (power-oriented person).

Although every individual possesses some combination of all three motivational drives, there are times when one stands out more clearly than the other two—when the individual is under stress. The need that is most clearly seen when a person is under stress is the need that drives most of that person's behavior.

An employment interview is a stressful situation for most candidates. That being the case, all you have to do is ask a few simple open-ended questions and listen carefully to how candidates frame their responses to discover their strongest motivational need. A candidate will use similar key words, phrases, or concepts in responding to many different questions. It is as if there is a musical theme playing in the background that they repeat over and over. This is what will tell you which motivational need has the strongest influence over the candidate's behavior and personality. (See Appendix B for a list of such questions.) During the interview, on that small piece of paper on which you are making your shorthand notes, print the letters *T, A,* and *P* across the top, standing for "task," "affiliation," and "power." Whenever the candidate says something that indicates a motivational bias toward either task, affiliation, or power motivation, put an *X* in the appropriate column. At the end of the interview, you will have marks in all three columns—because people are driven by combinations of all three motivations—but the majority of the marks will be in one column. Now you know which motivation is the primary driver of the candidate's behavior. You also have a fairly accurate picture of the relative strength of the other two motivations as well.

Task-oriented candidates are certain to tell you about their dedication to quality work—that they know how to do a job and get it done right, and that they are not afraid of a little hard work. Affiliation-oriented candidates will describe how they like people—that they have great human relations and get along well with everyone. Power people are certain to inform you about their leadership aspirations, as well as their potential to move up in the organization. Whatever the message, the candidate will reiterate it in various ways throughout the interview.

Once you have identified the primary factor that drives the candidate's behavior, it is a simple matter to predict how that motivation could be exhibited in the work situation and how such behavior will impact a particular work setting. It does not require a psychiatric background to develop such clarity of vision. From my personal experience with hundreds of clients, I have found that, armed with this knowledge, any manager who interviews can develop an accuracy rate of 98% in his or her assessment of personality fit regarding any candidate.

Please remember, however, that people reading is only about personality fit. It is *not* useful for determining professional qualifications, experience, probable longevity, skill set, learning ability, or effective management potential.

■ DETERMINING THE PERSONALITY-FIT NEEDS OF THE VACANCY

Before looking at the candidate, you should try to get a grasp on the personality-fit conditions of the vacancy. For this, you want to examine three specific areas:

1. The management style of the boss (that's you).
2. The nature of the work team already in place (your staff).
3. The requirements of the job itself.

You may really want to believe that anybody can work effectively with anyone if they try. Unfortunately, that is simply not true. You probably relish working with some people, whereas others drive you nuts. Because this candidate, if hired, will become a member of your staff, you want to be certain that his or her presence on your team will not create unnecessary stress for you.

For example, suppose you are a manager known as a perfectionist who expects superior performance from her people. You want your staff to concentrate on their work and leave any socializing for after hours. You would not want to add a person to your staff who sees work as an opportunity to widen his or her social circle and use the organization's communication systems for keeping in touch with friends and family.

On the other hand, if you are an outgoing, friendly, social person, you would likely feel some discomfort with a nose-to-the-grindstone type who rarely engages in the minimal courtesy protocols of saying "good morning" or exchanging basic pleasantries once in a while.

Some work teams require a great deal of internal interaction to meet goals that cannot be accomplished without the willing participation and active cooperation of every member. In other work teams, members are really not dependent on one another at all. Each team member has his or her own projects, goals, and customers; the work of one does not impact on the work of another.

If you characterize the group dynamics of your staff as a congenial and friendly group in which individuals go out of the way to help one another and where projects require the coordination of everyone's individual efforts, you would be ill-advised to hire an individual with a heavy task orientation into such a group. If such a person were added to that group, there would be complaints of noncooperation, unwillingness to share information, and lack of interpersonal skills. This would harm the overall effectiveness of the department.

Some jobs require a high level of precision and accuracy; there is no margin of error and no tolerance for deviation. Other jobs require a certain amount of adaptability and flexibility. If you were hiring a customer-service representative, for example, you would probably look for a person who felt comfortable being flexible with rules and regulations and who could adapt requirements according to the needs of the customers. On the other hand, if you were hiring a brain surgeon or a quality-control operator for a manufacturer of pacemakers, you would want a person who was obsessive about accuracy, precision, and doing things right.

Once you have a sense of the personality needs of the vacancy, note that information in the number-one spot on your matrix. This "personality-fit" matrix item should also indicate the combination of task, affiliation, and power most likely to be successful in the particular position. This is done while recognizing that, even when a candidate possesses all the skills, qualifications, experience, and knowledge required for the position, the candidate will likely fail in the position if the personality fit is off. In other words, if responsibilities require a power-oriented person and your "perfect" candidate is predominantly task oriented, the candidate may be wonderful, but not for this job.

Every candidate is part task oriented, part affiliation oriented, and part power oriented; no one is entirely driven by one single motivation. For the sake of simplicity, however, the candidate descriptions that follow depict candidates who are primarily driven by just one of the three motivations. This is done so that the differences between the three are dazzlingly clear.

■ THE ACHIEVEMENT- OR TASK-ORIENTED CANDIDATE

For the achievement- or task-oriented candidate, interviewing is a serious business. He or she will enter your office, offer you a straight-arm handshake (to keep you an appropriate distance), and then introduce him- or herself by full name and state the purpose for being there.

Candidate: How do you do. My name is Evan Rude, and I am here about the job for production manager that you advertised in Sunday's newspaper.

The candidate with a strong need for achievement wants a difficult, challenging job; the more difficult it is, the better. If it is next to impossible, this candidate will love it. If your ad in the newspaper reads "difficult, challenging position," this is the person who will show up at your door. He or she wants a job that will demand a lot of them. In answer to the question, "Why have you decided to leave your present employment?" it is typical to hear such responses as these:

- I could do so much more.
- They just aren't working me hard enough over there.
- The work isn't demanding enough.

Task-oriented candidates are famous for marrying the job. When you mention overtime, their eyes light up. No other candidate is willing to put in more hours of dedicated effort than this person. The problem, however, is that this candidate values the amount of effort rather than the results achieved:

Interviewer: What did you do at Ravings & Groan?

Candidate: I worked 50, sometimes 60 hours a week.

Interviewer: I see; but what type of work did you actually perform at Ravings & Groan?

Candidate: I managed the day-shift production line for the Y-Byit model.

Interviewer: So exactly how did you go about managing that responsibility?

Candidate: Well, it wasn't easy, I can tell you that. Even though the shift was over at 3:30, I rarely left the plant before 6:00 P.M.

Task-oriented candidates have a standard of excellence that far surpasses anything the organization will require of them. It is important for them to do everything right. To them, this means everything must be done thoroughly. These people believe in leaving no stone unturned. They find a plethora of paperwork comforting. This is the candidate who will produce an eight-page resume with a sizable stack of reference letters at the interview. This is the only candidate who will ask to see the job description. With affiliation- or power-oriented candidates, verbally describing the job is sufficient. The task-oriented candidate, however, needs to see it in writing.

It is also common for task-oriented candidates to bring concrete evidence of their work with them—diagrams, memos of commendation, articles, and so on. On one memorable occasion I was interviewing secretarial candidates for a position in my own office. One candidate arrived for her interview with a presentation folder containing examples of her photocopying ability.

No other candidate is more willing to assume a difficult, challenging task that requires an impeccable result. As you know, however, no candidate is perfect, and the problems that are likely to arise in the work setting are due to the fact that task-oriented people often have substandard human relations. This is because they value work effort and excellence and place a low priority on human relations.

Task-oriented people are primarily exceedingly competitive and win/lose oriented. Winning isn't everything; it's the only thing. Being right is important to them, often at the expense of those around them. For example, a client of mine hired a task-oriented person as part of her customer-service team. Inevitably there were complaints from the customers of argumentative behavior and nonresponsiveness. Upon investigating, I learned that this employee was totally uncompromising regarding the company's rules and regulations and often put the blame for any problems squarely on the shoulders of the poor customer, making comments such as, "Well, of course it's under warranty. That's not the point. None of our other customers have had this problem. You probably didn't follow the instructions." When I asked her if she ever argued with the customers, her response was, "Only if they're wrong or stupid, which is most of the time." Clearly, she was not a good personality fit for the job.

Task-oriented people tend to be exceptionally knowledgeable within the very narrow parameters of their work. It is routine in the interview to hear such remarks as these:

- I am a fast learner, a quick study.
- I knew more than my coworkers (or boss) did about that.
- I really dislike working with stupid (dumb, unsophisticated) people.

Whatever job they are in must be mentally stimulating or they will leave. This being the case, it is common to see a string of jobs of two to three years' duration on their resumes. In explaining their reason for leaving a particular position, it is typical to hear the following remarks:

- I was afraid of becoming technically (or professionally) obsolete.

- There was nothing more to learn.
- The work was no longer challenging.
- It was just the same old thing day after day.

Task-oriented people tend to be perfectionists. The downside of this is that their perfectionism causes them to be intolerant of others' mistakes or lack of knowledge. This causes much friction with coworkers. In the interview, however, they will speak at length about the quality of their work, excellence in performance, and their personal high standards of honesty, dedication, and ethical behavior. All of this is true and will be borne out in their work history and future performance. During the interview it is useful to ask them for specific examples of their dedication and high-quality standards. As they respond, listen for these candidates to compare themselves to others who obviously do not subscribe to those same standards of excellence.

For me, the most-difficult people to interview are those who suffer from verbal constipation. It may be that the candidate is nervous. Perhaps the candidate is shy. Whatever the problem, it seems that, no matter how good my questions may be, the candidate's response gives back very little. In fact, because this candidate only responds with one- or two-word answers, if I am not careful, he or she will condition me to ask only direct questions. It is the task-oriented candidate who plays this role of being timid and shy in the interview.

Asking open-ended questions in this situation usually brings forth a quantity of useful information. When that does not work, you always have the option of terminating the interview and asking the candidate to return at another time. Such a strategy is excellent when you think the candidate's reluctance may be due to nervousness. When the candidate returns, he or she will be experienced at finding the company's location, will know what your office looks like, and will already be somewhat familiar with you. You stand an excellent chance of seeing a reduction in the candidate's discomfort and an increase in their verbal participation.

The strategy for encouraging the reluctant task-oriented candidate to speak is to ask a very short question that requires a long response. If it appears that the candidate needs some time to frame a response, you must simply let the silence happen.

There are three types of questions that are useful in such a situation:

1. Asking for a list of something.
2. Requesting an explanation of a procedure.
3. Requiring the candidate to describe a typical day.

After asking one or two such questions back-to-back, the candidate is generally able to more adequately participate in the interview, as in this example:

Interviewer: What intrigued you about this job opening?

Candidate: [*Candidate squirms in the chair; hands twist in lap; responds with eyes averted downward in a very soft and hesitant voice.*] It sounded interesting.

Interviewer: Interesting? [*Parrot*]

Candidate: Yes.

Interviewer: What were the three most interesting items that attracted you to the job opening? [*Asking for a list*]

Candidate: [*After 20 seconds of silence*] Well . . . I've done somewhat-related work at other jobs and found it quite challenging . . . Ummm . . . I know this company has a good reputation. [*20 seconds of silence*]

Interviewer: Yes? [*Encouragement*]

Candidate: And I think I'll be able to learn a lot more skills here.

Interviewer: Since you've done related work before, please walk me through the procedure you used for qualifying a new customer for a credit account. [*Asking for explanation of a procedure*]

Task-oriented candidates prefer to work in a situation in which the responsibility for results is attributable to their efforts alone. These are loners who find that working in a team-based setting is a strain. They firmly believe that better results will be obtained if they can work by themselves. Although they may talk about working with a team, if you will ask more specific questions, you will learn that, for them, being a team player is beyond their understanding.

Interviewer: Tell me about a team assignment that you particularly enjoyed.

Candidate: There weren't any that I enjoyed.

Interviewer: Interesting. Why is that?

Candidate: It seems like a group can't get started on the task at hand until the leadership issue is sorted out. People argue and take sides. It just wastes time and leaves a lot of hard feelings hanging in the air. That makes it difficult to work together effectively.

Interviewer: What role did you play while all this jockeying for position was taking place?

Candidate: The wait-and-see role, I guess. If it was possible, I just rolled up my sleeves and got started on the task.

Interviewer: By yourself?

Candidate: Yes. That seemed to be the only way to get anything done.

Asking candidates to "describe for me what you consider to be the best or most-effective working environment" provides great data. Task-oriented candidates prefer to work by themselves physically. They would prefer an office with a door that locks from the inside—no cubicles with three-quarter walls, please. They have a low threshold for noise and may complain that their work location on a previous job was in the middle of a major traffic intersection between the coffee room and the copy machine. No other type of candidate will do that.

Task-oriented candidates like to be involved in the genesis of anything: new procedures, creative ideas, innovative products, and unconventional ways of doing things. They pride themselves on being the first to do something and will look for opportunities to boast about those activities during the interview.

Task-oriented people are also excellent problem solvers, which makes them ideal candidates for a troubleshooting assignment. They are frequently the candidates of choice for a corporate hatchet job. Because they place such a low priority on human relations, they are able to terminate people with ease.

In the interview, there is a significant lack of interest in anything relating to people. When you say to task-oriented candidates, "Tell me about your most recent job," they may list their activities in priority or even chronological order. If they used any equipment on the job, they may give you the name of the manufacturer and the model number. They will offer no information about bosses and/or coworkers unless it is to say that they were more knowledgeable, dedicated, and hard-working than their peers and/or manager.

Task-oriented people structure their nonwork time around solitary or highly competitive activities such as downhill skiing, tennis, or bridge. For them, reading and surfing the Internet are hobbies. Never will you hear about them being involved in a bowling league, alumni group, neighborhood interest group, or support group of some kind.

Sample Interview with an Achievement- or Task-Oriented Candidate

Interviewer: Why are you interested in a position with this company?

Candidate: I've been reading about the company's work in the development of noninvasive medical and surgical tools. It's an innovative field in which this organization is the leader.

Interviewer: What exactly have you read about us?

Candidate: You will be designing and manufacturing the tools yourselves rather than jobbing them out because you are concerned about the quality of the product. You will need engineers who are experienced in designing manufacturing equipment capable of extremely high-tolerance-level results.

Interviewer: And your experience is in engineering such equipment?

Candidate: Well, not exactly. I've been working in the medical instrumentation field for the past several years but not on high-tolerance equipment.

Interviewer: I see. So what do you think is the most-important quality I should look for in a candidate for this position?

Candidate: I think it's important that any new hire be knowledgeable in the field. More important, I think the person should be a fast learner who can ramp up quickly. You need someone who is willing to work hard and who is dedicated to producing superior results.

Interviewer: How would a person know whether he or she could ramp up quickly enough for such work?

Candidate: Past history and experience.

Interviewer: What would you say is the most-valuable quality you would be bringing to this position?

Candidate: My drive for perfection in whatever I do.

Interviewer: And why is that important, do you think?

Candidate: I believe that companies today cannot survive in the marketplace if they produce defective products and inferior service. It's unethical. It's like stealing from the customer. Companies need dedicated employees who will do whatever it takes to make certain that their job is done with meticulous precision. That's the way I believe a job should be done.

Interviewer: Besides your drive for perfection, why do you think you would be good in this job?

Candidate: I'm a very fast learner. As you can see from my paperwork, I've never really done anything exactly like this before. But the job sounds challenging, and I'd love the opportunity to learn something new that will expand my skills.

There are certain words, phrases, and ideas that are characteristic of the task- or achievement-oriented candidate. It is a rare event to hear the following from the affiliation- or power-oriented candidate:

- Efficient, effective.
- Practical, no-nonsense.

- Long, hard, steady hours.
- Do it right, check and recheck to be sure.
- Nose to the grindstone, shoulder to the wheel.
- Follow directions.
- Fast learner, quick study.
- Not wanting to work with stupid people.
- Difficult, challenging.
- New, different, novel.
- I was the first, never been done before.
- Quality, excellence.
- Thoroughly, leave no stone unturned.
- Loyalty, dependability, responsibility.
- Ethics, trust, honesty.
- Commitment, promise, keep my word.

In checking references, you may hear such things as the following:

- Quite a perfectionist.
- Not tolerant of others' mistakes.
- Very direct, no tact.
- Moody, mood swings, sometimes very angry.
- Blames others for their mistakes.
- Difficult for them to admit when they are wrong.
- Compulsive about time.
- Keeps to themselves.
- Not a team player.
- Human relations problems.
- Zero-sum mentality, take it or leave it, win/lose.
- Workaholic, type A personality.
- Complains about and criticizes other staff members.
- Not a great social communicator.

Body Language and Dress of the Achievement- or Task-Oriented Candidate

Task-oriented candidates will demonstrate stiff and formal body language. Often they find it difficult to sit still and may fidget. Because interviewing is for them a serious endeavor, they will rarely smile. They like to maintain a certain personal distance and will often choose to sit in the chair farthest away from you.

This candidate has a preference for dark colors and the regulation business dress. The task-oriented male candidate will probably be wearing a dark pin-striped suit with a plain button-down shirt—the conservative look. The task-oriented female candidate may also be wearing a dark suit along with sensible shoes (*not* high heels), with a noticeable absence of jewelry and makeup.

Hiring the Achievement- or Task-Oriented Candidate

If you decide to hire this type of candidate, there are a number of cautions to think about:

- Expect some problems with human relations.
- Expect overkill on paperwork (checking and rechecking; excessive design of forms to make sure all bases are covered).
- This employee may get into being right and be argumentative with others, customers included.
- He or she is a loner; be prepared to limit the amount of interface this employee has with others.
- He or she needs a supportive level of supervision (because this employee finds it difficult to admit he or she doesn't know or needs help).
- This employee may have problems taking responsibility for their mistakes (after all, perfectionists don't make mistakes).

■ THE AFFILIATION-ORIENTED CANDIDATE

In almost all respects the affiliation-oriented person is the antithesis of the task-oriented candidate. In general affiliates are not motivated to work. They see the job as a social situation. In fact, they see everything as a social situation. This is the candidate who will enter your office with a big smile and immediately attempt to engage you in a personal "let's-make-friends" conversation that has nothing to do with the interview.

Candidate: Gosh, is that a picture of your little boy?

Interviewer: Why, yes it is.

Candidate: My, he is a cutie. What's his name?

Interviewer: Charlie.

Candidate: I have a little boy also. Mine's name is Harold. We call him Harry, like Princess Di's youngest son. How old is your Charlie? . . .

You may ask yourself, "Is this candidate here for the interview or for my friendship?" The answer is friendship first, interview second.

Candidates with a strong need for affiliation will indicate a great interest in the human element of the vacancy. They will ask questions about the group dynamics of your staff and how your people get along with one another. These are the candidates who want to know about various non-work-related details of the job, such as benefits, personal-time allowances, the length of vacation, and so on. They will assure you that they understand the significance of going along in order to get along in the work situation. They will confirm many times during your conversation that they really like people and that they get along well with others. The theme that plays in the background of their conversation is that they recognize how critical it is that any new hire be willing to cooperate and do their best to fit into the employee group that is already in place. In describing their previous jobs, they may proudly relate how they took part in organizing the annual Christmas party or assumed the responsibility for passing the hat for Annie's baby gift, Mary's shower present, and flowers for Joe, who lost his mother.

The affiliation-oriented candidate is not an independent thinker or doer. In fact, should you give the affiliate candidate a job offer, this person will tell you that he or she will have to discuss it with the family (and perhaps their friends and neighbors) before giving you an answer. Affiliates may even bring a friend with them to the interview (as a kind of support group).

Affiliates gauge their behavior by what others in the immediate area are doing. The most-important goal in their work life is to fit into the work group of which they are a member. To them this means doing exactly what the others are doing. Task-oriented people, on the other hand, set their own standards regardless of what others are doing and no matter what others think—the boss included. Affiliates are committed to doing exactly what the person next to them is doing and not one iota more.

One sees the dramatic difference between task and affiliate behavior most clearly in a manufacturing setting. A group made up of affiliates will produce at the level of the lowest producer in the group. This is done to protect each member of the group from management's performance structure and consequences. If a task person is added to the group, the group will now have a "rate buster." The task person will outproduce his or her peers, only to be told by coworkers, "You're making the rest of us look bad."

Affiliates' desire to be an integral part of their group is so strong that it seems as if they are unable to exist apart from that group. This is why assuming a leadership role, no matter how minor, scares them. A leadership role would cause them to be amputated from their group: There will be no invitations to join the group for coffee or lunch; there will be no requests to take part in the Tupperware party or the Thursday-night poker game.

Interviewer: I'd be interested to learn why you did not want to become the lead person for your group.

Candidate: It would have been an uncomfortable situation. These people were my friends and . . . well . . . I've seen it happen before. You become the boss and suddenly your friends don't want to eat lunch with you any more.

When asked what they liked most in their previous jobs, affiliates will speak about the people with whom they worked and of projects in which they were involved with others. It soon becomes apparent that these candidates do not like to work alone, nor do they want to be solely accountable for an entire task. They are best suited to activities that involve lots of interaction with others. What they would like most is a job in a friendly, team-based environment in which responsibility is spread across the group.

Another strong message that plays through their conversation is a genuine dislike of change. In general affiliates find it difficult to adapt. This is the employee who wails, "But we've always done it this way." In the face of drastic organizational change, affiliates may quit or become physically ill and be absent for long periods of time. These candidates gravitate to jobs in which there is very little variation over time. They are certainly not interested in anything that may be a challenge. They are preservers of the status quo and are likely to remain in the same job for years as long as they have close warm relationships among their coworkers, good friends in the immediate work area, and job tasks that remain fairly stable. In answer to the question "Why have you decided to change jobs at this time in your career?" it is common to hear explanations such as these:

- A new management group took over, and things just didn't feel the same any more.
- My job kept changing all the time.
- The company fell on hard times, and a lot of my friends left.
- The company went out of business.
- I was laid off.

When you ask affiliation-oriented candidates about their nonwork activities and hobbies, you will learn that they are regular members of a bowling league or softball team and that they frequently get together with neighbors or family members for cookouts, outings, and parties. If they are involved with clubs, groups, and alumni associations, it is not in a leadership role. Frequently, they get involved in community volunteer work with the disabled or with elderly shut-ins. They love the idea of support groups and may be members of several. Whatever they join, the purpose is for camaraderie and friendship rather than advancing the goals of the group.

Affiliate candidates want you to like them, so they will try hard to tell you exactly what they think you want to hear. This is the candidate who plays the role of anxious-to-please. This means that you must assiduously avoid asking questions that telegraph a preferred response. Affiliates will make positive statements about everything you tell them, even when it is something negative.

Interviewer: Unfortunately, this job requires extensive overtime, especially in April, when our corporate year ends and . . .

Candidate: [*Interrupts.*] Oh, I don't mind overtime. It's fine with me.

Interviewer: And then, because our business is seasonal, sometimes, if we've had a poor year, there are layoffs in the fall but we . . .

Candidate: [*Interrupts.*] That won't be a problem. Fall is a nice time to take a vacation.

Because affiliates are so personable and friendly in the interview, they are a delight to interview. It feels similar to speaking with a close friend. If you relax and become less vigilant regarding your listening skills, you may not realize that your questions aren't really being answered. What affiliation-oriented candidates will give you—if they can get away with it—are shallow, noncommittal responses. In fact, the most-significant characteristic about the affiliates' anxious-to-please role is that they somehow manage to respond to your questions without giving any substantive information at all. You find that you must always follow up with clarifying questions of one sort or another in order to force them into giving you specific details:

Interviewer: Tell me about your involvement with project management on your previous job.

Candidate: I did all the usual things. It was challenging, fun, and interesting. Everyone always said I did a great job.

Interviewer: Please tell me specifically what you did.

Candidate: I organized everybody and coordinated assignments.

Interviewer: Because this position involves project management of multidimensional, multidepartmental endeavors with people who do not report directly to you, I'd be interested to learn what specific systems or strategies you have used to keep track of everyone's piece of the pie.

Candidate: I handled that stuff real well. Never had any problems.

Interviewer: Specifically, how did you keep track of assignments and project responsibilities?

If you ask whether they've had any problems on other jobs, of course they've never had a problem—mostly because they get along well with others.

Issues around quality of work output are not a priority concern for these candidates. They may talk about doing a fair day's work for a fair day's pay, but what they really mean is getting things done at a minimal acceptable level. This is why hiring an affiliate to work in an area managed by a task-oriented boss would be the worst kind of personality match:

Task-oriented boss:	Look at the typo on this letter. Didn't you use the spell checker?
Affiliation-oriented secretary:	Well. . . . [*Looking at her mistake*] It's close.
Task-oriented boss:	Close?? What kind of impression does this give the client about our dedication to quality?
Affiliation-oriented secretary:	Oh, he'll know what you mean.

On the job, affiliates have a difficult time saying "No." Instead, they will agree to do what you ask and then conveniently forget about doing it:

Boss:	[*At 1:30 P.M.*] Would you mind taking care of this report for me? It needs to be completed by the end of the day, and I'm not going to be able to get to it.
Affiliate:	Don't worry about a thing, boss. I'll take care of it. Just leave it right there.
Boss:	[*At 4:00 P.M.*] Where's that report I asked you to do for me?
Affiliate:	What report? Are you sure it was me that you asked?
Boss:	Yes. I put it right there on your desk.
Affiliate:	Oh, now I remember. *That* report. Where did I put it? Oh my gosh! I put something down on top of it. I forgot all about it. I'm so sorry. I can't do it now; it's almost time to go home. I'll come in early tomorrow and do it. Will that be all right?
Boss:	[Angrily] I guess it will have to be all right.

One guess who calls in sick the next day.

If your ad in the newspaper read, "Nice place to work, great benefits, call Suzie in personnel," this is the person who applied for the job.

Sample Interview with an Affiliation-Oriented Candidate

Interviewer: Why are you interested in a position with this company?

Candidate: I have friends who work here, and they said it was a nice place to work.

Interviewer: What exactly did your friends tell you?

Candidate: That your benefits are really good and the people here are very nice. Also, your location is a lot closer to my home than where I work now. I won't have to drive as far.

Interviewer: Drive as far? [*Parrot*]

Candidate: Yes. Then I'll have more time with my family.

Interviewer: I see. So what do you think is the most important quality I should look for in a candidate for this position?

Candidate: I think it's important that any new person be able to fit in and be willing to cooperate. They should also be willing to handle their fair share of the work.

Interviewer: How would a person know whether he or she was handling a fair share of the work?

Candidate: That's easy. Just look at what the others are doing and do the same amount.

Interviewer: What would you say is the most-valuable quality that you would be bringing to this position?

Candidate: Well, I like people, and I really get along well. People like me.

Interviewer: And why is that important, do you think?

Candidate: It's a lot easier at work when people like each other. There are opportunities to talk about things other than the job, so the day goes faster. People help each other with the work and with personal problems. It's like being with friends.

Interviewer: Other than your human relations skills, why do you think you would be good in this job?

Candidate: Well, I've done this sort of work before. That's why I applied. The duties sound exactly like my job at EZ Gear.

There are certain words, phrases, and ideas that are characteristic of the affiliation-oriented candidate but that would be rarely heard from the task- or power-oriented candidate. These include the following:

- Warm and friendly.
- Needed and helping.
- With a minimum of stress.
- Being part of a big happy family.
- Smooth, not make waves or upset any apple carts.
- Happy in my work.
- I like working with people.
- Nice.
- Cooperation and team effort.
- Pitching in and helping out.

In checking references, you may hear such things as these:

- Most-obvious quality is their warmth and friendliness.
- Tends to be casual about important details.
- Communication is vague and indirect, often impossible to get a straight answer.
- Runs away from problems.
- Has great difficulty making decisions.
- Not very independent, requires lots of personal interaction and support.
- Acts as if friendship is more important than work.
- Lacks good organization skills, somewhat disorganized.
- Overly sensitive, tends to take things personally.

Body Language and Dress
of the Affiliation-Oriented Candidate

Affiliation-oriented candidates will demonstrate relaxed and informal body language in the interview. These candidates like to touch. They will smile a good deal and nod "yes" often. It is typical for them to pull up the visitor's chair and reposition it so that the two of you are sitting cater-corner from one another rather than opposite one another. These candidates have a preference for bright colors and patterns. An affiliate male candidate may wear a blazer and slacks rather than a business suit. An affiliate female candidate may wear a dress rather than a suit, high heels, and a profuse amount of noisy jewelry (e.g., bangle bracelets).

Hiring the Affiliation-Oriented Candidate

If you decide to hire this type of candidate, there are a number of cautions to consider:

- Expect that friendly interaction with coworkers will take precedence over productivity.
- The affiliate will always tell you exactly what he or she thinks you want to hear but may do exactly as he or she wants (engaging in passive aggressive behavior).
- You may have a continuing problem regarding work output, quality, and productivity.
- He or she is not a good candidate for any sort of leadership responsibility. (Because of their overwhelming desire to be liked by others, affiliates are easily manipulated.)
- This employee requires close supervision with well-defined goals and expectations reviewed often (e.g., on a weekly basis).
- This employee has difficulty coping with change—any change.
- He or she may lack good organizational and time-management skills.

■ THE POWER-ORIENTED CANDIDATE

The third type of candidate, the power-oriented candidate, enjoys a leadership role and generally does very well with it. During the interview these candidates will express a preference for being in charge of things and/or people. They like responsibility, especially when there is status attached to it. Because status symbols are important to these candidates, they are hard bargainers on the issue of salary and job title.

In answer to the question "What would you like to know about this position?" power-oriented candidates will ask about the organizational structure of the department and the reporting relationships. In fact, these are the only candidates who want the organizational chart details so that they know who reports to whom. These are very astute political animals who want to know how the power flows in every situation. These are also the candidates who will ask how long their boss has been in his or her position and when does the interviewer think that person will be promoted to the next level of management. It is clear they wish to know how long it will be before they will be able to move into their boss's job.

Because they want to control every situation, the power-oriented candidate may name drop during the interview, saying things such as the following:

- Frank Bigcheze, your CEO, is my neighbor, and he suggested I stop by.
- Senator Gregory Spenditt, my cousin, recommended that I come by.
- I worked very closely with the person who is now your vice president of engineering.

Their message is clear: "You may think you have all the power in this situation, but I have some strings I can pull as well."

Power-oriented candidates enjoy working closely with those in authority, and if they have done so on previous jobs, they are certain to tell you about it in the interview. Those in authority will be identified by their job titles rather than by personality (affiliation-oriented) or job responsibilities (task-oriented). If they worked *with* others, they will create a picture of some type of reporting relationship, usually with them in the ascendent role. Upon asking follow-up questions, you will discover that they were at the same level as others. It is only in their minds that they were more important:

Interviewer: Tell me about the most-interesting project you worked on in your last job.

Candidate: I had to develop and organize a procedure for resolving production problems between three units in the plant.

Interviewer: Sounds awfully complex to be handled by one person. How much help did the organization give you to do this?

Candidate: There were actually six of us involved in the project, but I was the one who did most of the research. I was also responsible for the recommendations that were finally implemented.

Interviewer: What did the other five people in the group do?

Candidate: The others helped with the research and contributed ideas that were supposed to solve many of the issues. But I was really the "main man." You see, this problem-solving group was the plant manager's idea, and he asked me to direct the group.

Interviewer: So what I hear you telling me is that the plant manager made you the team leader on the project. [*Paraphrase*]

Candidate: Well . . . not really. No one was formally assigned to take that role. It was just that, with my experience and knowledge, I was able to influence the group to follow my lead.

Interviewer: So you were functioning as a peer professional; an equal among equals? [*Clarifying question*]

Candidate: Yes, sort of.

Interviewer: What exactly was the role you played in this group? [*Clarifying question*]

Candidate: I did some of the research, and I made some of the recommendations.

Interviewer: So you did the same things the others were doing. [*Paraphrase*]

Candidate: Well, more or less.

In asking power-oriented candidates to describe their work history, it often sounds as if they were the central figure in everything with which they were involved, from project team efforts to establishing or changing company policies. It is customary to hear the following types of phrases over and over:

- I did, I controlled, I was in charge of. . . .
- I impressed the others with the importance of. . . .
- It was through my efforts that. . . .
- I pushed them into doing. . . .
- I was the person who took the lead (or influenced them to . . .).
- As their leader, I felt it was important to mold them.

In response to "Tell me about your previous job," power-oriented candidates will lead with comments relating to their job title, what or who they controlled, or the titles of those with whom they worked. They will not respond by describing their actual duties, tasks, and responsibilities.

- My title was. . . .
- I controlled the activities of. . . .
- I assisted the supervisor of. . . .
- I worked very closely with the director of quality.
- My position reported directly to the executive vice president for commercial loans.

The power-oriented candidate has a clear sense of what his or her place ought to be in an organization. It is common to hear such things as these:

- That job was beneath me.
- A person of my caliber (or education or experience) should not be expected to. . . .
- What I'm looking for is a more-important job.
- It was not the kind of image I wanted to be associated with.
- Considering the responsibilities I was managing, my title should have been. . . .

Obviously, the power-oriented candidate has a tremendous ego. Top-level managerial candidates often come from this group. In answer to the question "Why have you decided to make a job change at this point in your career?" it is not unusual to hear the following responses:

- Because they decided to go outside the company to fill the vice president vacancy above me, there was really no other choice for me but to leave.

- They wouldn't give me the latitude I wanted to run my part of the organization.
- The additional compensation and title I requested was not forthcoming.
- As a result of the recent merger, my authority was curtailed.

The outside-of-work interests of power-oriented candidates seem to revolve around activities that they believe contribute to their status in the community. They may be involved in local politics not as a candidate necessarily but rather as a critical background person. They may express an interest in real estate, stocks, and bonds. These candidates do not buy a home; they "invest in property" and live on the premises of their investment.

The power-oriented candidate firmly believes in the strength of his or her own abilities as a natural-born leader. In the interview this candidate will ask for some assurance that promotional opportunities or training leading to more responsible assignments will be quickly available to him or her. Such a candidate is always seeking opportunities for self-aggrandizement. This is why issues of promotion, job title, and compensation are so important. Money is important only insofar as it is a reflection of the person's importance in the organization. So, if your newspaper ad placed salary or job title first, and in large print, this is the candidate who came through the door.

In salary discussions power-oriented candidates generally want to get more than the job is worth or than the company is willing to pay. It isn't because they need the extra dollars. It's really because they want to see if they can manipulate the situation. Power-oriented candidates are like the retail customer who tries to make these types of bargains:

> "How much will you charge me if I buy it without the frame?"
>
> "Suppose I purchase three at the regular price; how much will you give me off on the purchase of a fourth?"
>
> "Because this one has a scratch on it, what kind of a damage markdown are you offering?"

In the interview it might sound like this: "Well, that is a meager sum considering all the responsibilities attached to the position.

However, I'll take the job at the stated salary if you will agree to review my compensation relative to my performance at the end of six months. If you are pleased with my performance I'll expect a 15 to 20% increase. If you are not satisfied with my effectiveness, I'll resign immediately."

Even after everything is all set and agreed to, it is not uncommon for a power-oriented candidate to request additional changes and/or concessions to the offer of employment. It may be something minor such a request for a one-week delay in the start date or an assurance in writing regarding the date when they become eligible to take vacation. What the power-oriented candidate wants is for the company to do something just a little out of the ordinary for him or her.

These are the only candidates who will allow a ringing cell phone to interrupt the interview. Perhaps they wish to impress you with how very important they are to their present employer. Maybe this is a subtle, manipulative message to you that their skills are very much in demand, so you'd best make them an offer quickly. In fact, there have been a number of times when power-oriented candidates said something like. "I want you to know that I already have offers from three other firms. All of them have offered substantially more money (longer vacation period, higher signing bonus) than you have offered."

Because power-oriented candidates are manipulative, you can never be quite sure whether they are sincerely interested in your job opportunity. Such a candidate may just be looking for an offer letter to use to extort a sizable raise from his or her current employer.

Power-oriented candidates have a sense of the image they wish to convey. If they know the company is looking for a savvy business person, they will come to the interview with an expensive briefcase—probably empty—and a *Wall Street Journal,* folded so that the headline is prominently displayed. If they heard that the company is interested in Ivy League graduates, you can be sure that the class ring will be conspicuously flaunted with hand gestures. In the event they think you didn't notice the ring, they will be certain to sneak in the name of their college or university several times during the conversation.

At one point in my personnel career, I was involved in campus recruiting. The process is one in which interested students are invited to sign up for a 20-minute exploratory conversation with a company representative concerning the firm's job opportunities. Students arrive in all manner of dress because they are between classes. Some arrive in chemical-stained lab coats, others in sweats, some in sports gear, and a few in jeans. It is a rare event to see a student appropriately dressed in a regulation business suit for these interviews.

I was studiously making notes on a previous interview when I suddenly had a sense of another person being in the room. I looked up from my deliberations to find the smiling face of a clean, freshly shaven young man seated across from me at my desk. He was wearing a navy suit, a clean, pressed, light-blue shirt, and a red foulard tie with a matching handkerchief peeking out of his pocket. Was I impressed (halo effect)!

We interviewed for 20 minutes. He stood up, shook my hand, and started out of the room. It was only then that I noticed he was also wearing cutoff jeans with a large hole in the back—a naked cheek showing through—ripped-up sneakers, and no socks. As a power-oriented person, he had picked up on what was considered appropriate interview garb. He also knew that he would be sitting down for the interview. He only had to project the right image from the waist up. Because this was undoubtedly a power-oriented person, I immediately referred his application to the director of the company's management-trainee program.

Part of the political savvy of power-oriented people is that they very quickly learn what they have to do to be considered really competent in a situation, and that's all the effort they will make. Power-oriented employees are like race horses that always finish place or show. The task person comes in first—30 lengths ahead of the next horse—and drops dead on the finish line. The power person knows there are always other races to be run; no need to kill yourself on this one. Power people (and affiliates as well) never suffer burnout; that's a malady that only task-oriented people suffer.

Power-oriented candidates are generally looking for a job that will offer them more control over things and people. Whatever situation they are in, they always feel constrained in some manner. When you ask the question "What kinds of things make your work difficult?" it is customary to hear such things as the following:

- Not having enough authority to handle my responsibilities.
- When I can't hire and fire my own staff.
- If there's a lot of red tape and I can't do my own thing.
- When I'm being oversupervised.

If you have not properly initiated the interviewing exercise with a structuring statement, this is the candidate who will attempt to interview you. If you are not paying careful attention to the exchange, you will quickly lose control of the entire conversation and learn nothing at all about the candidate. Information on how to retain control in such instances is explained in Chapter 4.

With the right kind of supervision, the power-oriented candidate who is a novice in the business arena will become a strong potential candidate for a management role. Immature power people are an organization's management timber. In the early years of their employment experience, however, neophyte power-oriented candidates are the most difficult to supervise. This is due to their accomplished ability at manipulation, their acute sense of the politics in every situation, and their innate belief that all rules are meant to be exploited every now and then because it's just part of the game.

Power people quickly learn how easy it is for them to manipulate their task- and affiliation-oriented coworkers. It is common for them to get others to do their work and take the credit for it. It is also typical for them to take others' ideas and advertise them as their own. Should they report to a weak boss, power-oriented employees will quickly step into that power vacuum, assuming authority that is not theirs.

Unsophisticated power-oriented employees often function as if the rules do not apply to them or as though they deserve special treatment because they are exceptional. These are employees who presume that "no" isn't really "no"; it's just "no for right now." They assume that if they didn't obtain permission to do something today, they should ask again tomorrow; maybe things will appear somewhat different tomorrow, so the answer will be different. They examine every situation for possibilities of increasing their influence in the organization:

Manager:	I'd like you to manage this project for me.
Power-oriented employee:	Glad to! You know I'll do a great job. By the way, will I get a title change?
Manager:	A title change?? No! You will not get a title change.
Power-oriented employee:	Oh. . . . Well, I was just asking. . . . Will I get a pay increase?
Manager:	A pay increase?? For two weeks' work? Certainly not!
Power-oriented employee:	Oh. . . . Well, I just thought I'd ask. . . . Will you at least send out an official notice to everyone in the area that I am in charge of this project?
Manager:	Yes. I will do that.
Power-oriented employee:	Good. How soon?

Whereas the affiliation-oriented employee is more of a follower, the power-oriented employee is a natural-born leader. Should a power-oriented candidate join an area containing several affiliates, the power person will become the informal group leader. This happens very quickly. If the power-oriented candidate has a reasonable level of emotional maturity, the manager may realize some productivity gains within the affiliate group. On the other hand, if the power-oriented candidate is immature, serious problems may develop.

A power-oriented employee who lacks maturity, for example, may come to feel that the job is not furnishing him or her with sufficient status. This person will then foment dissension and dissatisfaction among the affiliate group. Besides complaining and filing grievances, the affiliate group will impede productivity with all kinds of delaying strategies. Because of a power person's ability to manipulate others in this manner, the only person who can effectively manage a power-oriented employee is a power-oriented manager. Such a manager will recognize the problem early on and take immediate action to stop it before it goes too far. Task- and affiliation-oriented managers generally fail to identify the problem until it has developed into a major catastrophe.

Sample Interview with a Power-Oriented Candidate

Interviewer: Why are you interested in a position with this company?

Candidate: I heard that you are relocating your Mexican operations to this area. Undoubtedly you will need some experienced managers.

Interviewer: What exactly have you read about us?

Candidate: Your experience in Mexico was less than successful due to a limited pool of experienced and competent managerial personnel. The company decided to relocate to the States in order to secure potent leadership talent.

Interviewer: And your experience is in directing the overall management of factory operations?

Candidate: Well, not exactly. I've been working closely with the general manager of manufacturing operations in my present position for the past two years. Before that I assisted the CEO of a small multinational in setting up his facility in the southwest.

Interviewer: I see. So what do you think is the most-important quality I should look for in a candidate for this position?

Candidate: I think it's important that your new hire be a strong leader, one who is able to lead by example. You also need someone who can rebuild the image of your manufacturing operation. More important, you want someone who can eventually join the ranks of the executive team in the home office.

Interviewer: How would a person know whether you could rebuild the image of an organization that had suffered serious setbacks in the past?

Candidate: From my past reputation and my level of confidence in my ability.

Interviewer: What would you say is the most-valuable quality you would be bringing to this position?

Candidate: My leadership ability.

Interviewer: And why is that important, do you think?

Candidate: Many companies today suffer from a lack of strong leadership at the helm. Sometimes tough decisions need to be made and made quickly. Fence sitters cause many good organizations to fail. In today's fast-moving business environment, leadership needs to be strong, nimble footed, and able to mold a staff that is action oriented. That's my strength.

Interviewer: Besides your ability to make tough decisions quickly, why do you think you would be good in this job?

Candidate: I have a strong sense of marketplace strategy where product success is often a matter of manipulating such things as advertising and public relations.

Certain words, phrases, and ideas are characteristic of the power-oriented candidate. It would be uncommon to hear such phrases as these from the task- or affiliation-oriented candidate:

- Make me look good.
- To be more in control of things, to be in a stronger position.
- Enhance the image of my resume.
- Appropriate for a person of my educational (or professional) status.
- Increase my influence.
- Good (or strong) reputation.
- A person of my caliber.
- It was beneath me to be doing. . . .

- A more-important job, more-important work.
- Caliber, status, image.
- Impress others.
- Power, control.
- Manage, be in charge of, mold, influence.

In checking references; you may hear the following phrases:

- Most-obvious quality is their manipulative behavior.
- Has quite an ego.
- Effective in a leadership capacity, troublesome as a follower.
- Sometimes does things just to impress others.
- A real salesman, that one.
- Always looking for a deal, likes to bargain and negotiate.
- Likes a good argument, often will challenge whatever you say.
- Open minded, willing to listen to suggestions.
- Delegates well, overdelegates, gets others to do their work.
- Has a good grasp of the big picture.
- Has flexible ethics, looks for ways around the rules.
- On occasion has violated the chain of command.
- Even temperament, never blows up.

Body Language and Dress of the Power-Oriented Candidate

Power-oriented candidates will, like affiliation-oriented candidates, demonstrate relaxed and informal body language in the interview. However, they will also spread out, taking up more space than necessary—overflowing the chair with expansive hand gestures. "Steepling" with the fingers is a common gesture among power-oriented candidates. These candidates treat themselves well; their hair looks to be professionally groomed, and even among male candidates the hands appear manicured. Power-oriented candidates are usually conservatively but expensively dressed. Even a candidate for a production job is likely to show up for the interview in designer jeans. Power-oriented candidates often wear their initials somewhere—perhaps a monogrammed shirt or a gold initial pin. These are the candidates who arrive for the interview carrying one or more of the following status props: a designer purse, a Rolex watch, a class ring from a well-respected university, a Phi Beta Kappa key, or a Mensa pin.

Hiring the Power-Oriented Candidate

If you decide to hire a power-oriented candidate, consider the following cautions:

- Expect that this employee will never work up to his or her full potential. This is because power-oriented employees very quickly learn exactly what they have to do to be considered good at the job, and that is all the effort you will ever get.
- Whatever it is he or she does, the power-oriented employee will make certain it is publicized and blown up out of proportion.
- The power-oriented employee may manipulate your other staff members into doing his or her work and then take the credit for any results.
- This employee may grab onto others' ideas and advertise them as his or her own.
- This employee will always ask for high-visibility assignments regardless of whether he or she is qualified to handle them.
- Whatever the level of responsibility you give to this employee, you can be certain he or she will push for more.
- You may see an overwhelming concern about status and reputation—about what others in the organization think of them (looking good in the eyes of others is important).

■ CONCLUSION

More than 90% of the candidates who perform at an unsatisfactory level because of deficient skills, inadequate motivation, poor attitude, or miserable interpersonal skills could have been easily spotted in the interview if only the interviewer knew the simple keys to *people reading.*

For example, a hiring manager states that he wants a person with an exceptional level of technical skill and knowledge. He interviews and hires such a person and then spends every coaching session beating the person about the head and shoulders for their poor interpersonal skills. The manager forgets that, when he went looking for an appropriate candidate, he did not ask for a person with good interpersonal skills. The poor candidate now finds she has to fight the manager and the organization in order to be who she is.

Manager:	How's the job going?
Task-oriented employee:	I think I'm doing great!
Manager:	Perhaps you'd better tell me what happened yesterday between you and Joe when I sent you over to help him.
Task-oriented employee:	Joe is stupid.
Manager:	Look, Joe doesn't know very much about writing framistans. You need to have patience with people.
Task-oriented employee:	Patience?? Do I do my job?
Manager:	Yes.
Task-oriented employee:	Do I do more work around here than anyone else?
Manager:	Well, yes.
Task-oriented employee:	So what do you want me to do—run a popularity contest or get the job done?
Manager:	I want you to get the job done. But part of getting the job done involves cooperating with the other people who work here.
Task-oriented employee:	If Joe needs my help, let him cooperate with me!

In order to create a good fit, it is important to place a task person in a task-oriented job, an affiliate in an affiliation-oriented job, and a power person in a power-oriented job. This is a matter of hiring to strengths. Then, if the person is comfortable in the job and isn't being criticized for who and what he or she is, the manager is now in a position of having this type of conversation with the employee:

Manager:	How do you think the job is going?
Task-oriented employee:	I think I'm doing great!
Manager:	I think so, too. How would you like to try something new and challenging?
Task-oriented employee:	Sounds interesting. What did you have in mind?
Manager:	How would you like to work with Joe and teach him how to write framistans? I know it won't be easy because Joe is pretty unsophisticated about these things. However, I am certain that with patience and effort you will do very well coaching Joe. What do you say?

If you survey those who have been successful and happy versus those who have been unsuccessful and miserable in a particular job, you will gain great insight into the issue of fit. You will see that fit is often a matter of someone's values. If a person feels that what he or she is being asked to do violates his or her values, good results on the job will not happen.

An illustration of this was provided by a client whose staff was made up of outside salespersons and administrative support personnel. My client had asked one of the clerical people to keep time records for the administrative staff. The sales staff came and went at various times, depending on their customer appointments; the administrative staff had set hours for being in the office. This clerical person (a task-oriented employee) simply could not understand why the rules were different for each group. She was very outspoken regarding what she felt were unethical practices by the company: "The rules should apply to everyone equally and with no exceptions."

Here is one last caution: Unenlightened interviewers tend to hire in their own image. An affiliation-oriented manager will most likely hire an affiliation-oriented candidate; a task-oriented manager will gravitate toward task-oriented candidates, and so on. Hiring in one's own image correlates with the halo effect: People are more comfortable around others who think and perceive in a manner similar to themselves. It is only the astute, educated interviewer who can look at the requirements of the position, independent of any personal preferences, and hire according to the specific needs of the job.

■ NOTES

1. David McClelland, *The Achieving Society* (New York: Irvington Press, 1985).

Chapter 9

What's Legal and What's Not

■ EQUAL OPPORTUNITY LEGISLATION

Until 1964 employers had great latitude to be subjective in deciding what qualifications they wanted in their potential candidates. Job requirements and candidate prerequisites were filled with personal preferences and prejudicial statements that effectively and unnecessarily limited employment opportunities for many Americans.

Over the years there have been a number of federal and state statutes, laws, court decisions, and administrative regulations that are designed to encourage those who are hiring to make their decisions based on an evaluation of the candidate's skills and abilities as they relate to the particular job. These laws and statutes address the overriding concern that every person should have an equal opportunity for employment.

Once it has been decided what qualifications are desirable in the ideal candidate for the job, it is important to examine those qualifications and determine if any of them eliminate certain groups or protected classes of possible candidates. If any of the listed qualifications remove a particular group from employment consideration, then a discrimination situation exists.

The term *protected classes* is used to identify those groups that are specifically protected by antidiscrimination legislation. Included are classes grouped by sex, race, national origin, religion, maternity, age (over 40 years old), handicap, and military service.

Organizations today have had several decades of experience with antidiscrimination regulations, so it is rare to find a blatant violation. There is also a sincere desire nationally to be fair; businesses have recognized that hiring the best necessitates looking at all the possibilities. What still occur, however, are the more subtle, unintentional violations of antidiscriminatory requirements that often appear innocuous to the company. Such carelessness, intentional or not, can cause legal problems for the organization. An intent to purposefully discriminate is not required—only the objective fact that what the employer required in terms of qualifications discriminated against a protected class. Here are a few examples:

Wanted: *Recent college graduate.*

("Recent graduate" suggests young, so this is age discrimination.)

Wanted: *Experienced, mature person for sales position.*

("Mature" signifies an older person, so this is age discrimination.)

Wanted: *Able-bodied person for construction work.*

("Able-bodied" indicates that a handicapped person should not apply, which makes this discriminatory under the Americans with Disabilities Act.)

Wanted: *Native-born German for translation of manuscripts.*

("Native-born German" discriminates by race and national origin.)

Wanted: *Drivers; must own car and have valid license.*

("Own car" is discriminatory because it targets personal finances.)

Wanted: *Outgoing, congenial woman for restaurant hostess position.*

("Woman" indicates sex discrimination.)

Wanted: *Male fitness trainer and instructor for city health club.*

("Male" indicates sex discrimination.)

The following is a brief outline of the federal statutes and acts that regulate the legal issues involved in interviewing and hiring.

Equal Pay Act of 1963

- Applies to organizations involved in interstate commerce.
- Prohibits discrimination in compensation based on the sex of the employee.

Title VII of the Civil Rights Act of 1964

- Applies to organizations involved in interstate commerce that have 15 or more employees.
- Prohibits employment discrimination on the basis of race, religion, national origin, and sex.

Age Discrimination Employment Act of 1967 (Amended in 1978 and 1986)

- Applies to organizations involved in interstate commerce that have 20 or more employees.
- Employers may not discriminate on the basis of age.
- Protected group are those from ages 40 to 70.

Rehabilitation Act of 1973

- Applies to organizations receiving federal funding and/or organizations doing at least $2,500 of business with the federal government.
- Prohibits discrimination by federal contractors based on disability.

Immigration Reform and Control Act of 1986

- Applies to all organizations with four or more employees.
- Prohibits discrimination based on national origin and citizenship status.
- Makes it a crime for employers to hire illegal aliens.

Americans with Disabilities Act of 1990

- Applies to organizations involved in interstate commerce that have 15 or more employees.

- Requires employers to provide reasonable accommodation for disabled employees.
- Makes it illegal to discriminate against handicapped employment candidates.

Civil Rights Act of 1991 (Amendment of the 1964 Act)

- Applies to organizations involved in interstate commerce that have 15 or more employees.
- Extends punitive damages to victims of discrimination based on disability.
- Shifts the burden of proof to the employer.

Here are a few good basic rules that promote sound and legal interviewing:

1. Treat all candidates equally.
2. If you would not ask the question of a male candidate, then you should not ask it of a female candidate.
3. Ask nothing about a candidate's personal life.
4. Focus on the candidate's skills and qualifications as they relate to the job.
5. Every question asked must have a direct and relevant relationship to the qualifications required for the job.
6. Any measurement or parameter used to evaluate anyone for anything in employment is subject to Equal Employment Opportunity (EEO) regulations—*everything.*

You may find it helpful to keep a list handy of the topics that should *not* be mentioned during the preemployment interview. (After the person is hired, of course, human resources needs some of this information to complete such documents as the W2, insurance forms, and so on.)

■ RESTRICTED AREAS OF INQUIRY IN THE INTERVIEW PROCESS

This section provides a list of topics that are restricted areas of inquiry under the law. Questions related to each topic that can be asked legally are followed by a sampling of questions that cannot be asked. Remember, however, that the legal landscape surrounding hiring practices is constantly changing. You would be well advised to seek legal guidance periodically so that your knowledge in this area is always current.

Age, Date of Birth

Legal: Are you 18 years of age or older?

If you are *not yet 18* years old, how old are you?

Illegal: How old are you?

What year did you graduate from high school?

When were you born?

What is your date of birth?

You seem awfully young to have had so much experience in the industry; how many years have you been working?

Availability for Saturday and Sunday Work

Legal: This job requires availability for Saturday and Sunday work.

Illegal: Does your religion prevent you from working weekends or holidays?

What religious holidays do you observe?

What church (or synagogue) do you go to?

Is Saturday a religious day for you?

Do you ever have to miss work because of your religion?

Does your religion prevent you from eating certain foods or drinking with customers?

That's a very attractive pendant; does it have some religious significance?

Citizenship

Legal: Are you a U.S. citizen?

If we decide to hire you, can you provide proof of citizenship?

If you are not a U.S. citizen, do you have proof that you can be legally employed here (e.g, have a "green card")?

How long have you been a resident of the United States (this state, this city)?

Illegal: What country are you from?

You have an interesting accent; where are you from?

Where are your people from?

Are you a native-born American or a naturalized citizen?

Are your parents (spouse, children) U.S. citizens?

I have a friend whose name is similar to yours and who is Armenian (Polish, Czech, Asian, Italian, etc.), is that what you are?

Race and National Origin

Legal: What foreign languages do you speak or write?

Illegal: What is your race (or nationality)?

What color is your skin (hair, eyes)?

Where are your ancestors (or parents) from?

What is the nationality of your spouse?

What language do you commonly speak at home?

What is your mother tongue?

You have a very distinctive (or unusual or unique) look about you; what is your racial background?

Do you consider yourself a person of color?

Would you characterize yourself as an Asian American (African American, Native American, etc.)?

Handicaps, Health, and Disabilities

Legal: This job requires lifting 60 pounds without a winch (using dangerous machinery, etc.). If we decide to hire you, can you perform these functions with or without reasonable accommodation?

Illegal: How's your health?

Do you have high blood pressure?

Are you overweight?

Are you on any type of medication?

Are you disabled in any way?

What is your height and weight?

Have you ever been treated for the following diseases?

Have you ever been tested for AIDS?

Have you ever collected workers' compensation?

Do you have a handicap that would prevent you from meeting the demands of this job?

Do you have a drug or alcohol problem?

Are under a physician's (or psychiatrist's) care at this time?

When did you have your most-recent physical exam?

How often do you see your regular doctor?

Marital Status

Legal: Are your employment records listed under any other name?

In checking your references and work records, are there any other names we should check under?

Illegal: What was your prior married name?

Have you ever worked under a different name?

What was your maiden name?

What is the name listed on your birth certificate?

Are you married (single, divorced, separated, living with anyone, engaged)?

How are you and your spouse getting along?

How is your family life?

Are you planning to get married (divorced, separated, engaged) in the near future?

Do you wish to be addressed as Miss, Mrs., or Ms.?

Spousal Information

Legal: None.

Illegal: What does your spouse do?

Does your spouse work?

How much money does your spouse make?

Does your spouse contribute to the family income?

Will your spouse object to you working overtime (or traveling)?

If your spouse is transferred, will you go with him/her?

Friends, Relatives, and Family

Legal: Do you have any relatives who are currently employed by this company?

What are their names?

Illegal: Who do you live with?

Do you live with your parents?

What did your family think about your last job?

Did your family interfere with your performance on your last job?

What do your parents do?

Do you have any brothers or sisters? How many?

Children, Child Care, and Sex

Legal: Is there anything that might prevent you from being here every day?

Illegal: Who looks after your children while you are at work?

Do you have to miss work at certain times of the month?

Do you suffer from monthly mood swings?

How many children do you have? What are their ages?

Do you have any children?

Are you planning to start a family?

How old is your youngest child?

If both of you are working, who takes care of the children when they get sick?

Do you ever have to miss work because of your children?

Are you pregnant?

Are you planning to have another child?

What are you doing to ensure that childbearing will not interrupt your career plans?

Criminal Record

Legal: Have you been convicted of a felony within the last seven years?

Illegal: Have you ever been arrested?

Have you ever had any trouble with the law?

Has a bonding company ever refused to bond you?

Have you ever filed an age (sex, race) discrimination case?

Have you ever had a sexual harassment case filed against you?

Have you ever been in jail?

Financial Information

Legal: We require that all employees in this job category be bonded; will that create any problems for you?

How will you be getting to work?

Illegal: Do you own a car?

Do you own your own home?

Have you ever been refused a bond or had a bond canceled?

Did you receive financial aid while attending school?

Who paid for your education?

Do you still owe money on your student loans?

How much in debt are you?

Do you think you live beyond your means?

Are your parents helping to support you?

Have you ever filed for bankruptcy?

Has your pay ever been garnished?

How's your credit rating?

Did you ever receive public assistance or collect unemployment?

Diversity Issues

Legal: What kind of people do you work best with?

Illegal: How do you get along with men (women, Asians, blacks, Muslims, etc.)?

Are you people good at working with numbers?

Most of our customers/clients are male (or female); will you have any problems interacting with them?

Your boss is female (or male); will that create any difficulties for you?

Your manager is an African American (Asian American, foreign-born, etc.); will that present a problem for you?

Your supervisor is considerably older (or younger) than you; will that be a problem for you?

How do you feel about working with people of different races (or cultures)?

How do you think you'll fit in with the younger (older, female, black, etc.) members of the staff?

You will be the only female (Asian, black, person over 50, etc.) in the department; do you think you can handle that?

This is a hectic job—lots of pressure; do you think you can keep up with the younger staff members?

Membership in Fraternal Organizations

Legal: In which professional organizations do you hold membership?

What organizations do you belong to that are relevant to your work?

What job-related professional associations do you belong to?

What community activities are you involved with?

Illegal: What social or fraternal organizations do you belong to?

Please list all the associations with which you are affiliated.

What political activist (religious, nationality) groups are you a member of?

How do you feel about labor unions?

What do you think about the women's movement?

What are your opinions about black (white, feminist) militant groups?

Are you member of the National Organization for Women (NOW)?

Are you a member of any support groups?

Are you a member of Alcoholics Anonymous (AA)?

Salary Requirements

Legal: What salary are you looking for?

What are your salary requirements?

How much were you getting at your most recent job?

Illegal: What is the lowest salary you will accept?

What is your minimum salary requirement?

How much money do you need?

■ THREE TALES FROM THE CRYPT

If you interview with any regularity, you probably have a few horror stories of your own. Here are my personal "tales from the crypt."

The Well-Meaning Receptionist

In the early 1970s, while I was working with a large insurance company, I learned that in this litigious society any casual, well-meaning remark can cause problems. A young woman was functioning as the receptionist for the human resources department. She had been an only child and hoped to marry and raise a very large family. I must have heard hundreds of times how lonely it was for her growing up and how she was going to have lots and lots of children so that everyone would have somebody to play with.

One day a man came in to inquire about one of our job openings. The receptionist handed him the standard application form and asked him to complete it. When he returned it to her, his address was missing. "Oh, sorry," he said. "I forget that. I have to look it up. I just moved into the area and only got my apartment yesterday." He pulled out his wallet to find the rent receipt, which displayed his new address. A long line of pictures in an accordion-style plastic folder tumbled out of his hands toward the floor. "Oh my gosh," exclaimed the receptionist. "What a lot of pictures! Is that your family?" "Yes," the candidate replied. "I have six brothers and eight sisters." "Wow! What a huge family! How lucky you were growing up; you always had someone to play with. Now, I was an only child and I think that's cruel. When I get married, I'm going to have tons of kids. . . ."

We did not hire the candidate because we found others with better qualifications. Several weeks later, however, we learned that the candidate was suing us for religious discrimination. He alleged that we didn't hire him because he was Catholic.

We were dumbfounded. We certainly never asked anything about religion; we knew better. Upon investigation, however, we realized that the basis of the suit was the candidate's conversation with the receptionist. Although we all protested, the director of human resources decided that our explanation would not protect us in court. The company settled out of court for $10,000.

Privileged Information

Because everything connected with employment is subject to legal review, it is critical that all the players who contribute to the process know the rules. When one person breaks those rules, it creates problems for all the others in the decision loop.

The manager of human resources in a regional bank was engaged in interviewing candidates for the position of vice president for commercial loans. A young man with a recent master's in business administration (MBA) from Stanford University was the leading candidate. What made him special was that he was related to that state's key political family. When the human resources manager shared this information with the president of the bank, the president immediately put the pressure on to complete the interview process and hire the candidate just as quickly as possible.

It was bank policy to put every executive-level candidate through a complete medical examination. The day after the candidate's medical exam, the bank's doctor called the human resources manager to report the results:

Doctor:	I think you should know that your candidate shoots up on the weekends, and he has been doing so for some time. I can tell you exactly which drugs he takes, how much he takes, and I can estimate how long this has been going on.
Human resources manager:	You're not supposed to tell me those things. That's personal, privileged information between you and the candidate. Just tell me whether he is physically capable of handling the demands of the job.
Doctor:	He is functional right now, but with drugs you never know when use levels will increase. I guess the question you have to ask yourself is whether you want a drug user managing your commercial loan department.

The human resources manager was in a quandary. The bank president, was pressing him to hire the candidate so that he could put the announcement in the local newspaper. This would have been an easy decision if the bank had a drug policy, but they did not. The human resources manager could not tell the president what he had learned from the doctor because it was privileged information.

After much deliberation, the human resources manager told his boss, "You'll just have to trust my judgment on this one. Believe me, we do *not* want this young man on our executive team." He then told the candidate that due to economic concerns the bank could not fill this position at the present time. He would, however, contact the candidate as soon as the situation improved. Four months later, when the candidate was happily employed elsewhere the human resources manager reactivated the interviewing process.

An Offer of Illegal Information

Sometimes the candidate will volunteer illegal information that the interviewer should not have (but may be delighted to know about). For example, a candidate may tell you:

> "I may be over 50, but I can still keep up with the younger folks."

> "I have four kids under the age of six, but, usually I can get a neighbor or my mother-in-law to baby-sit."

> "Even though I've had several workers' compensation claims over the years, I'm sure I can still handle the physical demands of the job."

Should this happen to you, speak up immediately and tell the candidate that your organization is *not* interested in that type of information because it has no bearing on your employment decisions. The candidate, however, can always assert that you never said anything like that. Once they provide that information, it is always possible that the candidate will later allege that they were discriminated against because of this information. Even though you did not ask for that data, the very possession of it puts you in a legally untenable position. Remember that, when it comes to employment law, you as the employer are presumed guilty until you prove yourself innocent. The candidate, however, can allege anything; you have to prove that what was alleged was not true.

One day, a candidate handed me the company's standard employment application. At the very top she had written in thick, bright red letters, "I am an epileptic." I made my usual speech about this having no bearing on the company's employment decisions and then asked her to redo her application *without* that piece of information.

In the end she was the successful candidate. I never shared the information with anyone. Because the job did not involve the operation of dangerous machinery, I believed that her medical situation would never come to light. Unfortunately, I was wrong. One year later she had a seizure while working with one of the company's largest customers. The customer was not very understanding, and the woman's boss was very upset with me: "You should have told me about her condition, so I could have reminded her to take her medicine. We could lose Butt, Head, & Beemis over this incident."

■ NONCOMPETE AGREEMENTS AND EMPLOYMENT CONTRACTS

Suppose you have a very successful salesperson; the customers like him, and his level of sales is phenomenal. As sales manager, you fear that one day this person will leave and—horror of horrors—take his customer base with him. You seize on the idea of a contract to prevent the salesperson from leaving.

Obviously, of course, there is no way to prevent a person from leaving a job. The salesperson is not a serf, bound for life to the company. Superior salespeople have a good deal of entrepreneurial fervor about them. That's precisely what makes them good. They believe they are working for themselves, not necessarily for the company. Commissions tend to substantiate that in their own minds. There is, however, a preventative measure available that can be taken to discourage a departing salesperson from taking the customer base with them. It is called an *employment contract* or *noncompete agreement.*

The purpose of such agreements is to prevent employees from taking a company's customers or customer-contact files when they go to a new employer or become self-employed. They are also used in cases where the employee will be privy to valuable and confidential information on which the company's business is based. A recent ruling by the Supreme Court broadened the definition of proprietary information to include any private information having commercial value. If the candidate in question will occupy a position of considerable importance in your organization, it may be wise for you to have a simple confidentiality agreement as a prerequisite to employment. Such agreements should be signed *before* the candidate starts work, as part of the interview process, rather than at the time of separation.

The courts have repeatedly demonstrated their dislike for these documents. In fact, the courts are predisposed to interpreting these documents in a manner most favorable to the employee. The rationale is that any ambiguities in it should be interpreted at the expense of the party who drafted the contract—which is the employer.

The courts recognize two reasons for enforcing employment contracts and noncompete agreements as legitimate:

1. To protect customer contacts and relationships.
2. To safeguard confidential information unavailable anywhere else.

A noncompete agreement whose main purpose is to prevent competition is not considered legitimate. The courts believe that it is not right to limit a person's opportunity to make a living. Noncompete agreements, however, can be made legally acceptable, and therefore enforceable, even though the judge involved may find the matter distasteful.

Because the legal statutes surrounding noncompete agreements differ somewhat from state to state, insist on having a local lawyer examine any noncompetition restrictions *before* you present the document to the candidate for signature. Second, put limits on the restrictions so that they will appear reasonable to the court. For example, a logical length of time in a noncompete restriction would be one year; anything over a year could be considered overkill. A reasonable geographical restriction would be a specific city or county. Anything larger than a county may be considered unreasonable. Courts look most favorably on those noncompete agreements that offer the employee some incentive—other than a threat of legal action—for agreeing to the employment restriction.

Courts are not just looking at whether the noncompete agreement is reasonable but whether it is unenforceable because it prevents a person from making a living.

■ WHAT EMPLOYMENT CONTRACTS AND NONCOMPETE AGREEMENTS SHOULD COVER

An employment contract or noncompete agreement is a legal business agreement that sets forth, in writing, the performance of services the salesperson is to provide. It should clearly state your expectations as the hiring manager regarding the following items:

1. How the work is to be done.

2. What the results are to be accomplished.

3. The basis of the compensation provided.

4. The duration of the employment (traditionally it is one year).

5. The territory allotted to the salesperson clearly delineated.

6. Description of the products to be sold. That leaves no room for disputes or claims.

7. A complete description of the duties of the salesperson.

   Whether full-time or part-time.

   Restriction on directly or indirectly accepting any other employment.

   Sales volume (quota) expected.

   Promotional activities.

   Customer-service activities, and so on.

8. The compensation offered, including a clear statement of the salary, commission basis, and/or drawing account, the time frame involved, and the payment of commissions after termination.

9. The paperwork to be done by the salesperson, such as the following:

   Daily or weekly reports to be submitted by the salesperson.

   What those reports should cover.

   Identification of the point at which orders are considered accepted and commissionable.

   Details of how commissions are processed; when earned; when paid.

10. The restrictions on the salesperson regarding price and quality concessions.

A clear statement regarding whether the salesperson is to be bound by certain constraints regarding issues of price, delivery, or quality or quantity.

11. The requirement of a fidelity bond, license, and so on.

12. The duration of employment.

If there is no stated term, the contract is cancelable by either party.

If the contract has a fixed duration, provide a specified time in which either party may cancel without cause and upon proper notice (usually 30 days). This is known as an escape clause.

Renewal clause.

A statement that company retains the right to terminate for cause (nonperformance) or economic reasons (downsizing).

13. The collection of accounts.

If the salesperson is to perform this function, a description of how it is to take place.

14. The restrictions after termination.

If the names of customers are to be treated as confidential information, state that here. If the salesperson will be restricted from accepting employment from a competitor or from going into business for him- or herself as a competitor, state that here. If you as the hiring manager intend to pay the salesperson through the contracted period *if* your salesperson leaves before the 12 months are up and *if* your salesperson agrees to maintain a noncompetitive stance for one year from the termination date, specify that here.

15. How disputes are to be handled.

Should there be a dispute, a statement that both parties agree to seek arbitration rather than litigation (it's quicker and cheaper).

■ THE OFFER-OF-EMPLOYMENT LETTER

Once you have decided on the candidate you want, it is important to move quickly. Delaying the offer can result in losing the candidate to another firm. Good people are hard to find. If you thought the candidate was good, so did others.

As the process of selection winds down to focus on one individual, it becomes critical that neither you nor anyone else involved in the selection process give the candidate any promises regarding the length of employment, the benefits, the working conditions, future raises, or any other sort of statement that could be construed as a guarantee. Even casual comments about the company's practice of giving exceptional raises to especially productive staff members can be considered a promise and therefore legally binding. This is definitely true if the candidate can show that such statements influenced him or her into accepting the job.

It is crucial to limit the number of people taking part in the hiring decision. The more people involved, the longer the process is going to take. Not only might the company lose the candidate to another organization, but the more decision makers there are in the loop, the more likely it is that a compromise candidate—rather than the best candidate—will be selected.

Set an early starting date. The longer the time frame between the job offer and the actual first day of employment, the more likely it is that the candidate will hear other offers, maybe more lucrative than yours, and you will lose the candidate.

As soon as you decide that a particular candidate is viable (during the 20-minute courtesy portion of the interview), you can tell him or her that any offer if made, will be contingent upon the successful outcome of the reference-checking process. Clients who have handled the reference-checking matter in this way have reported that, in every case in which they later found something suspect in the background check, the candidate, when contacted for a second interview, declined the invitation.

Once the decision to hire is made, it is time for you to create an offer in writing. The offer letter puts forth the terms and conditions of employment. Because of liability concerns, you may be reluctant to put anything in writing. A properly written offer letter, however, can help prevent miscommunication, misunderstandings, and lawsuits down the road.

The offer letter is a contract and can be enforced verbatim by the courts. It is a good idea to have the company lawyer examine the offer letter *before* it is presented to the candidate.

Even a cordial introductory sentence such as, "Welcome to the BrainDrain, Inc., family, Jim. I know you will find the work here challenging and that you will be with us for many years to come" can be interpreted as a guarantee of lifetime job security.

In addition, always list the salary in either biweekly or monthly terms. The courts have ruled that a salary figure shown as an annual figure implies that the candidate is guaranteed the job for one full year.

Perhaps the most-important provision in any offer letter is a statement protecting the organization's rights as an employer-at-will. Although putting this in an offer letter sounds totally out of place, it is there to protect the company against any implied guarantee of job security.

The following elements should be included in an offer letter:

1. The starting date of employment.

2. The official job title that will be given to the employee.

3. A statement that the company retains the right to terminate employment for any reason or no reason.

4. A statement that this offer letter represents the complete understanding between the company and the candidate regarding the terms and conditions of employment.

5. A statement that whatever is contained in this offer letter supersedes any oral statements that may have been made.

6. A statement regarding the company's policy on discrimination and sexual harassment.

7. A section concerning the terms of the probationary period, which also states that permanent employment is not necessarily guaranteed at the completion of that period.

8. A list of the benefits that accrue with employment, with references to the appropriate manuals or documents that fully describe the extent and limits of those benefits.

9. A place for you and the candidate to sign, signifying acceptance and agreement of the terms and conditions set forth in the letter.

The issues listed below should be discussed with the candidate prior to creating the offer letter. Although the following items can be included in the offer letter, it is not common practice to do so:

1. A list of the main tasks and responsibilities of the job.
2. The standards of performance for each task.
3. The conditions under which the tasks are to be performed.
4. Performance-review periods.
5. Compensation-adjustment periods.
6. Expectations regarding overtime and overtime compensation.
7. Policies regarding rest periods, lunch breaks, religious holidays, jury duty, national guard duty, and family leave.

Any confidentiality or competition restrictions should be delineated in a separate document (the employment contract or noncompete agreement).

One of my clients, a multinational manufacturing company, goes through the offer process every year with each of its senior executives. Included in the offer letter is a statement of goals that the executive is to accomplish in the coming year, along with a list of responsibilities that the person is to manage. The CEO of the company explained that jobs can change radically each year, depending in large part on what is occurring in its marketplace. Job descriptions, therefore, are of little use. Moreover, his expectations change as well. Because each year presents new challenges and virtually a different job, the CEO concluded that a new employment contract was a positive way of acknowledging the changes. His executive staff agrees. They appreciate the clarity of expectations that results from the redefining of their responsibilities.

Chapter

The Quagmire of Reference Checking, Negligent Hiring, Employer Liability, and Termination

■ REFERENCE CHECKING

A significant part of prudent hiring is reference checking. As the hiring manager, you want to know all the pertinent facts about this person who is going to be a part of your team. You don't want any ugly surprises waiting for you in the underbrush. Today it is more difficult than ever to obtain candid, reliable references because, in this litigious society everyone is worried about protecting themselves from lawsuits.

There are two myths regarding reference checking. The first is that the candidate will provide names that will yield only positive information and that it is therefore a waste of time to use them. The second is that *only* the references provided by the candidate can be checked.

Candidates often supply names of people who give negative as well as positive information. In addition, reference data can be obtained from any number of sources *not* mentioned by the candidate. You can use the contacts you have at the organizations where the candidate has had prior work experience. You can ask for and use the names of people that the candidate's references give you. You can always speak with consultants or temporary employees who may have worked with the candidate. You can also talk with coworkers and peers of the candidate, as well as the candidate's immediate supervisor.

The references that the candidate chooses to give you provide you with another interesting piece of information. If the candidate does *not* offer the names of his or her immediate bosses, always ask why.

When talking to references listen carefully for such things as long pauses, hesitations, evasive or noncommittal responses, deliberate choice of wording, and so on. To get the most information from references, begin with one all-encompassing open-ended question and wait to hear how the other person responds. Here is a sample: "We are in the process of interviewing Ann Briggs for a position as accounts-receivable supervisor. How do you think she'll do for us?"

Asking more closed-ended questions, such as the following, gives respondents too much time to think, revise, and restrict their information:

How many days was Ann absent during last year?

How often was she late to work?

How did she get along with the staff?

What was her title?

What did she do?

Should your respondent be willing to provide you with quality information, be ready with a prepared list of additional questions. Such questions should reflect the needs listed on your MMM, as well as those areas in which you feel the candidate may have some shortcomings in terms of the position's requirements. The following questions are useful for reference checking:

What characteristics did you look for (or will you be looking for) in the person you hired to replace Ann?

If Ann was doing so well in that position, why didn't you encourage her to stay?

I'd like to read you the description of her job that is on her resume and have you comment on it.

What is the most-significant quality Ann brought to the job?

What kind of job would make the best use of Ann's apparent abilities as well as her innate capabilities?

How did the staff react to Ann?

In what areas was Ann less effective?

What contribution did Ann make to the organization during the time she was with you?

There is a widely held belief that any attempt to probe into a candidate's work history and employment performance is a swift and guaranteed route to expensive litigation. Companies have been cautioned by their corporate attorneys not to give out information, even on dangerous former employees, for fear of being sued and/or for fear of violating a former employee's right to privacy.

There is no such thing as a "right to privacy" specifically guaranteed by the U.S. Constitution. Courts have, however, implied that every individual has a common-law right to be free from unreasonable intrusions, especially into his or her private life. The courts also frown on any general rule that automatically eliminates a candidate from consideration based on negative background information.

Based on those two issues, an increasing number of people have sued their former employers for slander, libel, and defamation of character for providing prospective employers with negative information. As a result, it has become common practice for companies to provide only the dates of employment when responding to requests for references.

The term *defamation* covers both slander (a spoken statement) and libel (a written statement). A statement is considered defamatory if (1) it is untrue, (2) it harms the person's reputation in the community (placing their employability in question), and (3) it was communicated to someone other than the employee.

Employers who reveal information about former employees to potential future employers do have protection under the law. The statements they make, however, must be (1) true (i.e., verifiable with documentation), (2) not intentionally designed to ruin the person's reputation, (3) given only to those who need to know, (4) limited to the specific inquiry, (5) free of references to the employee's personal life (invasion of privacy) unless it interfered with his or her job, and (6) related to the requirements of the position.

There are some measures you can take to make sure you are protected.

1. Ask that the candidate sign a release that is directed at his or her former employer. State in the release that the candidate holds the former employer legally harmless for the information to be provided.

2. Do not ask about discriminatory or personal issues such as age, religion, race, national origin, marital status, sexual preference, and so on.

3. Keep the information obtained confidential and on a need-to-know basis.

4. Reference checking is a do-it-yourself project. The best ones (i.e., the most candid and honest) are obtained when the manager for whom the candidate will work (that's you—*not* human resources) calls the executive for whom the candidate used to work. Peers tend to be more open with peers.

5. Reference checking should be done by phone or face-to-face. Requesting references in writing will generally net the dates of employment and nothing else.

6. The least-candid reference resource will be the human resources department. They have not had day-to-day contact with the candidate, and they are primarily concerned about protecting the company from possible legal problems.

7. Asking someone to give a reference is asking that person a favor. Plan the questions ahead of time; be brief, polite, and considerate of the person's time. Above all, place the call yourself.

Because the issue of reference checking is fraught with all sorts of legal issues, your organization may decide to implement a policy of *not* checking references. The company may fear treading on the candidate's mythical right of privacy; it may be concerned that obtaining negative information from a previous employer could cause the candidate to sue the former employer for defamation of character. Not checking references could, however, put your company smack in the middle of a negligent-hiring lawsuit.

■ NEGLIGENT HIRING

Negligent-hiring lawsuits are legal actions taken against a company and are made by third parties (customers, clients, etc.) who have been harmed by the company's employees.[1] The basis of such lawsuits is that the company hired someone who was likely to injure others. Had the employer done a proper job of reference checking, they would have discovered the candidate's dangerous tendencies. The employer's negligence was the proximate cause of the injury to people with whom it was reasonable to assume the new employee would come into contact.

The company may allege that it didn't know this candidate was a problem (because no references were checked or perhaps because the references it obtained were not truthful). The legal answer, however, is that, had the company been diligent in its reference-checking efforts, it would have uncovered the information that this employee was dangerous, prior to hiring him or her.

Refusal to disclose negative reference information is a legal paradox. Although it is in the public interest for the previous employer to provide the succeeding employer with any critical information, many former employers will limit any disclosure to the dates of employment or provide inaccurate written and spoken references because they fear being sued by the former employee. Such a practice makes legal sense for the previous employer, but it exposes the succeeding employer to negligent-hiring lawsuits.

The courts have come down hard on companies who did not make the proper reference checks before hiring a person who later harmed a third party while in the process of discharging his or her job responsibilities. What follows are a few horror stories.

A company hired a truck driver with a record of drunk-driving offenses. The previous employer would only verify employment dates, which spanned five years. The new truck driver subsequently smashed into a passenger car while making a delivery in a company truck. He totaled the passenger car and seriously injured the family inside. The family sued the trucking company for negligent hiring. The courts upheld the suit, stating that the succeeding employer should have checked into the employee's driving history, which was a matter of public record, before hiring him.

A hotel hired a bellhop who had been in similar positions at several nearby hotels for very short periods of time. The previous employers were reluctant to provide the succeeding employer with any reference information other than the dates of employment. The newly hired bellhop broke into a guest's room and raped her. The guest sued the hotel for negligent hiring. The court upheld her suit, stating that, as a guest in the hotel, the woman had a right to assume that she would be safe from harm at the hands of the hotel's personnel. The hotel was responsible for carefully checking the background of those employees who would have access to guests' rooms.

A large community hospital hired a surgeon based on the glowing written references given by peers at the previous hospital at which he had worked. After two years in his new job, this surgeon was convicted of involuntary manslaughter and negligent homicide in the deaths of several patients. Peers at the community hospital described the doctor as technically incompetent and totally lacking in judgment. The families whose relatives suffered at the hands of this doctor sued the hospital for negligent hiring. The court agreed that the hospital's failure to investigate the surgeon's background was responsible for the tragedies. Although the court cases never uncovered the truth about those reference letters, there was some speculation that they had been created by the surgeon himself.

■ GIVING REFERENCES

If the organization you work for allows you to provide references, there are some simple guidelines you can follow that will prevent legal problems later on:

1. Tell the caller to give you his or her number so that you can call back.

2. Verify the identity of the caller and that this request for information is legitimate.

3. Discuss what you intend to say with one person in the company (perhaps someone from human resources) who has been well schooled on the legal ramifications of providing reference information.

4. When you are asked to provide a reference, tell the prospective employer to secure a written release from the employee holding you harmless for the information you will provide. Have the release in hand before you say anything else.

5. Stipulate that the information is confidential and is to be used by professional hiring authorities and specialists for employment purposes only.

6. Do not volunteer information; respond only to specific queries that relate to the job and to the performance in it.

7. When providing a reference, stick to the facts; leave out hearsay or personal opinions. Make no vague, judgmental, or clever statements such as "When Bill opens his mouth, it's only to change feet" or "Betty would be out of her depth in a parking-lot puddle."

8. When an employee has been fired, provide a reason for the dismissal that can be substantiated with specific evidence and fact. Create a file of specific documentation to substantiate any negative statements made in reference giving.

9. A manager providing a reference to a potential employer in good faith—even a negative reference—has some legal protection. Gossiping with customers and other staff members about a dismissal is not protected by law, however, and *is* grounds for a defamation suit.

10. Remember that where employment is concerned, no piece of information is ever off the record legally.

■ TERMINATION

The one area for which a manager can create the most problems for his or her company is around the issue of termination.

Even when an employee's performance is seriously deficient, the situation may have been allowed to continue far too long before it was addressed. When the manager finally does confront the problem, the frustration level is so great that he or she often loses control. In a fit of anger, the manager fires the employee without adequate documentation and without consulting others to ensure an objective analysis of the situation. Don't let this happen to you.

Perhaps managers delay addressing problems because they do not want to admit they made a hiring or promotional mistake. Maybe it is because the manager believes a termination reflects negatively on his or her ability as a leader. The longer a deficient performance is allowed to continue, however, the harder it is to justify terminating the employee, as illustrated in the following example.

One company terminated a 28-year employee for "deficient performance." The employee sued the company, claiming that, in all his 28 years, no one had ever told him his performance was anything less than fully satisfactory. He was able to produce many years worth of appraisal forms substantiating that fact. "If I had been told something was wrong with my performance," he stated, "I would have made every effort to improve. But I didn't know anything was wrong."

The company lawyer put eight different supervisors and managers on the stand for whom, at one time or another, this employee had worked during his 28 years with the company. Each manager testified that the employee had been marginal at best. Each one admitted that in order to convince another department to take the employee, they made him look attractive on paper so he would be transferred.

The judge ruled in favor of the employee. Because none of his many supervisors and managers had confronted him with the truth about his performance, he had not been given the opportunity to remedy the situation. The company was forced to reinstate the employee at his former position and salary, fund the employee's legal fees, and pay his wages and benefits retroactively for the three years between his termination and reinstatement.

If you are like most managers, you hate to give an employee the bad news. You may instead engage in hinting, suggesting, and alluding to your dissatisfaction with the employee's performance. You may be so accomplished at being tactful that the employee never really gets the message that he or she is in trouble. Then when the ax falls, it is a total surprise. The employee says he or she was never *really* told that there were serious problems and sues the company for wrongful discharge.

More than 25,000 wrongful-discharge cases are dragged through the courts each year, and when employees sue they usually win. The average award is $500,000.[2] In addition, the employee may also receive a sizable punitive-damages award for pain and suffering. In the cases where the company wins, legal fees and expenses can run even higher. Unless it has clearly defined job descriptions, precisely written expectations, and specific job performance standards against which the employee was judged, a company can face expensive litigation.

As a manager, it is critical that you document problem performances so that there is a factual basis on which to make a termination judgment. It is not sufficient to write, "Tom is one slice short of a sandwich when it comes to accuracy." You must be able to state in writing, "Tom made four errors in calculating client billings during the week of July 12, 1999, seven errors during the week of July 19, 1999, and six errors during the week of July 26, 1999."

Where executives are concerned, laying out a paper trail with specific data becomes very difficult. Executives are often fired because the chemistry between them and the company is poor and/or because their judgment has been faulty.

Termination is the most-punishing action an organization can inflict on an employee. The impact and emotional trauma associated with getting fired ranks as one of the highest sources of stress. It comes in fourth, right after the death of a close family member, serious personal injury, and the imposition of a jail sentence. Therefore, you should give careful deliberation before taking such a drastic step. There must be just and sufficient cause for termination and only after all practical steps at saving the employee have been taken. In order to ensure objectivity, it is best to discuss your decision to dismiss with several other people (perhaps someone from human resources and certainly your boss) so that your decision is evaluated by those who may not be as close to the situation as you.

Reasons for termination should be clearly and specifically defined by the organization and included in the employee handbook. The following is a list of sanctioned grounds for dismissal:

- Persistent, unsatisfactory performance: failure to meet normal job requirements or perform the assigned duties or meet the proscribed standards for the job.
- Excessive absenteeism or tardiness as established by company guidelines.
- Economic cutbacks or other valid business reasons.
- Providing false or misleading information on the original employment application.
- Adverse attitude toward the company, manager, coworkers, or established policies and procedures.
- Deliberate misconduct: willful violation of company or departmental rules, dishonesty, sleeping on the job, conducting personal business during work hours, rowdyism, destruction of company property or numerous accidents.
- Serious undesirable and dangerous behavior (to others): physically attacking or threatening another employee, fighting, drinking, or taking and/or selling drugs on the job, bringing firearms into work (these should be grounds for instant termination).

■ PREVENTIVE MEASURES FOR AVOIDING LEGAL PROBLEMS DUE TO WRONGFUL DISCHARGE

The following are some things you can do to limit your exposure to charges of wrongful discharge:

1. Make certain that all employment application forms, company handbooks, and policy declarations do not contain any statements that can be interpreted as a promise of continuous employment.
2. Establish definitive written standards for terminations.
3. Maintain periodic and accurate performance ratings and records of each employee's work effectiveness.
4. Ensure rating consistency among your supervisors; discourage them from giving unwarranted and excessively high appraisals.
5. Warn, counsel, and discuss the troublesome issues with problem employees prior to any discharge action.
6. Ensure fairness, evenhandedness, and objectivity in all termination decisions.

7. Produce a strong paper trail of documentation for any discharge decisions.

8. Make sure that you and any of your staff who are involved in the employment interviewing process avoid making promises of future employment.

9. In cases for which there is a concern regarding the legal propriety of some action that you wish to take, consult a legal expert before you do anything.

10. When terminating for incompetence, it is always best to do so during the probationary period; after the probationary period it is better to offer the employee a demotion *first*.

11. Unless required by state law, do *not* provide written reasons for discharge even if the employee requests it.

12. In order to avoid a possible suit, assist (or at least do not hinder) terminated employees to locate new jobs.

13. During the exit interview ask the employee to put in writing what he or she wants the company to confirm should a potential employer call for a reference. Have a form available for the employee to complete (see Figure 10.1).

■ FEDERAL GUIDELINES AND SUGGESTIONS REGARDING TERMINATION DOCUMENTATION

The federal guidelines state that an employer must have three separate pieces of documentation in file stating clearly (1) what was wrong with the employee's performance, (2) what the employee had to do to correct the situation, (3) proof that the employee had been given this information, (4) a reasonable time frame in which correction could be made, and (5) what was likely to occur if corrective action did not take place. This three-step documentation procedure should be preceded by a verbal warning that you formalize with a written memo for your own files.

Step One: Verbal Warning Memo

If an issue is important enough that you have to make the time for a serious discussion, then a piece of documentation should be created to indicate that such a conversation took place. That

I, _____, hereby authorize _____

      Employee's name   Company's name

You may verify the following information to those who may call seeking reference information about me:

_____   Current salary

_____   Length of employment

_____   Position and/or title

_____   No information may be given

_____

               Signature of employee

_____

                    Date

Figure 10.1 Sample Form to Authorize Release of Information.

document should state what was discussed and what was agreed to as the result of that discussion. At the top of the memo, write the date and the words "Verbal Warning" and put it in a special file (*not* the employee's personal file).

In your verbal-warning discussion with the employee, explain clearly and in specific terms (1) what is wrong with the employee's performance and (2) how you want things to be corrected. Then give the employee a specific time frame in which to improve.

The conventional recommendation for this time frame is 30 working days, depending on the nature of the job. For example, it is appropriate for a salesperson to be given "the next quarter" as a time frame for improvement of his or her call-to-close ratio, but a clerical-support person might be given only 20 working days as a time frame for improving a tardiness problem.

Many times the performance problem ends here. Once the employee sees you documenting the conversation, he or she realizes that this is a serious issue and wants to ensure that you destroy the verbal-warning memo as soon as possible.

Step Two: First Written Warning

On the 30th day after the verbal-warning meeting (or after the quarter for the salesperson or on the 20th day for the clerical person), you proceed to the next step if necessary, the second serious discussion on this employee's problem issue. This second discussion takes place if you have not seen any improvement in the situation.

Once again you explain clearly and in specific terms (1) what is wrong with the employee's performance and (2) how you want things to be corrected. This time you give the employee a shorter specific time frame in which to improve. The recommended time frame in this instance is 20 days. For the salesperson it might be 30 days; for the clerical person 10 days.

As a part of this discussion, you create a written memo entitled "First Written Warning," documenting the content and commitment results of this meeting. This document, however, must be signed by both you and the employee. It is then placed in the employee's personnel file, not your special file. The employee is given a copy of the signed memo.

Should the employee refuse to sign the memo or refuse to accept a copy of the signed memo, you must ask another manager at your level to sign the memo, witnessing that the conversation took place and that the employee in question was offered (or did receive) a copy of the memo detailing the content and commitment results of the meeting.

Step Three: Second Written Warning

On the 20th day after the meeting for the first written warning (the 30th day for the salesperson or the 10th day for the clerical person), you proceed to step three: the third serious discussion with the employee about his or her performance problem. This third discussion takes place because you have not seen any improvement in the situation.

At this stage you want to repeat step two exactly, with one exception: Give a shorter time frame during which improvement must take place. The usual time frame here is 10 days. For the salesperson it might be 14 days; for the clerical person perhaps 5 days. This time the employee is told that if improvement does not occur, he or she will be terminated at the end of this time period.

Step Four: Termination

On the 10th day after the meeting at which you created the second written warning (the 14th day for the salesperson or the 5th day for the clerical person), you move to step four and hold the fourth and final meeting with this employee on his or her performance problem. You explain clearly and in specific terms (1) what was wrong with the employee's performance, (2) how you wanted things to be corrected, and (3) the various time frames that you gave the employee in which to effect correction. This final memo, however, concludes with a statement that, because no improvement has occurred, you have made the decision to terminate effective this date.

■ THE TERMINATION INTERVIEW

Part of treating everyone with dignity and respect requires that the termination interview come as no surprise to the employee. If you have followed the steps as just detailed, you have already had several previous discussions in which the gravity of the situation was explicitly defined for the employee. The only action for this meeting is the announcement of the termination, and it is best done quickly.

The termination discussion should take place in your office with you standing up behind your desk. The desk serves as a symbol of the formality of the meeting. Quiet surroundings with no interruptions are a must. The employee should have the courtesy of your undivided attention. It is a good idea to set aside one-half hour even though 10 minutes is all that should be necessary.

Friday afternoon at 4:15 P.M. seems to be the favorite time for most executives to deliver the bad news of termination. That ruins the employee's weekend. It does, however, provide the person an opportunity to avoid the embarrassment of facing his or her colleagues. It also gives the employee the weekend to rewrite his or her resume. On the other hand, having the termination discussion on a Monday morning gives the person a chance to visit a number of potential employers companies or employment agencies right away.

Whenever the discussion takes place, it is important that you do *not* beat around the bush. Attempting to soften the blow will only create misunderstandings and an assumption by the employee that there is still a chance, despite everything, that employment will continue. No amount of verbiage is going to compensate for your feelings of guilt or the employee's shock. The purpose of this conversation is to gently but firmly inform the employee that his or her career with the company is over. The termination message itself can be effectively handled in a 30-second speech. The following is a list of items you should include in this discussion, together with a sample speech.

1. *State the problem with quantitative details.*

   "Over the past three months, you and I have discussed the problem of your abusive language and actions toward the office clerical staff four times. There has been, however, no change in your behavior."

2. *State your feelings in the matter clearly.*

   "This has been very frustrating for me because, except for this issue, you are a very fine manager with a lot of creative energy and good ideas."

3. *Declare your decision clearly and with conviction.*

   "I have decided that today will be your last day with Stress & Strain, Incorporated."

4. *Ask for those things that make the employee a part of the company.*

   "Please give me your identification badge, garage pass, and your property keys so that I can give you a severance check and benefits continuation (or unemployment) information." (This information should be already written out on official company stationery so that verbalization of the data is not necessary.) This is the point at which you ask the employee to complete the *Authorization to Release Information* form (see Figure 10.1).

5. *End with a statement of positive concern for the person's future employment.*

   "I wish you the very best in whatever you decide to do in your future employment endeavor."

It is a prudent practice to have a member of the security staff standing by to escort the employee from your office to his or her desk (to collect any personal items) and from there, straight out the door. Once the employee is told he or she been terminated, he or she should not be left alone for a single moment. In recent years there have been a number of situations where terminated employees claimed they were too upset to gather up their things at the moment. They asked if they could take care of it on Monday (when security would *not* be standing right there). On Monday they arrived with a gun and killed their immediate supervisor.

■ CONCLUSION

How strange that a book on interviewing ends with information on how to terminate a staff member! If you use the interviewing strategies and techniques contained in this book, however, you may never have to refer to these last few pages. No matter how many years you work and how many people you hire and supervise over those years, the memories that will remain the clearest and most painful will be those involving the poor performers you had to terminate. You want those painful memories to be as few as possible.

■ NOTES

1. See Kenneth Sovereign, *Personnel Law,* 3rd ed. (Englewood Cliffs, NJ: Prentice Hall, 1998).
2. Walter Olson, *The Excuse Factory: How Employment Law Is Paralyzing the American Workplace* (New York: Free Press, 1997).

Appendix

Common Errors in Conducting the Interview

Without appropriate training and preparation, even the most well-meaning person will fall prey to the following common interviewing errors. The unfortunate result is the hiring of a candidate who should have not been hired at all.

1. *Failing to establish rapport with the candidate.*

    You establish rapport by stating at the outset how the interview will be structured. The interview is not about making friends with the candidate. Neither is it about playing psychologist to the candidate's anxieties.

2. *Not knowing exactly what abilities are required; not working from a meticulously developed list of requirements.*

    Job descriptions list duties, activities, and responsibilities; they do not detail expectations or results to be achieved. Without this other kind of information, there is no way to analyze or measure a candidate's past performance against the needs of the vacant position.

3. *Becoming a victim of the halo effect.*

    This can occur in two ways. The first is when the interviewer finds something in the candidate's background that matches something in his or her own (e.g., attending the same university or having grown up in the same state). That similarity gives the entire interview a golden glow so that, when negative information surfaces, the tendency is to play it down or ignore it. The second way the halo effect can occur is when the interviewer finds the candidate possesses outstanding abilities in one area and then assumes the person is equally superior in other areas.

4. *Doing most of the talking.*

Most untrained interviewers talk too much and therefore fail to obtain meaningful information about the candidate. The most-important skill in interviewing is listening. The only time one can listen to a candidate is when he or she is speaking.

5. *Not allowing silences to occur.*

The only way the interviewer can influence a reluctant candidate to speak is by keeping silent with body language that says, "I'm awaiting your next words." More often that not, the reason for the silence is that the candidate is thinking. When the interviewer fills that silence, he or she has effectively derailed the candidate's train of thought.

6. *Using too many direct questions (questions answerable by "yes" or "no").*

This type of question minimizes the amount of information received, discourages the candidate from speaking freely, and prevents the interview from flowing smoothly. The most-significant issue of all is that direct questions prevent the interviewer from learning how the candidate thinks.

7. *Asking questions that serve no purpose.*

Without adequate preparation—which includes a preselected battery of questions to be asked—the interviewer may ask irrelevant questions just to take up airtime while trying to conjure up the next question. Not only does this waste time, but candidates recognize that the interviewer is engaged in question generation rather than listening to them.

8. *Poor sequencing of questions.*

Without designing a structure beforehand, the interviewer will jump around from area to area in his or her questioning. The result is superficial information from many areas of the candidate's background but no in-depth knowledge of any single area.

9. *Making impulsive conclusions and generalizations based on some assumed characteristic.*

   Interviewers' biases may work against them by influencing them to recommend hiring the candidate based on their appearance (e.g., "looks the part"), verbal facility (e.g., "thinks well on her feet"), and apparent values (e.g., "honest and forthright," "looked me straight in the eye").

10. *Repeating the information on the application or resume.*

    Repeating information already in hand wastes everyone's time, but it is an excellent ploy for someone who is not prepared to conduct an interview. Unfortunately, such an approach signals the candidate that the organization has no interest in him or her.

11. *Selling the organization too soon.*

    Telling the candidate all the things that the interviewer believes make the position challenging, rewarding, advantageous, and exciting will not make it attractive to the candidate no matter how enthusiastically the interviewer imparts the information. The only way to find out what excites candidates about a job—any job—is to allow them to tell their own story.

12. *Ignoring intuition (gut feelings)*

    Intuitive feelings are the result of facts, observation (of the candidate's body language), and experience coming together on a subconscious level. If the message from your gut feelings is negative, it is vital that you substantiate intuitive messages with more incisive data before going any further. A cardinal rule in interviewing is "When in doubt, don't hire." Intuition is a signal that more definitive information is needed.

13. *Asking questions that don't give worthwhile information.*

    Included in this category are (1) questions that telegraph the desired responses (e.g., "This job requires exceptionally good listening skills. Are you a good listener?"), (2) apparent choices where there are none (e.g., "Do you get emotional and overreact, or can you keep a cool head?"), and questions where the answers, although obvious, cannot be checked for truthfulness (e.g., "Do you have good common sense?").

14. *Asking "magic" questions.*

   Questions of this nature are supposed to provide penetrating information about the candidate's personality (e.g., "If you could be an animal, which one would you choose?" or "What do you think is the meaning of life?") Such questions are an excuse for not doing the real investigative work required for an effective interview.

15. *Not being knowledgeable about the legal restrictions regarding interviewing.*

   There are two problems here. Should the interviewer ask an illegal question, the company could face an expensive lawsuit. On the other hand, if the interviewer is unclear about what can and cannot be asked, he or she may fail to do a thorough interview out of fear of delving into an illegal topic.

16. *Giving evaluative feedback; exchanging opinions with the candidate.*

   It is not the function of the interviewer to hold up his or her end of the conversation by commenting on or evaluating what the candidate has said. The interview is not a social event; the interviewer's opinions are not a concern here.

17. *Asking multiple-choice (laundry-list) questions.*

   Questions that contain too many queries elicit only partial responses. In addition, they allow the candidate to escape the task of thinking by simply selecting a response from the list of choices provided by the interviewer.

18. *Excessive note taking.*

   Voluminous notes make it impossible to cull out the important data afterward. Moreover, when an interviewer's attention is consumed with note taking, there is little eye contact and therefore scant opportunity to relate to the candidate. At the end of the dialogue, the interviewer may have no sense of the character or personality of the candidate.

19. *Giving commitments; making promises.*

Even innocent comments such as "I think you would be very good in this job" can be interpreted as a hiring commitment and as an inducement to quit the current job. If not hired, the candidate may then have grounds for filing a lawsuit alleging he or she was guaranteed employment.

Appendix B

Sample Interview Questions

The interview questions that follow are a combination of both behavioral and puzzle questions listed according to the attributes you may be seeking in a candidate. As you might expect, a particular question may be useful under several different attribute headings. For example, a query such as "What mechanisms have you put in place so that the typical problems likely to occur on your job do not surface again? could be used to assess time-management awareness, management competence, decision-making and analytical skills and initiative-taking and enterprising skill.

■ ABILITY TO INFLUENCE OTHERS

It is easy to persuade others when you are in charge; the difficult task is to influence others when you are not in control. Such an ability requires a talent for building relationships with people by appealing to common goals and values. It requires a knowledge of the currencies of influence that are typically valued in organizations, such as information, contacts, visibility, support, and so on. Candidates who possess the ability to influence others are able to induce coworkers and clients to support their ideas and objectives. The following questions will help assess a candidate's strength in this area.

- Describe a time when you succeeded in getting someone to go along with something he or she was strongly opposed to doing. [*Behavioral question*]
- Tell me about an occasion when you captured the involvement, participation, and support of others to work on and achieve a particular goal. [*Behavioral question*]
- Let's say you discovered that a coworker was doing something that you considered to be unethical. What would you do to influence the coworker to change his or her actions? [*Puzzle question*]
- Suppose management was going to make a procedural change that would have a detrimental effect on your job. What steps would you take to influence management that the change should *not* be made? [*Puzzle question*]
- Tell me about a time when you worked for a manager who assigned work at the last possible minute. What attempts did you make to influence a change in that manager's modus operandi? [*Behavioral question*]
- I'd like to hear how you influenced a staff member to assume more responsibility or to take on a task that you knew would be difficult for him or her to do. [*Behavioral question*]
- Tell me about a time when you came up with an idea that would solve a departmental problem. How did you go about selling your idea to your boss? [*Behavioral question*]
- I'd like to hear about a time when one team member did not carry his or her own weight. What efforts did you make to influence that situation? [*Behavioral question*]
- Tell me about a time when you had to introduce an unpopular change to your staff. What steps did you take so that negative reactions would be minimized? [*Behavioral question*]
- Describe a situation in which you were supervising a mediocre performer. What strategies did you use to motivate that person to increase his or her effectiveness? [*Behavioral question*]

■ CUSTOMER-SERVICE ORIENTATION

Service providers need a special attitude and a psyche that is not tied to the importance of being right in every situation.

Candidates interested in providing superior customer service to both internal and external clients must be able to identify and understand the needs of others. They strive to surpass the expectations of their clients. They realize that without customers there is no business; and without an adequate level of service, the customer will not return. They can differentiate the fine line between extraordinary customer service, resulting in a delighted client, and maintaining a healthy business (not giving the store away). Here are some questions that will explore the candidate's understanding and ability to serve others.

- Please describe a situation in which you were able to turn a negative customer around. What was the issue? How did you accomplish the turnaround? [*Behavioral question*]
- Tell me about a time when you made a personal sacrifice in order to attain a work-related objective. [*Behavioral question*]
- What do you think is the difference between quality and customer service? [*Puzzle question*]
- Most customer-service efforts focus on handling complaints. What problems do you see with such a strategy? [*Puzzle question*]
- Tell me about a time when you were dealing with a customer who wanted his or her problem resolved in a way that was detrimental to the company. What did you do? [*Behavioral question*]
- What role should company policies and procedures play in customer service? [*Puzzle question*]
- Please describe four qualities a good customer-service representative should demonstrate. Why do you think those qualities are important? [*Puzzle question*]
- Describe a situation when the customer's perception of what occurred was clearly wrong. How did you go about resolving the problem? [*Behavioral question*]
- Statistics tell us that for every customer who complains 18 others will go away dissatisfied saying nothing. How can a customer-service representative encourage the silent customers to speak up? [*Puzzle question*]
- What is an acceptable level of customer dissatisfaction? [*Puzzle question*]

■ TEAM-PLAYER AWARENESS

Working with others in a team setting requires strong human-relations skills and a good deal of old-fashioned common sense. Many people find their way onto teams without either quality. As a result, they cause all kinds of problems that eventually affect the group's productivity. Experience on a team does not automatically qualify a candidate as a *good* team player. You want a person who can help motivate individuals to achieve shared objectives, who knows how to collaborate and who consistently demonstrates enthusiasm about the organization. Here are some questions that can help the assessment process.

- What do you consider to be the main attribute of a good supervisor whose people work in teams? Why? [*Puzzle question*]
- Tell me about the most-creative challenge you were involved with in a team setting. What incentives were used to motivate you and the group? [*Behavioral question*]
- Should a supervisor be able to ask a staff member to do something without giving an explanation? Why or why not? [*Puzzle question*]
- Tell me what you like most/least about working in a team setting. Why? [*Behavioral question*]
- Tell me about the most-difficult situation you faced as a team member. How was that situation was resolved? What role did you play in the resolution process? [*Behavioral question*]
- Describe for me the circumstances under which you have worked most effectively on a team. [*Behavioral question*]
- What is your idea of a good team player? [*Puzzle question*]
- What are the major differences between being an effective employee and being an effective team member? [*Puzzle question*]
- In your experience, what kinds of problems is a team likely to experience when one member is excessively late, absent, or does not carry his or her own weight? How were those issues dealt with? As a member of that team, what did you try to do to ameliorate the situation? [*Behavioral question*]

■ EFFECTIVE COMMUNICATION SKILLS

No matter what the job, communication is part of it. In fact, the greater the responsibilities, the more critical it is that the person in that job be a competent communicator. The interview process is a great opportunity to assess a candidate's communication skills. You have the chance here to evaluate the candidate's ability to express his or her ideas persuasively, describe concepts clearly, organize his or her thoughts sequentially, use appropriate vocabulary and diction, hold the listener's interest, and establish and maintain good eye contact. You want someone who listens well to others and is able to communicate clearly, concisely, and directly with people at all levels of the organization. The following questions are aimed at testing the candidate's communication skills.

- Describe an occasion when you really had to listen to someone who was not communicating clearly. How were you able to respond effectively? [*Behavioral question*]
- What do you think are the characteristics of an effective communicator? [*Puzzle question*]
- Describe yourself as you are seen by other people. [*Puzzle question*]
- Describe a time when you were working closely with a peer who had a very annoying habit. How did you influence that person to moderate his or her behavior? [*Behavioral question*]
- Tell me about a time when you were in the middle of a very complicated project and your boss assigned an untrained person to help you. How did you obtain worthwhile assistance from this person? [*Behavioral question*]
- If you were assigned the task of making a presentation to the board of directors of this company, what steps would you take to prepare yourself for that speech? [*Puzzle question*]
- I'd like to hear about the most-challenging communication situation you have ever come up against. Tell me what made it challenging and how you handled it. [*Behavioral question*]
- What kind of communication situations are most difficult for you? Why? [*Behavioral question*]

- What do you think are the keys to good communication? [*Puzzle question*]
- Suppose two of your peers were locked in a conflict that impacted the entire group, and you were asked to mediate and help the combatants resolve their problem. How would you go about doing that? [*Puzzle question*]

■ ABILITY TO DEVELOP PEOPLE

If an organization is to survive and grow, leadership positions must be staffed with people willing and able to develop their staff members into the organization's future leaders. This means making room for the maximum contribution possible from each staff member. It requires an ability to inspire and coach one's people to fulfill and then exceed their individual potential. It also means encouraging and rewarding responsible risk taking. The following questions target this area.

- Describe a time when you encouraged and rewarded employees for taking initiative. How did you encourage them? How did you reward them? [*Behavioral question*]
- What has been one of the most-difficult pieces of performance-related feedback you had to give an employee? [*Behavioral question*]
- What strategies have you used to encourage your people to develop their capabilities? [*Behavioral question*]
- How would you determine which tasks get delegated to whom? [*Puzzle question*]
- What techniques have you used to monitor the progress (or lack thereof) of tasks you have delegated? [*Behavioral question*]
- How would you assess the development needs of one of your employees? [*Puzzle question*]
- Describe a situation where an employee was having a performance problem. What kind of assistance did you provide to him or her? [*Behavioral question*]
- How have you ensured objectivity when evaluating the performance of your staff? [*Behavioral question*]
- Tell me about a time when you had to motivate an employee who was afraid to make decisions. What did you do? [*Behavioral question*]

- How often and under what circumstances should a supervisor engage in a formal coaching session with an individual employee? [*Puzzle question*]
- Suppose you had an employee who totally resisted all efforts at development. What steps would you take to change his or her attitude? [*Puzzle question*]
- How would you determine that one of your people was ready to assume a leadership role? [*Puzzle question*]

■ SALES ORIENTATION

Of all the jobs in an organization, the job of salesperson is the most complex of all. Perhaps it is because customers must first buy into the salesperson before they will agree to purchase the product or service. Maybe it is because the approach to selling has changed so drastically over the past decade (from adversarial to consultative). Then again, it may be because a good salesperson needs to possess so many diverse and contradictory skills: (1) listening and speaking skills, (2) product knowledge and people savvy, (3) selling acumen and market-penetration strategies, (4) compelling but nonmanipulative communication skills, (5) motivation to achieve high levels of individual performance along with a desire to serve the customer, (6) resiliency and integrity, and (7) being a self-starter who enjoys interacting with others. Here are some questions to help assess sales candidates.

- Tell me about the toughest sale you ever made. Describe how you convinced your client to buy. [*Behavioral question*]
- What are the three major reasons why a person might purchase our product? [*Puzzle question*]
- What do you know about our product line and about our customer base? [*Puzzle question*]
- What do you like (or dislike) most about sales? Why? [*Puzzle question*]
- How do you like to be rewarded? [*Behavioral question*]
- How do you typically plan your day? [*Behavioral question*]
- Please describe four qualities a good salesperson must have in order to be successful. Why do you think those qualities are important? [*Puzzle question*]

- How does selling over the telephone differ from selling face-to-face? What special skills and techniques are necessary to be successful in selling by phone? [*Puzzle question*]
- In your previous job what techniques did you use to develop and maintain existing customers? [*Behavioral question*]
- If you were developing a salesmanship course for new recruits, what topics would you include? Why? [*Puzzle question*]
- Walk me through the typical selling strategy or approach you would have used with a new customer on your previous job. [*Behavioral question*]
- Tell me about a time when you were given a sizable sales goal and a relatively short time frame in which to produce results. What steps did you take to ensure that the goal was achieved? [*Behavioral question*]
- I'd be interested to hear about a time when you exceeded your sales goal. How did you achieve those results? [*Behavioral question*]
- Typically, how long does it take you from the initial contact to close a sale? [*Behavioral question*] How might that time frame be shortened? [*Puzzle question*]
- How would you turn an occasional buyer into a regular buyer? [*Puzzle question*]
- Tell me about a time when you took over an existing territory or group of customers. How did you go about making it yours—putting your personal stamp on things? [*Behavioral question*]
- What steps did you take to prepare for a sales call? [*Behavioral question*]
- How do you handle the paperwork and other assorted non-selling activities for which you are responsible? [*Behavioral question*]
- Sell me this pen. [*Puzzle question*]
- What do you think are the most-critical aspects of a sales call? Why? [*Puzzle question*]
- Which do you prefer—dealing with existing customers or working with new ones? Why? [*Puzzle question*]
- Describe how you influenced a customer to purchase your higher-priced product when they had been buying a similar, lower-priced product from a competitor. [*Behavioral question*]
- What qualities and skills make you unique among salespeople? [*Puzzle question*]

- Tell me about a situation in which the customer acknowledged that your product or service was what the organization needed but that internal politics were pushing for an inferior, substandard product. The customer asked for your help. What did you do? [*Behavioral question*]

■ ABILITY TO TAKE THE INITIATIVE

An important attribute to look for in candidates is that of taking the initiative. Such individuals have an entrepreneurial spirit that is always searching for better ways of doing things. In their search for continuous improvement, they pursue innovative, imaginative projects with energy and enthusiasm. Such enterprising people contribute to an organization's long-term success. They help foster a challenging (and sometimes chaotic) workplace because they bring fresh approaches to solving problems. The following questions aim at assessing this attribute.

- Tell me about a time when you went above and beyond the call of duty. What motivated you to make that extra effort? [*Behavioral question*]
- Relate an incident where you secured resources that were difficult to obtain but which were necessary in order for you to achieve a goal. [*Behavioral question*]
- What specific activities were you involved with in your last job that drew on your creative skills? [*Behavioral question*]
- Describe a time when you responded to rejection by trying an alternative approach. [*Behavioral question*]
- On previous jobs what organizational problems did you try to solve that were not specifically related to your job responsibilities? [*Behavioral question*]
- What have you done recently to become more effective at your present position? [*Behavioral question*]
- What typically gives you the most satisfaction on a job? [*Behavioral question*]
- Tell me about some of the changes that occurred on your last job because of something you did. [*Behavioral question*]
- What in your opinion qualifies as a risky situation at work? Why? [*Puzzle question*]

- When was the last time you broke the rules? [*Behavioral question*]
- If you took this job, how would you determine if changes needed to be made? [*Puzzle question*]
- What kinds of experiences have contributed most to your development? [*Behavioral question*] How would you ensure that such opportunities are available to you here? [*Puzzle question*]
- How do you get support for the things you want to do that are outside of your normal job responsibilities? [*Behavioral question*]

■ ADAPTABILITY AND FLEXIBILITY

Every company is continuously changing and growing; you want to hire people who do the same. You need candidates who invite and welcome change, people who understand that change is a part of the everyday life of an organization that believes in continuous improvement. Such people adjust quickly and positively to change. In addition, they are open-minded when presented with perspectives different from their own. Here are some questions that can help identify such individuals.

- Some people are said to roll with the punches. Describe a situation in which you demonstrated this sort of skill in dealing with people. [*Behavioral question*]
- Some work situations require that we work with people we dislike. Tell me about an occasion in which you overcame a personality conflict to achieve results. [*Behavioral question*]
- Please describe a situation that demonstrates your flexibility. [*Behavioral question*]
- What do you do when what you are doing isn't working out? [*Behavioral question*]
- Tell me about a time when your boss presented you with a task that was unrelated to your job and which put you behind in terms of you own work. What did you do? [*Behavioral question*]
- Suppose you were involved in a task that was estimated to reach completion with one week's worth of effort, and

halfway through you realized that, even with three weeks of effort, the project would not be completed. What options might be available to you for dealing with that situation? Which one would you choose? Why? [*Puzzle question*]

- Tell me about the circumstances under which you accepted assistance from someone outside your area on something that was distinctly your personal responsibility? [*Behavioral question*]
- What responsibility—if any—do you believe you have to-ward people in other areas of the company? How should those responsibilities be carried out? [*Puzzle question*]
- Describe a situation in which you dealt successfully with unwanted changes that organization had thrust upon you. [*Behavioral question*]
- Describe a situation for which there was a good deal to learn before you were up to speed and you were facing a tight time frame. What strategies did you use to learn and then accomplish the task within the assigned time frame? [*Behavioral question*]

■ INTEGRITY

Integrity is not something you can teach an adult. It becomes an integral part of an individual's makeup at a very early age. In adults it permeates their every decision and action. When the work involves handling other people's money, organizations are particularly careful to select candidates who conduct themselves with honesty and integrity in both their business and personal activities. You too should look for candidates who can be relied on to act in the best interests of customers, coworkers, and the organization. Here are some questions that can help identify such individuals.

- Describe a situation in which you had to challenge someone who was not acting in the best interests of the organization and its guiding principles. [*Behavioral question*]
- Tell me about a time when you resolved to pursue a course of action you believed in, despite opposition from others. [*Behavioral question*]

- In a normal, everyday working situation, what actions or behaviors show others that a person has integrity? [*Puzzle question*]
- Suppose you knew that others in your area (or your employees) were pilfering minor office supplies. Would you do anything about it, and if so, what would you do? [*Puzzle question*]
- Tell me about a time when your integrity was challenged. [*Behavioral question*]
- Suppose the organization had a rule that prohibited gambling on the premises. You are a new supervisor with an inherited staff of great employees who organize and bet on a sports pool every week. This practice has been going on for years. What would you do? [*Puzzle question*]
- Describe a situation when you were asked to tell a customer a little white lie (perhaps that an order had been shipped, even though it was still sitting on the warehouse floor). What did you do? [*Behavioral question*]
- Suppose a coworker told you something critical and swore you to secrecy. You thought it was important that your boss have the information. What would you do? [*Puzzle question*]
- Describe a situation when you made a reasonable request for time off—maybe for a doctor's appointment—and the boss refused your request. What did you do? [*Behavioral question*]
- Please give me a good illustration of unethical behavior on the part of an employee. Why do you believe that behavior is unethical? [*Puzzle question*]

■ CONFIDENCE

Confidence is the one attribute that makes a candidate extremely appealing to an interviewer. These are people who demonstrate conviction in their ideas and judgments and evidence a strong belief in themselves and their capabilities. They accept responsibility for the outcomes of their decisions and the results of their actions. In addition, they look at conflict as an opportunity for growth. The following questions target this area.

- Tell me about one of the most-challenging assignments you have undertaken during the last year. How did you meet those challenges? [*Behavioral question*]
- What experience have you had with conflict-resolution techniques that would enable you to do well in a supervisory role? [*Behavioral question*]
- Tell me about a time when you and your boss didn't agree on how a situation should be dealt with. How did you resolve your differences? [*Behavioral question*]
- Describe a situation when your work priorities were in conflict with those of your boss. How did you resolve the problem? [*Behavioral question*]
- Tell me about a decision you made where things did not turn out as well as you had anticipated they would. How did you rescue the situation? [*Behavioral question*]
- I'd be interested to learn what kinds of circumstances or events at work have influenced you the most. [*Behavioral question*]
- What have you learned about yourself in the past three years? [*Behavioral question*]
- How do you get new ideas? [*Behavioral question*]
- What do you think are the most-important issues that will face this industry in the next 10 years? How are you preparing yourself to deal with those changes? [*Puzzle question*]
- During the past six months, how many times have you stepped outside the normal bounds of your knowledge, authority, and responsibility to take on an unfamiliar task? Why? How did things work out? [*Behavioral question*]

■ VERSATILITY

A candidate who is versatile has superior communication abilities and knows how to alter his or her style while at the same time maintaining personal and organizational goals. Such candidates recognize that people are different and that to gain cooperation they must often vary their customary approach. Versatile people are also effective at managing their time, able to balance multiple priorities. Here are some questions that target these abilities.

- Tell me about a time when you modified your style so that you could respond more effectively to a difficult situation. [*Behavioral question*]
- Tell me about a time when your boss volunteered you for a task in another area that was unrelated to your current responsibilities and that would put you behind in terms of you own assignments. How did you manage that situation? [*Behavioral question*]
- What type of person have you found is most difficult to work with? What have you done to work successfully with such a person? [*Behavioral question*]
- Describe an occasion when you had to juggle multiple priorities. What did you do so that everything was accomplished? [*Behavioral question*]
- Describe how you schedule your time on an unusually hectic day. [*Puzzle question*]
- How do you plan your day (or week)? [*Puzzle question*]
- What is your strategy for approaching a huge workload that is to be accomplished within an inadequate time frame? [*Puzzle question*]
- How do you determine your priorities? [*Puzzle question*]
- Tell me about a time when a short-term crisis clashed with long-term and important responsibilities. How did you determine which took priority? [*Behavioral question*]
- Interruptions are a fact of life at work. What strategies have you used in the past for dealing with them? [*Behavioral question*]
- Please tell me about the kinds of activities you were involved with on previous jobs that were *not* a part of your regular work responsibilities. I'd be interested to learn how you happened to become involved with those particular tasks. [*Behavioral question*]

■ CONTINUOUS LEARNING

Today, with such fast technological changes, a person's skills can rapidly become obsolete. A good candidate for *any* job is one who makes an effort to keep his or her knowledge and skills current. Self-development is something a person does for him- or herself, not because the boss or the organization requires it. It is done because the individual is motivated by a desire to improve. In the interview, also listen for situations for which learning was possible if the candidate accepted responsibility for errors in judgment or actions. When candidates blame others or the organization for what went wrong, they show you they cannot learn from their experiences. Here are some questions that may shed some light on this area.

- Share with me an experience of learning something new about yourself in the course of a project or assignment. [*Behavioral question*]
- What have you done recently to become more effective in your present position? [*Behavioral question*]
- Describe a situation that turned out badly for you but from which you learned a great deal. [*Behavioral question*]
- Over the past 12 months, how much of your own time and/or money have you invested in your own personal development and for what specific purposes? [*Behavioral question*]
- Tell me how you have purposefully attempted to strengthen your skills, knowledge, and capabilities on the job. What strategies did you use? [*Behavioral question*]
- I'd be interested to learn what kinds of circumstances or events have influenced you to learn something totally new. [*Behavioral question*]
- In what ways have you shared your desire for additional growth (or challenge) with your present (previous) boss? [*Behavioral question*]
- What do you think are the most-important issues that will face this industry in the next 10 years? How are you preparing yourself to deal with those changes? [*Puzzle question*]
- What self-development goals have you set for yourself in the past three years? Why those particular goals? [*Behavioral question*]
- What educational experiences have you had recently that will help you on this job? [*Behavioral question*]
- What have you done to prepare yourself for a job of this type? [*Behavioral question*]
- Let's say your boss gave you some feedback regarding skills or knowledge he or she felt you did not have but should have.

Suppose you felt that the boss's suggestions were not relevant to your situation. What would you do? [*Puzzle question*]

■ DECISION-MAKING AND ANALYTICAL SKILL

Decision making, the process of making a conscious choice of one alternative from a group of alternatives, is one of the measures of a superior candidate. In today's world you certainly would not give someone an important job without first considering whether he or she could gather facts, analyze data, and reason things out systematically. The astute candidate knows that decisions cannot be made in a vacuum; attention must be given to how each decision may impact others in the organization. The following questions assist you with assessing such abilities.

- Would you describe yourself as a logical or intuitive problem solver? [*Puzzle question*] Please give me an example from your previous job that illustrates your choice. [*Behavioral question*]
- Describe a situation in which you had to be analytical and thorough in making a decision. Walk me through the process you followed. [*Behavioral question*]
- Suppose it turns out that we offer you the position. How will you decide whether to accept? [*Puzzle question*]
- How is that you are pursuing this line of work rather than some other? [*Puzzle question*]
- Describe for me the most significant decision you have made in your life. What made it significant? How did you go about making it? [*Behavioral question*]
- When you are deciding whether to try something totally new, what weight do you give to the probability of success? [*Puzzle question*]
- On previous jobs what was the basis on which you determined to take on tasks, projects, or responsibilities that were not assigned to you or even expected of you? [*Behavioral question*]
- What influenced you to seek a new employment opportunity at this point in your career? [*Behavioral question*]
- Suppose you were in the process of hiring yourself an assistant and you had two equally qualified and acceptable

candidates. How would you choose one over the other? [*Puzzle question*]

- Tell me about a time when an employee from another department was disrupting the productivity of your staff. What alternatives did you assume you had for handling the situation? Which alternative did you choose? Why? [*Behavioral question*]

■ STRATEGIST (SEEING THE BIG PICTURE)

Candidates who are good strategists never lose sight of the larger objectives associated with their jobs. They identify complex situations and seek big-picture solutions. They work toward achieving the organization's overall objectives rather than just their own personal goals. If hired, they would focus on increasing quality service, expanding growth, and improving profitability. Here are some questions that may help in identifying such individuals.

- Tell me about a time when you identified a fundamental problem or misconception underlying your organization's policy and/or practice. What did you prescribe as a more effective approach [*Behavioral question*]
- Describe some organizational objectives that were given to your department. How did you and your staff realize some of those objectives? [*Behavioral question*]
- How would you ensure that the company's vision, mission, and purpose were reflected in any goals set by you for you and your staff? [*Puzzle question*]
- Describe a situation in which you participated in problem-solving efforts to rectify a dilemma that was impacting the entire organization. [*Behavioral question*]
- When you are making decisions, how do you go about determining how those decisions will impact other parts of the organization? [*Behavioral question*]
- Suppose management told you to downsize your staff by 20%. On what basis would you decide who remained and who to let go? [*Puzzle question*]
- Tell me about a time when you were faced with a crisis while you were simultaneously involved in something else

that was extremely important. How did you decide what to do? [*Behavioral question*]

- What do you think are the most-important issues that will face this industry in the next 10 years? How are you preparing yourself to deal with those changes? [*Puzzle question*]
- On previous jobs, what was the basis on which you determined to take on tasks, projects, or responsibilities that were not assigned to you or even expected of you? [*Behavioral question*]
- Suppose you made a decision and things did not turn out well. How would you determine what piece you missed in your original analysis? [*Puzzle question*]

■ SELF-APPRAISAL QUESTIONS

Questions of this type ask candidates to analyze their behavior, experiences, and skills from their point of view. It provides an opportunity to discover what the candidate thinks of him- or herself. In addition, these questions can yield some insight into the candidate's self-image, level of self-esteem, self-awareness, and self-knowledge.

- What qualities made you a valuable employee on your last job? [*Puzzle question*]
- How would you describe yourself? [*Puzzle question*]
- What skills and personal resources do you feel have been the major contributors to your success up to now? [*Puzzle question*]
- When people describe you, what qualities do they usually mention first? [*Puzzle question*]
- How do you evaluate your effectiveness? [*Puzzle question*]
- What are the basic factors that motivate you? [*Puzzle question*]
- What would you say are your most-important contributions to a job? [*Puzzle question*]
- If hired, what would you contribute to this job that other candidates could not? [*Puzzle question*]
- What do you consider your greatest strengths to be? [*Puzzle question*]

- What are the special characteristics that make you unique? [*Puzzle question*]
- Why do you feel you would be good for this position? [*Puzzle question*]

■ QUESTIONS FOR THE RECENT GRADUATE

When looking at recent graduates (i.e., candidates with little or no work experience), you hope to find a person with the ability to learn quickly and/or someone with leadership (management) potential. You want a candidate who exhibits decision-making ability, perseverance (time plus effort equal results), and some level of insight about people. The following questions target those issues.

- What influenced you to seek a college degree? [*Puzzle question*]
- What led you to choose_____College (or University)? [*Puzzle question*]
- What prompted you to pick_____as your major course of study? [*Puzzle question*]
- If you had any part-time jobs while in school or college, which one(s) did you find most interesting? Why? [*Behavioral question*]
- What was your favorite course? Why? What was your least-favorite course? Why? [*Behavioral question*]
- What do you think will be the most-valuable contribution your education will make to your life? [*Puzzle question*]
- How do you feel about the importance of grades in school? Of what value are grading systems? What do they show? [*Puzzle question*]
- What subjects did you do best in? Why? [*Behavioral question*]
- What subjects did you not handle as well as you would have liked? Why? What, if anything, did you do to strengthen your proficiency with those subjects? [*Behavioral question*]
- What was it about the subjects in your major that made them especially appealing to you? [*Behavioral question*]
- I'd be interested to learn about the most-challenging situation you faced during your school (or college) years. What made it challenging? [*Behavioral question*]

- Tell me about your extracurricular activities. How did you happen to choose those particular areas of involvement? What did you learn about yourself from engaging in those activities? [*Behavioral question*]

■ QUESTIONS TO DETERMINE THE CANDIDATE'S GOALS

Most candidates will paint a rosy picture regarding their skills, value, and abilities. You find yourself wondering, "If they are so fantastic, how come the current employer doesn't see their marvelousness?" The candidate assures you that he or she is *not* being forced out by the present employer due to poor performance or economic belt tightening; it is the candidate who has made the decision to leave. The assumption then is that the present job is somehow no longer meeting this person's needs or goals. In order to properly assess the candidate's suitability for your job, you must find out what his or her goals are and then decide if your position will satisfy those goals. Here are some questions designed to evaluate that issue.

- Why are you interested in working for us? [*Puzzle question*]
- What are some of the reasons you are considering leaving your present job? [*Puzzle question*]
- What do you hope to find here that you haven't found at your present job? [*Puzzle question*]
- Please describe what constitutes a conducive work atmosphere for you? [*Behavioral question*]
- In what ways do you consider your movement from position to position representative of your ability? Why? [*Puzzle question*]
- Under what circumstances would you remain at your present (previous) job? [*Puzzle question*]
- What are some things you would want to avoid in future jobs? Why? [*Behavioral question*]
- What would you say was the most promising job you ever had? Why? [*Behavioral question*]
- Tell me about the specific events or incidents that contributed the most to your development. Please describe

what you learned and how you put that knowledge to work on succeeding jobs. [*Behavioral question*]

- What two or three things do you feel you learned about yourself from your last position? [*Behavioral question*]
- What did you particularly like (or dislike) about your last position? [*Behavioral question*]

■ DRONE OR FAST TRACKER

Isn't it interesting that no interviewer will admit to needing drones? Everyone wants candidates who express a desire to move up, to become managers, to be promotable. Certainly you would agree, however, that you also need drones—people who want to work at the same dull job year after year after year; people who have no desire whatsoever for promotion or additional responsibilities, people who would never leave for a better opportunity because that better opportunity is right here. These questions can help sort out the drones from the fast-track candidates.

- If you had all the money you could ever use and you still wanted to keep busy, what would you do with your time? [*Puzzle question*]
- What did you hope to be when you were in school? [*Puzzle question*]
- If you could write your own job description, what would it include? [*Puzzle question*]
- What would you personally like to accomplish here for yourself? [*Puzzle question*]
- What does a job have to entail in order to satisfy you? [*Behavioral question*]
- Tell me about any goals you set for yourself over the past 12 months. How did you happen to select those particular objectives? [*Behavioral question*]
- How have you kept track of your progress toward the achievement of your goals? [*Behavioral question*]
- How have you gained support for your goals from your present (previous) bosses? [*Behavioral question*]
- Please tell me about the best job you ever had. What made it the best? How did you get the job in the first place? [*Behavioral question*]

- Tell me about a time when you volunteered to do something totally outside your normal responsibilities. Why did you volunteer? How did it work out? [*Behavioral question*]
- Describe a work situation in which you felt really motivated. [*Behavioral question*]

■ QUESTIONS FOR SELLING THE JOB

The ideal candidate is seated before you; he or she has the right background, education, training, and attitude. How will you entice this candidate to join your company? Most interviewers jump right in by explaining how great they think their organization is, without ever trying to discover what it is that the candidate thinks is appealing. Unless you find out what is important to the candidate, there is no way you will be able to sell the candidate on joining your organization. Here are some questions that will uncover what is important to the candidate. (Remember, however, that if your organization cannot provide those things to the candidate and you manipulate the candidate into accepting the position anyway, you have guaranteed a turnover statistic.)

- What do you hope to find here that you haven't found at your previous organization? [*Puzzle question*]
- Why is it important to you to have that in a job? [*Puzzle question*]
- How would you know that this organization could provide those opportunities for you? [*Puzzle question*]
- What would it look like to you if this organization had the potential of giving you that kind of challenge (responsibility, freedom, etc.) you want? [*Puzzle question*]
- What would you need to know in order to be confident that this job would give you those things? [*Puzzle question*]
- What has gotten in the way of other jobs being able to give you these things? [*Behavioral question*]
- What kind of effort did you make to initiate those opportunities for yourself at other jobs? [*Behavioral question*]
- What were the typical obstacles that prevented other organizations from offering those kinds of opportunities to you? [*Behavioral question*]

- If you could construct this job exactly the way you would want it, what would it look like? [*Puzzle question*]
- What would convince you that we have the ideal job for you? [*Puzzle question*]

■ TIME-MANAGEMENT AWARENESS

It is not possible to *manage* time. In effect, time management is about managing oneself. This important resource is often squandered or poorly utilized because the person has no concept of how critical that resource is. Effective use of time separates the adequate employee or manager from the superior one. In the interview situation you want to look for the candidate who has formulated some overall strategy for time use. The following questions can help you determine this.

- Give me an example of how you traditionally plan your day (or week). [*Behavioral question*]
- What do you think is the most-significant piece of information regarding time management that a person ought to understand? [*Puzzle question*]
- What has been your basic strategy for approaching a huge workload that is to be accomplished within an inadequate time frame? [*Behavioral question*]
- How should an effective person (manager, supervisor) determine his or her priorities? [*Puzzle question*]
- Tell me about a time when you were faced with a crisis while you were involved in something that was extremely important. How did you apportion your time? [*Behavioral question*]
- Interruptions are a fact of life at work. What strategies have you used in the past for dealing with them? [*Behavioral question*]
- What was the toughest time-management problem you ever faced? Why did you find it so difficult? How did you attempt to deal with it? [*Behavioral question*]
- Tell me about a time when you worked for a boss who assigned work at the last possible minute. How did you deal with the difficulties that this created? [*Behavioral question*]
- Tell me about a time when your boss volunteered you for a task in another area that was unrelated to your current re-

sponsibilities and which would put you behind in terms of you own assignments. How did you manage that situation? [*Behavioral question*]

■ Suppose you were involved in a task that was estimated to reach completion with one week's worth of effort. Halfway through, you realized that, even with three weeks of effort, the project could not be accomplished. What options might be available to you for dealing with that situation? Which one would you choose? Why? [*Puzzle question*]

■ SELF-STARTER AND INDEPENDENT THINKER

Sometimes you will find yourself looking for people who can function with a minimum of supervision—people who can be relied upon to see what needs to be done and, without depending on someone or something else to provide structure, will move ahead and get it done. These people are called self-starters. Here are some questions designed to help you ascertain if the candidate can work comfortably and effectively without structure and who fully demonstrates independent thinking.

■ Suppose you were pressured to make a decision that was outside the normal limits of your authority and your boss was unavailable. What would you do? [*Puzzle question*]

■ Tell me about a situation when you were presented with a project that had no history, guidelines, or structure other than a due date. How did you start? [*Behavioral question*]

■ Do you want greater responsibility? Why? [*Puzzle question*]

■ Describe a situation when more responsibility was thrust upon you unexpectedly. [*Behavioral question*]

■ In previous jobs what organizational problems have you tried to solve that were not specifically related to your job responsibilities? [*Behavioral question*]

■ What typically gives you the most satisfaction in a job? [*Puzzle question*]

■ In your present position what problems have you identified that had been previously overlooked? [*Behavioral question*]

■ Tell me about some of the changes that occurred in your last job because of you. [*Puzzle question*]

- What do you consider to be a risky situation at work? Why? [*Puzzle question*]
- Describe a situation when you found it necessary to go above and beyond the call of duty in order to get something done. [*Behavioral question*]

■ INTERPERSONAL SKILLS

The quality of a candidate's interpersonal skills plays an important role in determining his or her eventual job success. The most-significant reason employees are terminated is their inability to get along with coworkers. When asked, candidates will assert that they have good people skills. It is important to look at two areas: (1) their basic attitude toward other people and (2) their ability to establish and maintain productive relationships with others whose deficiencies and irritating behavior they acknowledge. Here are several questions that may help in this assessment.

- How have you handled the frustration of working closely with an annoying person? [*Behavioral question*]
- Tell me about a time when you had to influence someone higher up in the organization who had a reputation for being hardheaded? [*Behavioral question*]
- What type of person do you like to work with? Why? [*Puzzle question*]
- In previous jobs what type of person have you found is most difficult to work with? What did you do in order to work productively with such a person? [*Behavioral question*]
- What are some of the things previous supervisors did that you particularly disliked? [*Puzzle question*]
- Consider all the bosses you've ever had. What were their most-common weaknesses? What were their most-common strengths? [*Behavioral question*]
- How do you feel you've been treated by your coworkers over the years? [*Puzzle question*]
- Tell me some of the things about which you and your manager disagreed. How did you handle those disagreements? [*Behavioral question*]

- Working closely with others on a team can be difficult. Describe for me the major challenges you've experienced as a team member. [*Behavioral question*]
- Suppose your manager asked you tell one of your peers that he or she had better "shape up or ship out." How would you handle that situation? [*Puzzle question*]

■ MANAGEMENT COMPETENCE

Managing others requires strong human relations skills and a good deal of old-fashioned common sense. Many people find their way into leadership roles without either and consequently cause much strife and the loss of talented staff. If you are looking for a candidate who will hold a leadership role (e.g., supervisor, team leader, lead person), understand that experience as a supervisor does not automatically qualify a candidate as a *good* leader. The following questions may help your assessment process.

- What do you consider to be the most-important attribute of a person functioning in a leadership role? Why? [*Puzzle question*]
- In your opinion, under what circumstances should a supervisor be able to ask a staff member to do something without giving an explanation? Why? [*Puzzle question*]
- Describe a situation in which you believed the violation of the chain of command was necessary and would be condoned? [*Behavioral question*]
- How do you quantify your effectiveness as a manager? [*Puzzle question*]
- Tell me about a time when you had to introduce an unpopular change to your staff. What steps did you take so that negative reactions would be minimized? [*Behavioral question*]
- What has happened to those staff members who left your supervision? [*Puzzle question*]
- Describe the circumstances under which you have supervised most effectively. [*Behavioral question*]
- How would you characterize your management style? [*Puzzle question*]

- In the past how have you recognized your staff for their contributions? [*Behavioral question*]
- What kinds of things demotivate employees? [*Puzzle question*]
- Tell me about a time when you were supervising a mediocre performer. What strategies did you use to motivate that person to increase his or her effectiveness? [*Behavioral question*]
- In the past how have you ensured that your people trust and respect you? [*Behavioral question*]

■ USE OF GOALS AS A MANAGEMENT STRATEGY

The competent management candidate understands that goal setting is a crucial leadership strategy. Goal setting moves an employee to higher levels of competence. It is also a key ingredient for empowering a person to direct his or her career. The clearer the notion employees have about what they need to accomplish (in their job or career), the greater the chances are that it will happen. Having a clear end result in mind is not enough, however. People must be able to gauge their progress toward that end result by including measurement markers along the way. This is what will sustain the employee's motivation. It is the manager who must set the process in motion. Here are some questions that target a candidate's understanding of this process.

- What role, if any, have goals and goal setting played in your management strategy? Why? Please give me some examples. [*Behavioral question*]
- What are the elements of an effective goal? [*Puzzle question*]
- Should a manager influence his or her staff to set goals for themselves? Why? How should a manager do that? [*Puzzle question*]
- Tell me about the process you have used to establish the unit's goals. [*Behavioral question*]
- Please describe the role have you played in the development of the individual goals of your staff. [*Behavioral question*]

- What steps have you taken to ensure that each employee knows how to write effective goals (i.e., goals that are challenging, achievable, measurable, realistic, manageable, and compatible)? [*Behavioral question*]
- How have you motivated your staff to achieve their goals? [*Behavioral question*]
- How have you ensured that the goals are realistic? [*Behavioral question*]
- Describe for me the process you have used for reviewing employees' progress toward the achievement of their individual goals. I'd be interested in learning how often you reviewed their progress and about any special techniques you initiated. [*Behavioral question*]
- Describe a situation when you had an employee who set easily achievable goals. How did you influence him or her to set more challenging goals? [*Behavioral question*]
- In what way have you ensured that the company's vision, mission, and purpose are reflected in the goals set by you for the department and in the personal goals set by your staff? [*Behavioral question*]

■ ABILITY TO ENCOURAGE CREATIVITY AND INNOVATION

Innovation depends on hiring people with creative capabilities. It also depends upon management personnel that know how to develop and maintain a working environment that encourages and nurtures change and risk-taking. People with imagination and ingenuity need leadership that understands the needs of the inventive mind and how to inspire it. The following questions target this ability in candidates.

- I'd be interested to learn how you have rewarded risk takers whose results were dubious versus those risk takers whose results were successful. [*Behavioral question*]
- How would you determine whether a person is creative? [*Puzzle question*]
- How would you encourage an employee to be more imaginative? [*Puzzle question*]

- What kinds of things tend to kill a person's creative energy? [*Puzzle question*]
- Describe a time when you knew that one of your people was suffering burnout. How did you identify the problem? What did you do to help him or her? [*Behavioral question*]
- In your previous jobs how did you typically introduce significant changes to your staff? I'd be interested in hearing some specific examples. [*Behavioral question*]
- Please describe the techniques or strategies you have found most helpful in encouraging the creativity of your staff. [*Behavioral question*]
- Tell me about the changes made in your area in the past three months. I'd be interested to learn what created the focus on those particular areas and how you made those changes work. [*Behavioral question*]
- If you took this job, how would you determine if changes needed to be made? [*Puzzle question*]
- Please describe the creative-management strategies you have implemented with your people. For what specific purposes did you use these strategies? [*Behavioral question*]

■ ABILITY TO WORK INDEPENDENTLY

There is a category of jobs that requires specific knowledge, skills, technical education, and self-supervision. Such jobs do not involve supervision of other people. For this type of job, you want an employee who is more comfortable working alone than as part of a team. You need someone who functions independently but who also knows when to seek assistance from others. Such candidates are distinguished by their intensity and drive. They like an environment that values achievement. Here are some questions for discovering this type of candidate.

- Tell me about a time when you had an idea that would solve a serious departmental or organizational problem but you knew your boss was not interested in putting any new ideas to work. How did you handle that situation? [*Behavioral question*]
- How do you know when you've done a good job? [*Puzzle question*]

- What have you found to be the most-difficult challenge in dealing with people? What techniques have you used to help yourself in situations when these challenges threatened to get in the way of what you had to do? [*Behavioral question*]
- Describe a situation in which you were participating in a team project. I'd be interested to learn about the problems you encountered and how they were resolved. [*Behavioral question*]
- Tell me about a time when you were in the middle of one project and the organization required your expertise on another assignment. What happened to the first project? [*Behavioral question*]
- Describe a situation for which there was a good deal to learn before you were up to speed and you were facing a tight time frame. What strategies did you use to learn and then accomplish the task within the assigned time frame? [*Behavioral question*]
- Suppose you were working on something where you had a good deal of knowledge about the issues involved but were stuck on some portion of the problem. How would you make the judgment as to when someone else's input is necessary? [*Puzzle question*]
- What do you do when something you are working on isn't working out? [*Behavioral question*]
- Please describe the physical work setting in which you have been the most productive. Why? [*Behavioral question*]
- What kind of management style or supervisory techniques do you find are the most motivational for you? Why? [*Puzzle question*]

■ CLERICAL SUPPORT SKILLS

Competent clerical-support persons are among the most-important assets an organization has; they are the key to managerial effectiveness. By assuming the bulk of the administrative trivia and bureaucratic paperwork, they free their bosses to concentrate on the more-critical issues of the business. The key ingredient to a successful placement depends on the personality fit between the assistants and the executives for whom they work so that they can forge a highly cohesive partnership. These questions can be useful in determining the effectiveness of a clerical-support candidate:

- How would you go about establishing a relationship with a new boss? [*Puzzle question*]
- Tell me about a time when you had to juggle multiple priorities for a number of bosses, all of whom thought their work was the most important and should be done first. How did you sort that out? [*Behavioral question*]
- Please explain how you typically organize your day. I'd be interested to hear about the tools and strategies you like to use. [*Behavioral question*]
- What system do you typically use for setting your work priorities? Why? [*Behavioral question*]
- Describe a situation when you had to complete an important project for a very senior executive. At some point on the project, you needed your boss's input but he or she was unavailable. How did you determine what to do? [*Behavioral question*]
- What kind of people do you find are the most trying in terms of your patience? [*Puzzle question*]
- Please describe the best boss you ever had. What made him or her so special? [*Behavioral question*]
- Please describe the worst boss you ever had. What made him or her so terrible? What techniques did you use to make your relationship function effectively? [*Behavioral question*]
- Please tell me about the kind of activities you were involved with in previous jobs that were *not* a part of your regular work responsibilities. I'd be interested to learn how you happened to become involved with those particular tasks. [*Behavioral question*]
- Tell me about a time when a boss asked you to work overtime and your personal plans required that you leave work at the regular time. How did you manage your boss's expectations without sacrificing your plans? [*Behavioral question*]

■ CONFLICT-MANAGEMENT SKILLS

One seldom works strictly alone, and so the issue of human relations becomes important in evaluating the suitability of a candidate. Typically, that issue surfaces with the closed-ended question "Do you get along well with other people?" which brings forth the response, "Yes." Under the pressure of work, human relations can become strained. It may become extremely difficult to keep relationships smooth. What you need to ascertain during the interview is whether the candidate can manage conflict effectively. Here are some questions that may provide some insight on this issue.

- Tell me about a situation when you and a peer from somewhere else in the organization were in conflict over some interdepartmental work situation. How was the problem resolved? What role did you play in its resolution? [*Behavioral question*]
- Suppose you were a member of a seven-person work team, and three of the members could not get along with one another. Suppose this situation was destroying the group's effectiveness. What—if anything—would you do? Why? [*Puzzle question*]
- What experience have you had with conflict-resolution techniques that would enable you to do well in a management role? [*Behavioral question*]
- Tell me about a time when you and your boss didn't agree on how a situation should be handled. How did you resolve your differences? [*Behavioral question*]
- Describe a situation when your work priorities were in conflict with those of your boss. How did you resolve the problem? [*Behavioral question*]
- Tell me about a time when you needed critical information from another department in order to complete your work. The other department, however, did not think the gathering of your data was a priority. How did you work things out? [*Behavioral question*]
- What circumstances or situations make your work difficult? Please give me an example of how, when faced with such a situation, you resolved it. [*Behavioral question*]
- Please describe a common type of conflict situation you experienced in your previous job. What resolution techniques did you use to deal with such situations? [*Behavioral question*]

- What's the biggest problem you are wrestling with at work right now? [*Behavioral question*] How do you plan to resolve it? [*Puzzle question*]
- What strategies does a person have for dealing with conflict? [*Puzzle question*]

■ SUBORDINATE COMPETENCE

If you are hiring an employee who will become a part of your staff, that person will have to answer to you concerning his or her actions at work. Although it is important that the candidate be able to work comfortably and cooperatively within the immediate environment, it is essential that he or she be able to get on well with you. Some candidates have a history of authority-based friction; they hate being told what to do. They may claim that they were just being independent and entrepreneurial but that their bosses wanted an automaton. The following questions are designed to give you some insight regarding how the candidate typically handles authority relationships at work.

- How do you like to be supervised? [*Puzzle question*]
- Describe a situation in which you and your boss disagreed on some issue. What techniques did you use to turn your boss around? [*Behavioral question*]
- Tell me about the worst manager you ever had. I'd be interested in learning what made the situation so uncomfortable and how you attempted to deal with it. [*Behavioral question*]
- What have you done to get support for the things you want to do? [*Behavioral question*]
- Tell me about the best manager you ever had. I'd be interested in hearing about the qualities and techniques that made him or her so effective. [*Behavioral question*]
- Let's say your manager made a change in your job—without first discussing that change with you. Suppose that change would have a detrimental effect on your ability to meet job expectations. What would you do? [*Puzzle question*]
- I'd be interested to learn how you and your previous bosses typically exchanged information. [*Behavioral question*]
- What element about being managed bothers you the most? Why? [*Puzzle question*]

- What do you think are the most-important factors in establishing and maintaining a good relationship with your immediate boss? [*Puzzle question*]
- Tell me about a situation when you believed your boss was about to make a very serious error in judgment. What did you do? [*Behavioral question*]
- It's been said that managing others is a skill but that functioning as a subordinate is an art. What do you think are the major challenges in functioning as a subordinate? [*Puzzle question*]

■ ABILITY TO BUILD COLLABORATIVE RELATIONSHIPS

If you are looking for a candidate who will hold a leadership role in your organization, you will need someone with the ability to build and maintain collaborative working relationships. Trust is the essential ingredient in building such relationships. The new hire must be able to generate confidence in his or her brand of leadership and must provide each staff member with a sense of stability and consistency. At the same time, this person must sustain that sense of mutual accountability and individual responsibility that you have established among the staff. These questions can help you find that type of person.

- What strategies have you used to maintain a strong relationship between yourself and each one of your individual staff members? [*Behavioral question*]
- What techniques have you used to encourage your people to give you the bad news when they screw things up? [*Behavioral question*]
- Tell me about a time when changes that are likely to be unpopular with your staff were imminent. What means did you use to inform your staff of those changes? How far in advance did you inform them? Why? [*Behavioral question*]
- What have you done to encourage the full sharing of information among individual staff members? [*Behavioral question*]
- How would you go about building and maintaining an atmosphere of trust in your department? [*Puzzle question*]

- How often and under what circumstances should a supervisor involve the staff in his or her decision-making and problem-solving efforts? [*Puzzle question*]
- What role have you played in managing conflicts that arise between staff members? Please share with me some specific examples of when your intervention was necessary and when it was not. [*Behavioral question*]
- Under what circumstances have you accepted assistance from your staff members in matters that are distinctly your personal responsibility? [*Behavioral question*]
- On previous jobs, how did you go about establishing your leadership role with an inherited staff? [*Behavioral question*]

■ ASSESSING BELIEFS, VALUES, AND PHILOSOPHY

Because ultimately people base their decisions on their beliefs, values, and philosophy, the compatibility of these elements with those of the organization becomes a critical factor in the hiring process. An executive who believes that people are disposable and interchangeable will, in the face of downsizing, make different decisions from one who believes that every employee is unique and that those individual differences are the key to the organization's future success. A salesperson who believes that his job is to assist a customer in buying the best product for his or her needs will behave differently from one who believes that her job is to "make my numbers and push product." Here are some questions to help you explore the candidate's beliefs, values, and philosophy.

- How would you describe what has been your basic business philosophy? [*Behavioral question*]
- Please describe your overall philosophy regarding the management of other people. I'd be interested to learn how your philosophy guided some of your decisions on previous jobs. [*Behavioral question*]
- What specific work experience has done the most to shape your personal beliefs, values, and philosophy? [*Behavioral question*]

Appendix

Personality Fit: Key Questions and Responses

Chapter 8 presented you with some tools for assessing personality fit and suggested that you use several very open-ended and minimally structured questions to prompt candidates into revealing their personality. Here are 10 such questions with an indication of the likely responses from each of the three personality types described in Chapter 8.

1. Tell me about your most recent job.

   Task-oriented candidate: Item-by-item description of the job activities.

   Affiliation-oriented candidate: Description of the personalities of coworkers.

   Power-oriented candidate: Control, in-charge-of issues.

2. What kinds of things make your work difficult?

   Task-oriented candidate: People who are stupid, slow, dumb, or won't listen.

   Affiliation-oriented candidate: Too much work, long hours, working alone.

   Power-oriented candidate: Not enough control over the job, too much red tape.

3. What do you consider your greatest strengths to be?

   Task-oriented candidate: Excellence, quality work, doing a good job.

Affiliation-oriented candidate: Getting along well with people.

Power-oriented candidate: Being able to take charge, to run the show.

4. At work, what kinds of things did you enjoy doing most?

Task-oriented candidate: Paperwork (detail work), working on the computer, keeping the place tidy.

Affiliation-oriented candidate: Dealing with people, helping others.

Power-oriented candidate: Managing, supervising others, leadership role.

5. Why does this kind of work interest you?

Task-oriented candidate: Challenge, working without supervision, something new to do.

Affiliation-oriented candidate: Near my home, something I can handle, did it before.

Power-oriented candidate: Step to the future, advancement, leadership role.

6. Give me an example of a difficult problem you solved or decision you had to make.

Task-oriented candidate: Will talk about a technical problem.

Affiliation-oriented candidate: Will describe a people problem, perhaps a personal one.

Power-oriented candidate: Taking over, taking charge, making a leadership decision, or influencing others.

7. What do you think are the most-important qualities I should look for in a person for this type of work? (The candidate will describe him- or herself.)

Task-oriented candidate: Dependable, hard worker, self-starter, honest.

Affiliation-oriented candidate: Helpful, friendly, likes people, cooperative.

Power-oriented candidate: Leadership potential, wants to move up, grow, take control.

8. What do you think are the most-important qualities in a boss or supervisor?

   Task-oriented candidate: To see that the job gets done right, to be tough but fair.

   Affiliation-oriented candidate: To help the employees, to be a friend.

   Power-oriented candidate: To be a strong leader, to help mold people.

9. What do you do in your spare time?

   Task-oriented candidate: Does competitive activities (like tennis) with one other person, attends night school, reads, surfs the Internet.

   Affiliation-oriented candidate: Participates in bowling league or softball team, likes spectator sports, support groups.

   Power-oriented candidate: Interested in politics and world affairs, leader of a group, team, or club, interested in investments and money.

10. Describe a situation in which you successfully handled people in a service-type role.

    Task-oriented candidate: Analyzed a difficult, challenging problem and solved it.

    Affiliation-oriented candidate: Helped, nurtured, assisted.

    Power-oriented candidate: Convinced someone to do something my way, leading, influencing.

Index